50% OFF
Online HSPT Prep Course!
By Mometrix

Dear Customer,

We consider it an honor and a privilege that you chose our HSPT Study Guide. As a way of showing our appreciation and to help us better serve you, we are offering **50% off our online HSPT Course.** Many HSPT courses are needlessly expensive and don't deliver enough value. With our course, you get access to the best HSPT prep material, and **you only pay half price**.

We have structured our online course to perfectly complement your printed study guide. The HSPT Online Course contains **in-depth lessons** that cover all the most important topics, **170+ video reviews** that explain difficult concepts, over **1,450 practice questions** to ensure you feel prepared, and more than **350 digital flashcards**, so you can study while you're on the go.

Online HSPT Prep Course

Topics Covered:

- Verbal Skills
  - Synonyms and Antonyms
  - Logical and Verbal Classifications
- Reading Comprehension
  - Informational and Literary Texts
  - Figurative Language
- Language
  - Foundations of Grammar
  - Structure and Purpose of a Sentence
- Mathematics and Quantitative Skills
  - Fractions, Decimals, and Percentages
  - Polygons and Triangles

Course Features:

- HSPT Study Guide
  - Get content that complements our best-selling study guide.
- Full-Length Practice Tests
  - With over 1,450 practice questions, you can test yourself again and again.
- Mobile Friendly
  - If you need to study on the go, the course is easily accessible from your mobile device.
- HSPT Flashcards
  - Our course includes a flashcards mode with over 350 content cards for you to study.

To receive this discount, visit our website at <u>mometrix.com/university/hspt</u> or simply scan this QR code with your smartphone. At the checkout page, enter the discount code: **hspt50off**

If you have any questions or concerns, please contact us at <u>support@mometrix.com</u>.

Sincerely,

FREE Study Skills Videos/DVD Offer

Dear Customer,

Thank you for your purchase from Mometrix! We consider it an honor and a privilege that you have purchased our product and we want to ensure your satisfaction.

As part of our ongoing effort to meet the needs of test takers, we have developed a set of Study Skills Videos that we would like to give you for <u>FREE</u>. These videos cover our *best practices* for getting ready for your exam, from how to use our study materials to how to best prepare for the day of the test.

All that we ask is that you email us with feedback that would describe your experience so far with our product. Good, bad, or indifferent, we want to know what you think!

To get your FREE Study Skills Videos, you can use the **QR code** below, or send us an **email** at studyvideos@mometrix.com with *FREE VIDEOS* in the subject line and the following information in the body of the email:

- The name of the product you purchased.
- Your product rating on a scale of 1-5, with 5 being the highest rating.
- Your feedback. It can be long, short, or anything in between. We just want to know your impressions and experience so far with our product. (Good feedback might include how our study material met your needs and ways we might be able to make it even better. You could highlight features that you found helpful or features that you think we should add.)

If you have any questions or concerns, please don't hesitate to contact me directly.

Thanks again!

Sincerely,

Jay Willis
Vice President
jay.willis@mometrix.com
1-800-673-8175

HSPT®

SECRETS

Study Guide
Your Key to Exam Success

Written and edited by the Mometrix School Admissions Test Team

Mometrix offers volume discount pricing to institutions. For more information or a price quote, please contact our sales department at sales@mometrix.com or 888-248-1219.

Mometrix Media LLC is not affiliated with or endorsed by any official testing organization. All organizational and test names are trademarks of their respective owners.

Paperback
ISBN 13: 978-1-60971-867-1
ISBN 10: 1-60971-867-4

Ebook
ISBN 13: 978-1-62120-307-0
ISBN 10: 1-62120-307-7

Hardback
ISBN 13: 978-1-5167-0803-1
ISBN 10: 1-5167-0803-2

DEAR FUTURE EXAM SUCCESS STORY

First of all, **THANK YOU** for purchasing Mometrix study materials!

Second, congratulations! You are one of the few determined test-takers who are committed to doing whatever it takes to excel on your exam. **You have come to the right place.** We developed these study materials with one goal in mind: to deliver you the information you need in a format that's concise and easy to use.

In addition to optimizing your guide for the content of the test, we've outlined our recommended steps for breaking down the preparation process into small, attainable goals so you can make sure you stay on track.

We've also analyzed the entire test-taking process, identifying the most common pitfalls and showing how you can overcome them and be ready for any curveball the test throws you.

Standardized testing is one of the biggest obstacles on your road to success, which only increases the importance of doing well in the high-pressure, high-stakes environment of test day. Your results on this test could have a significant impact on your future, and this guide provides the information and practical advice to help you achieve your full potential on test day.

Your success is our success

We would love to hear from you! If you would like to share the story of your exam success or if you have any questions or comments in regard to our products, please contact us at **800-673-8175** or **support@mometrix.com**.

Thanks again for your business and we wish you continued success!

Sincerely,
The Mometrix Test Preparation Team

Need more help? Check out our flashcards at:
http://MometrixFlashcards.com/HSPT

TABLE OF CONTENTS

Introduction

Thank you for purchasing this resource! You have made the choice to prepare yourself for a test that could have a huge impact on your future, and this guide is designed to help you be fully ready for test day. Obviously, it's important to have a solid understanding of the test material, but you also need to be prepared for the unique environment and stressors of the test, so that you can perform to the best of your abilities.

For this purpose, the first section that appears in this guide is the **Secret Keys**. We've devoted countless hours to meticulously researching what works and what doesn't, and we've boiled down our findings to the five most impactful steps you can take to improve your performance on the test. We start at the beginning with study planning and move through the preparation process, all the way to the testing strategies that will help you get the most out of what you know when you're finally sitting in front of the test.

We recommend that you start preparing for your test as far in advance as possible. However, if you've bought this guide as a last-minute study resource and only have a few days before your test, we recommend that you skip over the first two Secret Keys since they address a long-term study plan.

If you struggle with **test anxiety**, we strongly encourage you to check out our recommendations for how you can overcome it. Test anxiety is a formidable foe, but it can be beaten, and we want to make sure you have the tools you need to defeat it.

1

Secret Key #1 – Plan Big, Study Small

There's a lot riding on your performance. If you want to ace this test, you're going to need to keep your skills sharp and the material fresh in your mind. You need a plan that lets you review everything you need to know while still fitting in your schedule. We'll break this strategy down into three categories.

Information Organization

Start with the information you already have: the official test outline. From this, you can make a complete list of all the concepts you need to cover before the test. Organize these concepts into groups that can be studied together, and create a list of any related vocabulary you need to learn so you can brush up on any difficult terms. You'll want to keep this vocabulary list handy once you actually start studying since you may need to add to it along the way.

Time Management

Once you have your set of study concepts, decide how to spread them out over the time you have left before the test. Break your study plan into small, clear goals so you have a manageable task for each day and know exactly what you're doing. Then just focus on one small step at a time. When you manage your time this way, you don't need to spend hours at a time studying. Studying a small block of content for a short period each day helps you retain information better and avoid stressing over how much you have left to do. You can relax knowing that you have a plan to cover everything in time. In order for this strategy to be effective though, you have to start studying early and stick to your schedule. Avoid the exhaustion and futility that comes from last-minute cramming!

Study Environment

The environment you study in has a big impact on your learning. Studying in a coffee shop, while probably more enjoyable, is not likely to be as fruitful as studying in a quiet room. It's important to keep distractions to a minimum. You're only planning to study for a short block of time, so make the most of it. Don't pause to check your phone or get up to find a snack. It's also important to **avoid multitasking**. Research has consistently shown that multitasking will make your studying dramatically less effective. Your study area should also be comfortable and well-lit so you don't have the distraction of straining your eyes or sitting on an uncomfortable chair.

 The time of day you study is also important. You want to be rested and alert. Don't wait until just before bedtime. Study when you'll be most likely to comprehend and remember. Even better, if you know what time of day your test will be, set that time aside for study. That way your brain will be used to working on that subject at that specific time and you'll have a better chance of recalling information.

Finally, it can be helpful to team up with others who are studying for the same test. Your actual studying should be done in as isolated an environment as possible, but the work of organizing the information and setting up the study plan can be divided up. In between study sessions, you can discuss with your teammates the concepts that you're all studying and quiz each other on the details. Just be sure that your teammates are as serious about the test as you are. If you find that your study time is being replaced with social time, you might need to find a new team.

2

Secret Key #2 – Make Your Studying Count

You're devoting a lot of time and effort to preparing for this test, so you want to be absolutely certain it will pay off. This means doing more than just reading the content and hoping you can remember it on test day. It's important to make every minute of study count. There are two main areas you can focus on to make your studying count.

Retention

It doesn't matter how much time you study if you can't remember the material. You need to make sure you are retaining the concepts. To check your retention of the information you're learning, try recalling it at later times with minimal prompting. Try carrying around flashcards and glance at one or two from time to time or ask a friend who's also studying for the test to quiz you.

To enhance your retention, look for ways to put the information into practice so that you can apply it rather than simply recalling it. If you're using the information in practical ways, it will be much easier to remember. Similarly, it helps to solidify a concept in your mind if you're not only reading it to yourself but also explaining it to someone else. Ask a friend to let you teach them about a concept you're a little shaky on (or speak aloud to an imaginary audience if necessary). As you try to summarize, define, give examples, and answer your friend's questions, you'll understand the concepts better and they will stay with you longer. Finally, step back for a big picture view and ask yourself how each piece of information fits with the whole subject. When you link the different concepts together and see them working together as a whole, it's easier to remember the individual components.

Finally, practice showing your work on any multi-step problems, even if you're just studying. Writing out each step you take to solve a problem will help solidify the process in your mind, and you'll be more likely to remember it during the test.

Modality

Modality simply refers to the means or method by which you study. Choosing a study modality that fits your own individual learning style is crucial. No two people learn best in exactly the same way, so it's important to know your strengths and use them to your advantage.

For example, if you learn best by visualization, focus on visualizing a concept in your mind and draw an image or a diagram. Try color-coding your notes, illustrating them, or creating symbols that will trigger your mind to recall a learned concept. If you learn best by hearing or discussing information, find a study partner who learns the same way or read aloud to yourself. Think about how to put the information in your own words. Imagine that you are giving a lecture on the topic and record yourself so you can listen to it later.

For any learning style, flashcards can be helpful. Organize the information so you can take advantage of spare moments to review. Underline key words or phrases. Use different colors for different categories. Mnemonic devices (such as creating a short list in which every item starts with the same letter) can also help with retention. Find what works best for you and use it to store the information in your mind most effectively and easily.

3

Secret Key #3 – Practice the Right Way

Your success on test day depends not only on how many hours you put into preparing, but also on whether you prepared the right way. It's good to check along the way to see if your studying is paying off. One of the most effective ways to do this is by taking practice tests to evaluate your progress. Practice tests are useful because they show exactly where you need to improve. Every time you take a practice test, pay special attention to these three groups of questions:

- The questions you got wrong
- The questions you had to guess on, even if you guessed right
- The questions you found difficult or slow to work through

This will show you exactly what your weak areas are, and where you need to devote more study time. Ask yourself why each of these questions gave you trouble. Was it because you didn't understand the material? Was it because you didn't remember the vocabulary? Do you need more repetitions on this type of question to build speed and confidence? Dig into those questions and figure out how you can strengthen your weak areas as you go back to review the material.

 Additionally, many practice tests have a section explaining the answer choices. It can be tempting to read the explanation and think that you now have a good understanding of the concept. However, an explanation likely only covers part of the question's broader context. Even if the explanation makes perfect sense, **go back and investigate** every concept related to the question until you're positive you have a thorough understanding.

As you go along, keep in mind that the practice test is just that: practice. Memorizing these questions and answers will not be very helpful on the actual test because it is unlikely to have any of the same exact questions. If you only know the right answers to the sample questions, you won't be prepared for the real thing. **Study the concepts** until you understand them fully, and then you'll be able to answer any question that shows up on the test.

It's important to wait on the practice tests until you're ready. If you take a test on your first day of study, you may be overwhelmed by the amount of material covered and how much you need to learn. Work up to it gradually.

On test day, you'll need to be prepared for answering questions, managing your time, and using the test-taking strategies you've learned. It's a lot to balance, like a mental marathon that will have a big impact on your future. Like training for a marathon, you'll need to start slowly and work your way up. When test day arrives, you'll be ready.

Start with the strategies you've read in the first two Secret Keys—plan your course and study in the way that works best for you. If you have time, consider using multiple study resources to get different approaches to the same concepts. It can be helpful to see difficult concepts from more than one angle. Then find a good source for practice tests. Many times, the test website will suggest potential study resources or provide sample tests.

Practice Test Strategy

If you're able to find at least three practice tests, we recommend this strategy:

UNTIMED AND OPEN-BOOK PRACTICE

Take the first test with no time constraints and with your notes and study guide handy. Take your time and focus on applying the strategies you've learned.

TIMED AND OPEN-BOOK PRACTICE

Take the second practice test open-book as well, but set a timer and practice pacing yourself to finish in time.

TIMED AND CLOSED-BOOK PRACTICE

Take any other practice tests as if it were test day. Set a timer and put away your study materials. Sit at a table or desk in a quiet room, imagine yourself at the testing center, and answer questions as quickly and accurately as possible.

Keep repeating timed and closed-book tests on a regular basis until you run out of practice tests or it's time for the actual test. Your mind will be ready for the schedule and stress of test day, and you'll be able to focus on recalling the material you've learned.

Secret Key #4 – Pace Yourself

Once you're fully prepared for the material on the test, your biggest challenge on test day will be managing your time. Just knowing that the clock is ticking can make you panic even if you have plenty of time left. Work on pacing yourself so you can build confidence against the time constraints of the exam. Pacing is a difficult skill to master, especially in a high-pressure environment, so **practice is vital**.

Set time expectations for your pace based on how much time is available. For example, if a section has 60 questions and the time limit is 30 minutes, you know you have to average 30 seconds or less per question in order to answer them all. Although 30 seconds is the hard limit, set 25 seconds per question as your goal, so you reserve extra time to spend on harder questions. When you budget extra time for the harder questions, you no longer have any reason to stress when those questions take longer to answer.

Don't let this time expectation distract you from working through the test at a calm, steady pace, but keep it in mind so you don't spend too much time on any one question. Recognize that taking extra time on one question you don't understand may keep you from answering two that you do understand later in the test. If your time limit for a question is up and you're still not sure of the answer, mark it and move on, and come back to it later if the time and the test format allow. If the testing format doesn't allow you to return to earlier questions, just make an educated guess; then put it out of your mind and move on.

On the easier questions, be careful not to rush. It may seem wise to hurry through them so you have more time for the challenging ones, but it's not worth missing one if you know the concept and just didn't take the time to read the question fully. Work efficiently but make sure you understand the question and have looked at all of the answer choices, since more than one may seem right at first.

Even if you're paying attention to the time, you may find yourself a little behind at some point. You should speed up to get back on track, but do so wisely. Don't panic; just take a few seconds less on each question until you're caught up. Don't guess without thinking, but do look through the answer choices and eliminate any you know are wrong. If you can get down to two choices, it is often worthwhile to guess from those. Once you've chosen an answer, move on and don't dwell on any that you skipped or had to hurry through. If a question was taking too long, chances are it was one of the harder ones, so you weren't as likely to get it right anyway.

On the other hand, if you find yourself getting ahead of schedule, it may be beneficial to slow down a little. The more quickly you work, the more likely you are to make a careless mistake that will affect your score. You've budgeted time for each question, so don't be afraid to spend that time. Practice an efficient but careful pace to get the most out of the time you have.

6

Secret Key #5 – Have a Plan for Guessing

When you're taking the test, you may find yourself stuck on a question. Some of the answer choices seem better than others, but you don't see the one answer choice that is obviously correct. What do you do?

The scenario described above is very common, yet most test takers have not effectively prepared for it. Developing and practicing a plan for guessing may be one of the single most effective uses of your time as you get ready for the exam.

In developing your plan for guessing, there are three questions to address:

- When should you start the guessing process?
- How should you narrow down the choices?
- Which answer should you choose?

When to Start the Guessing Process

Unless your plan for guessing is to select C every time (which, despite its merits, is not what we recommend), you need to leave yourself enough time to apply your answer elimination strategies. Since you have a limited amount of time for each question, that means that if you're going to give yourself the best shot at guessing correctly, you have to decide quickly whether or not you will guess.

Of course, the best-case scenario is that you don't have to guess at all, so first, see if you can answer the question based on your knowledge of the subject and basic reasoning skills. Focus on the key words in the question and try to jog your memory of related topics. Give yourself a chance to bring the knowledge to mind, but once you realize that you don't have (or you can't access) the knowledge you need to answer the question, it's time to start the guessing process.

It's almost always better to start the guessing process too early than too late. It only takes a few seconds to remember something and answer the question from knowledge. Carefully eliminating wrong answer choices takes longer. Plus, going through the process of eliminating answer choices can actually help jog your memory.

Summary: Start the guessing process as soon as you decide that you can't answer the question based on your knowledge.

7

How to Narrow Down the Choices

The next chapter in this book (**Test-Taking Strategies**) includes a wide range of strategies for how to approach questions and how to look for answer choices to eliminate. You will definitely want to read those carefully, practice them, and figure out which ones work best for you. Here though, we're going to address a mindset rather than a particular strategy.

Your odds of guessing an answer correctly depend on how many options you are choosing from.

Number of options left	5	4	3	2	1
Odds of guessing correctly	20%	25%	33%	50%	100%

You can see from this chart just how valuable it is to be able to eliminate incorrect answers and make an educated guess, but there are two things that many test takers do that cause them to miss out on the benefits of guessing:

- Accidentally eliminating the correct answer
- Selecting an answer based on an impression

We'll look at the first one here, and the second one in the next section.

To avoid accidentally eliminating the correct answer, we recommend a thought exercise called **the $5 challenge**. In this challenge, you only eliminate an answer choice from contention if you are willing to bet $5 on it being wrong. Why $5? Five dollars is a small but not insignificant amount of money. It's an amount you could afford to lose but wouldn't want to throw away. And while losing

$5 once might not hurt too much, doing it twenty times will set you back $100. In the same way, each small decision you make—eliminating a choice here, guessing on a question there—won't by itself impact your score very much, but when you put them all together, they can make a big difference. By holding each answer choice elimination decision to a higher standard, you can reduce the risk of accidentally eliminating the correct answer.

The $5 challenge can also be applied in a positive sense: If you are willing to bet $5 that an answer choice *is* correct, go ahead and mark it as correct.

Summary: Only eliminate an answer choice if you are willing to bet $5 that it is wrong.

8

Which Answer to Choose

You're taking the test. You've run into a hard question and decided you'll have to guess. You've eliminated all the answer choices you're willing to bet $5 on. Now you have to pick an answer. Why do we even need to talk about this? Why can't you just pick whichever one you feel like when the time comes?

The answer to these questions is that if you don't come into the test with a plan, you'll rely on your impression to select an answer choice, and if you do that, you risk falling into a trap. The test writers know that everyone who takes their test will be guessing on some of the questions, so they intentionally write wrong answer choices to seem plausible. You still have to pick an answer though, and if the wrong answer choices are designed to look right, how can you ever be sure that you're not falling for their trap? The best solution we've found to this dilemma is to take the decision out of your hands entirely. Here is the process we recommend:

Once you've eliminated any choices that you are confident (willing to bet $5) are wrong, select the first remaining choice as your answer.

Whether you choose to select the first remaining choice, the second, or the last, the important thing is that you use some preselected standard. Using this approach guarantees that you will not be enticed into selecting an answer choice that looks right, because you are not basing your decision on how the answer choices look.

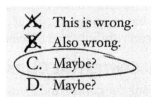

This is not meant to make you question your knowledge. Instead, it is to help you recognize the difference between your knowledge and your impressions. There's a huge difference between thinking an answer is right because of what you know, and thinking an answer is right because it looks or sounds like it should be right.

Summary: To ensure that your selection is appropriately random, make a predetermined selection from among all answer choices you have not eliminated.

9

Test-Taking Strategies

This section contains a list of test-taking strategies that you may find helpful as you work through the test. By taking what you know and applying logical thought, you can maximize your chances of answering any question correctly!

It is very important to realize that every question is different and every person is different: no single strategy will work on every question, and no single strategy will work for every person. That's why we've included all of them here, so you can try them out and determine which ones work best for different types of questions and which ones work best for you.

Question Strategies

☑ READ CAREFULLY

Read the question and the answer choices carefully. Don't miss the question because you misread the terms. You have plenty of time to read each question thoroughly and make sure you understand what is being asked. Yet a happy medium must be attained, so don't waste too much time. You must read carefully and efficiently.

☑ CONTEXTUAL CLUES

Look for contextual clues. If the question includes a word you are not familiar with, look at the immediate context for some indication of what the word might mean. Contextual clues can often give you all the information you need to decipher the meaning of an unfamiliar word. Even if you can't determine the meaning, you may be able to narrow down the possibilities enough to make a solid guess at the answer to the question.

☑ PREFIXES

If you're having trouble with a word in the question or answer choices, try dissecting it. Take advantage of every clue that the word might include. Prefixes can be a huge help. Usually, they allow you to determine a basic meaning. *Pre-* means before, *post-* means after, *pro-* is positive, *de-* is negative. From prefixes, you can get an idea of the general meaning of the word and try to put it into context.

☑ HEDGE WORDS

Watch out for critical hedge words, such as *likely, may, can, sometimes, often, almost, mostly, usually, generally, rarely,* and *sometimes*. Question writers insert these hedge phrases to cover every possibility. Often an answer choice will be wrong simply because it leaves no room for exception. Be on guard for answer choices that have definitive words such as *exactly* and *always*.

☑ SWITCHBACK WORDS

Stay alert for *switchbacks*. These are the words and phrases frequently used to alert you to shifts in thought. The most common switchback words are *but, although,* and *however*. Others include *nevertheless, on the other hand, even though, while, in spite of, despite,* and *regardless of*. Switchback words are important to catch because they can change the direction of the question or an answer choice.

⊘ Face Value

When in doubt, use common sense. Accept the situation in the problem at face value. Don't read too much into it. These problems will not require you to make wild assumptions. If you have to go beyond creativity and warp time or space in order to have an answer choice fit the question, then you should move on and consider the other answer choices. These are normal problems rooted in reality. The applicable relationship or explanation may not be readily apparent, but it is there for you to figure out. Use your common sense to interpret anything that isn't clear.

Answer Choice Strategies

⊘ Answer Selection

The most thorough way to pick an answer choice is to identify and eliminate wrong answers until only one is left, then confirm it is the correct answer. Sometimes an answer choice may immediately seem right, but be careful. The test writers will usually put more than one reasonable answer choice on each question, so take a second to read all of them and make sure that the other choices are not equally obvious. As long as you have time left, it is better to read every answer choice than to pick the first one that looks right without checking the others.

⊘ Answer Choice Families

An answer choice family consists of two (in rare cases, three) answer choices that are very similar in construction and cannot all be true at the same time. If you see two answer choices that are direct opposites or parallels, one of them is usually the correct answer. For instance, if one answer choice says that quantity x increases and another either says that quantity x decreases (opposite) or says that quantity y increases (parallel), then those answer choices would fall into the same family. An answer choice that doesn't match the construction of the answer choice family is more likely to be incorrect. Most questions will not have answer choice families, but when they do appear, you should be prepared to recognize them.

⊘ Eliminate Answers

Eliminate answer choices as soon as you realize they are wrong, but make sure you consider all possibilities. If you are eliminating answer choices and realize that the last one you are left with is also wrong, don't panic. Start over and consider each choice again. There may be something you missed the first time that you will realize on the second pass.

⊘ Avoid Fact Traps

Don't be distracted by an answer choice that is factually true but doesn't answer the question. You are looking for the choice that answers the question. Stay focused on what the question is asking for so you don't accidentally pick an answer that is true but incorrect. Always go back to the question and make sure the answer choice you've selected actually answers the question and is not merely a true statement.

⊘ Extreme Statements

In general, you should avoid answers that put forth extreme actions as standard practice or proclaim controversial ideas as established fact. An answer choice that states the "process should be used in certain situations, if..." is much more likely to be correct than one that states the "process should be discontinued completely." The first is a calm rational statement and doesn't even make a definitive, uncompromising stance, using a hedge word *if* to provide wiggle room, whereas the second choice is far more extreme.

11

⊘ BENCHMARK

As you read through the answer choices and you come across one that seems to answer the question well, mentally select that answer choice. This is not your final answer, but it's the one that will help you evaluate the other answer choices. The one that you selected is your benchmark or standard for judging each of the other answer choices. Every other answer choice must be compared to your benchmark. That choice is correct until proven otherwise by another answer choice beating it. If you find a better answer, then that one becomes your new benchmark. Once you've decided that no other choice answers the question as well as your benchmark, you have your final answer.

⊘ PREDICT THE ANSWER

Before you even start looking at the answer choices, it is often best to try to predict the answer. When you come up with the answer on your own, it is easier to avoid distractions and traps because you will know exactly what to look for. The right answer choice is unlikely to be word-for-word what you came up with, but it should be a close match. Even if you are confident that you have the right answer, you should still take the time to read each option before moving on.

General Strategies

⊘ TOUGH QUESTIONS

If you are stumped on a problem or it appears too hard or too difficult, don't waste time. Move on! Remember though, if you can quickly check for obviously incorrect answer choices, your chances of guessing correctly are greatly improved. Before you completely give up, at least try to knock out a couple of possible answers. Eliminate what you can and then guess at the remaining answer choices before moving on.

⊘ CHECK YOUR WORK

Since you will probably not know every term listed and the answer to every question, it is important that you get credit for the ones that you do know. Don't miss any questions through careless mistakes. If at all possible, try to take a second to look back over your answer selection and make sure you've selected the correct answer choice and haven't made a costly careless mistake (such as marking an answer choice that you didn't mean to mark). This quick double check should more than pay for itself in caught mistakes for the time it costs.

⊘ PACE YOURSELF

It's easy to be overwhelmed when you're looking at a page full of questions; your mind is confused and full of random thoughts, and the clock is ticking down faster than you would like. Calm down and maintain the pace that you have set for yourself. Especially as you get down to the last few minutes of the test, don't let the small numbers on the clock make you panic. As long as you are on track by monitoring your pace, you are guaranteed to have time for each question.

⊘ DON'T RUSH

It is very easy to make errors when you are in a hurry. Maintaining a fast pace in answering questions is pointless if it makes you miss questions that you would have gotten right otherwise. Test writers like to include distracting information and wrong answers that seem right. Taking a little extra time to avoid careless mistakes can make all the difference in your test score. Find a pace that allows you to be confident in the answers that you select.

⊘ KEEP MOVING

Panicking will not help you pass the test, so do your best to stay calm and keep moving. Taking deep breaths and going through the answer elimination steps you practiced can help to break through a stress barrier and keep your pace.

Final Notes

The combination of a solid foundation of content knowledge and the confidence that comes from practicing your plan for applying that knowledge is the key to maximizing your performance on test day. As your foundation of content knowledge is built up and strengthened, you'll find that the strategies included in this chapter become more and more effective in helping you quickly sift through the distractions and traps of the test to isolate the correct answer.

Now that you're preparing to move forward into the test content chapters of this book, be sure to keep your goal in mind. As you read, think about how you will be able to apply this information on the test. If you've already seen sample questions for the test and you have an idea of the question format and style, try to come up with questions of your own that you can answer based on what you're reading. This will give you valuable practice applying your knowledge in the same ways you can expect to on test day.

Good luck and good studying!

14

Verbal Skills Test

Synonyms and Antonyms

When you understand how words relate to each other, you will discover more in a passage. This is explained by understanding **synonyms** (e.g., words that mean the same thing) and **antonyms** (e.g., words that mean the opposite of one another). As an example, *dry* and *arid* are synonyms, and *dry* and *wet* are antonyms. There are many pairs of words in English that can be considered synonyms, despite having slightly different definitions. For instance, the words *friendly* and *collegial* can both be used to describe a warm interpersonal relationship, and one would be correct to call them **synonyms**. However, *collegial* (kin to *colleague*) is often used in reference to professional or academic relationships, and *friendly* has no such connotation. If the difference between two words is too great, then they should not be called synonyms. *Hot* and *warm* are not synonyms because their meanings are too distinct. A good way to determine whether two words are synonyms is to substitute one word for the other word and verify that the meaning of the sentence has not changed. Substituting *warm* for *hot* in a sentence would convey a different meaning. Although warm and hot may seem close in meaning, warm generally means that the temperature is moderate, and hot generally means that the temperature is excessively high.

Antonyms are words with opposite meanings. *Light* and *dark*, *up* and *down*, *right* and *left*, *good* and *bad*: these are all sets of antonyms. Be careful to distinguish between antonyms and pairs of words that are simply different. *Black* and *gray*, for instance, are not antonyms because gray is not the opposite of black. *Black* and *white*, on the other hand, are antonyms. Not every word has an antonym. For instance, many nouns do not: What would be the antonym of chair? During your exam, the questions related to antonyms are more likely to concern adjectives. You will recall that adjectives are words that describe a noun. Some common adjectives include *purple*, *fast*, *skinny*, and *sweet*. From those four adjectives, *purple* is the item that lacks a group of obvious antonyms.

> **Review Video: What Are Synonyms and Antonyms?**
> Visit mometrix.com/academy and enter code: 105612

SYNONYM AND ANTONYM EXAMPLES

For this section, you will have one word and four choices for a synonym or antonym of that word. Before you look at the choices, try to think of a few words that could be a synonym or antonym for your question. Then, check the choices for a synonym or antonym of the question. Some words may seem close to the question, but you are looking for the best choice. So, don't let your first reaction be your final decision.

EXAMPLE 1

Insatiable most nearly means:
- A. Compensated
- B. Content
- C. Fulfilled
- D. Unsatisfied

15

EXAMPLE 2

Adherent means the opposite of:

    A. Antagonist
    B. Disciple
    C. Piquant
    D. Submissive

EXAMPLE 3

Protrude most nearly means:

    A. Contract
    B. Evocative
    C. Secede
    D. Swell

EXAMPLE 4

Unkempt means the opposite of:

    A. Disorder
    B. Flaunt
    C. Unblemished
    D. Volatile

ANSWERS

Example 1: D, Unsatisfied (Synonym)

Example 2: A, Antagonist (Antonym)

Example 3: D, Swell (Synonym)

Example 4: C, Unblemished (Antonym)

Analogies

DETERMINE THE RELATIONSHIP

As you try to decide on how the words in question are connected, don't jump to understand the meaning of the words. Instead, see if you can find the **relationship** between the two words. To understand the relationship, you can start by creating a sentence that links the two words and puts them into perspective. At first, try to use a simple sentence to find a connection. Then, go through each answer choice and replace the words in the answer choices with the parts of your simple sentence. Depending on the question, you may need to make changes to your sentence to make it more specific.

EXAMPLE:

Wood is to fire as

Simple Sentence: *Wood* feeds a *fire* as

Wood is to fire as

> A. Farmer is to cow
> B. Gasoline is to engine

Using the simple sentence, you would state "Farmer feeds a cow" which is correct. Yet, the next answer choice "Gasoline feeds an engine" is also true. So, which is the correct answer? With this simple sentence, we need to be more **specific**.

Specific Sentences: "Wood feeds a fire and is consumed" / "Wood is burned in a fire"

These specific sentences show that answer choice (A) is incorrect and answer choice (B) is clearly correct. With the specific sentences, you have "Gasoline feeds an engine and is consumed" is correct. Also, "Farmer feeds a cow and is consumed" is clearly incorrect. If your simple sentence seems correct with more than one answer choice, then keep making changes until only one answer choice makes sense.

ELIMINATING SIMILARITIES

This method works well in the Analogies section and the Synonyms/Antonyms section. You can start by looking over the answer choices and see what clues they provide. If there are any common relationships between the pairs of terms, then those answer choices have to be **wrong**.

EXAMPLE:

Tough is to rugged as
> A. Soft is to hard
> B. Clear is to foggy
> C. Inhale is to exhale
> D. Rigid is to taut

In this example, tough and rugged are synonyms. Also, the first three answer choices are antonyms. You may not realize that taut and rigid are synonyms. However, it has to be correct. The reason is that you know the other answer choices all had the **same relationship** of being antonyms.

Mometrix

Word Types
EXAMPLE:
Gardener is to hedge as

> A. Wind is to rock
> B. Woodcarver is to stick

In this example, you could start with a simple sentence of "Gardener cuts away at hedges." Now, both answer choices seem correct with this sentence. For choice (A), you can say that "Wind cuts away at rocks" due to erosion. For choice (B), you can say that a "Woodcarver cuts away at sticks." The difference is that a gardener is a person, and a woodcarver is a person. However, the wind is a thing, which makes answer choice (B) correct.

Face Value

When you are not sure about an answer, you should try to accept the problem at **face value**. Don't read too much into it. These problems will not ask you to make **impossible comparisons**. The test writers are not trying to throw you off with cheap tricks. If you have to make a stretch of the question to make a connection between the two terms, then you should start over and find another relationship. Don't make the problem more difficult. These are normal questions with differences in difficulty. Sometimes the terms that go together and their relationships may not be very clear. So, you will want to read over the question and answer choices carefully.

EXAMPLE:
Odor is to smell as flavor is to
> A. believe
> B. know
> C. feel
> D. taste

Would a flavor be "known", "felt", "tasted", or "believed"? The analogy is about a synonym. So, answer choice D, which is "taste," is a synonym of flavor and is the best answer.

Read Carefully

To understand the analogies, you need to read the terms and answer choices **carefully**. You can miss the question because you misread the terms. Each question here has only a few words, so you can spend time reading them carefully. Yet, you cannot forget your time limit of the section. So, don't spend too much time on one question. Just focus on reading carefully and be sure to read all of the choices. You may find an answer choice that seems correct. Yet, when you finish reading over the choices, you may find a better choice.

Logic and Verbal Classification

LOGIC

These questions will provide you with three statements and then ask you that if the first two are true, what must the third statement be, whether true, false, or uncertain.

LOOK FOR THE OBVIOUS

Usually the nature of the first two statements will give a **clue** about what a truthful third statement will look like. Example: John runs faster than Mary. Bob runs faster than John.

Ask yourself what is probably going to be the true statement that you should expect to see as the third statement. It will likely be "Bob runs faster than Mary." Both of the given statements seem to be leading up to that statement.

If you expect that to be the third statement, then you can quickly look at the third statement and see if you are correct. If so, you know the third statement is true. If not, you will have to determine whether or not it is false or uncertain.

WATCH FOR INVERSIONS

Not only does the statement "Bob runs faster than Mary" seem to be a likely possibility, but also the **inverse**, which is "Mary runs slower than Bob".

Don't get caught off guard and think that your predicted answer isn't the third statement. It's inverse, which is equally true, may be provided.

Example 1:

John throws faster pitches than Kyle. Greg throws faster pitches than John. Kyle throws faster pitches than Greg. If the first two statements are true, then the third is:

    A. True
    B. False
    C. Uncertain
    D. An opinion

Example 2:

Allen sent in his taxes one day after Phil. Phil sent in his taxes before Blake. Blake sent in his taxes after Allen. If the first two statements are true, then the third is:

    A. True
    B. False
    C. Uncertain
    D. A contradiction

ANSWERS

Example 1: B: We can diagram the first two sentences as follows: John > Kyle and Greg > John. In other words, Greg throws faster pitches than John and Kyle. If those statements are true, then the third statement is certainly false.

Example 2: C: We can diagram this sentence as follows: Phil > Allen; Phil > Blake. In other words, Phil sent in his taxes before Allen and before Blake. We do not have enough information to determine whether Allen > Blake is true.

VERBAL CLASSIFICATION

These questions will give you a list of four words and ask you to determine which does not belong with the others.

FIND THE COMMON GROUND

The common ground is the characteristics that all of the words have in common. All but one that is. Once you've identified the **common characteristic** shared by three of the words, you know which is your correct answer, because it does not share that same characteristic.

Example:

   A. bass
   B. salmon
   C. moose
   D. tuna

In the example above, answer choices a, b, and d all share one thing in common. They are fish. The lone exception is answer choice c, which is moose and is not a species of fish.

WATCH OUT FOR GENERIC TYPES

Usually the answer choices will provide **specific** examples of a certain thing. If the more **generic** name of the common characteristic is given, it is usually wrong.

Example:

   A. bass
   B. salmon
   C. fish
   D. tuna

At first glance these all seem the same. They are all fish, right? Wrong. Three of them are species of fish. Answer choice c, "fish" is not a species of fish, but is rather the name of the category the other answer choices fall into.

Example:

   A. football
   B. basketball
   C. tennis
   D. sports

Notice the similarity in examples. Here again all four answer choices seem similar. The first three are types of sporting activities. The last is the name of the category the others fall into. Choice d does *not* belong.

Reading Comprehension Test

Informational Text

PARTS OF A PASSAGE

An **introduction** has a summary of the passage and the thesis statement. The purpose of the introduction is to grab the reader's attention. To win the reader's attention, authors may use a quote, question, or strong opinion. Some authors choose to use an interesting description or puzzling statement. Also, the introduction is the place that authors use to explain their reason for writing.

Following the introduction, **body paragraphs** are used to explain the thesis statement. A body paragraph has a topic sentence that may be found in the first sentence. In these paragraphs, there is evidence that helps the argument of the paragraph. Also, the author may have commentary on the evidence. Be careful because this commentary can be filled with bias.

> **Review Video: How to Write a Body Paragraph**
> Visit mometrix.com/academy and enter code: 724590

The **topic sentence** gives the paragraph's subject and the main idea. The rest of the body paragraph should be linked to the topic sentence. Again, the topic sentence should be explained with facts, details, and examples.

The topic sentence is general and covers the ideas in a body paragraph. Sometimes, the topic sentence may be implied (i.e., the sentence is not stated directly by the author). Also, the topic sentence shows the connections among the supporting details.

The **conclusion** should provide a summary on the passage. New material is not given in the conclusion. The conclusion is the final paragraph that may have a call to action (i.e., something the writer wants readers to do) or a question for the reader to think about.

ORGANIZATION OF THE PASSAGE

The way a passage is organized can help readers to understand the author's purpose and his or her conclusions. There are many ways to organize a passage, and each one has an important use.

Some nonfiction texts are organized to **present a problem** followed by a solution. For this type of passage, the problem is explained before the solution is given. When the problem is well known, the solution may be given in a few sentences at the beginning. Other passages may focus on the solution, and the problem will be talked about only a few times. Some passages will outline many solutions to a problem. This will leave you to choose among the possible solutions. If authors have loyalty to one solution, they may not describe some of the other solutions. Be careful with the author's plan when reading a problem-solution passage. When you know the author's point of view, you can make a better judgment of the author's solution.

Sometimes authors will organize information clearly for you to follow and locate the information. However, this is not always the case with passages in an exam. Two common ways to order a passage are cause and effect and chronological order. When using **chronological order** (i.e., a plan that moves in order from the first step to the last), the author gives information in the order that the event happened. For example, biographies are written in chronological order. The person's birth and childhood are first. Their adult life is next. The events leading up to the person's death are last.

In **cause and effect** passages, an author shows one thing that makes something else happen. For example, if one were to go to bed very late and wake up very early, then they would be tired in the morning. The cause is a lack of sleep, with the effect of being tired the next day.

Finding the cause-and-effect relationships in a passage can be tricky. Often, these relationships come with certain words or terms. When authors use words like *because, since, in order*, and *so*, they are describing a cause and effect relationship. Think about the sentence: *He called her because he needed the homework.* This is a simple causal relationship. The cause was his need for the homework, and the effect was his phone call. Yet, not all cause and effect relationships are marked like this. Think about the sentences: *He called her. He needed the homework.* When the cause-and-effect relationship does not come with a keyword, the relationship can be known by asking why. For example, *He called her*. Why did he call her? The answer is in the next sentence: He needed the homework.

> **Review Video: Rhetorical Strategy of Cause-and-Effect Analysis**
> Visit mometrix.com/academy and enter code: 725944

When authors try to change the minds of readers, they may use cause-and-effect relationships. However, these relationships should not always be taken at face value. To read a persuasive essay well, you need to judge the cause-and-effect relationships. For example, imagine an author wrote the following: *The parking deck has not been making money because people want to ride their bikes.* The relationship is clear: the cause is that people want to ride their bikes. The effect is that the parking deck has not been making money. However, you should look at this argument again. Maybe there are other reasons that the parking deck was not a success: a bad economy, too many costs, etc.

Many passages follow the **compare-and-contrast** model. In this model, the similarities and differences between two ideas or things are reviewed. A review of the similarities between ideas is called comparison. In a perfect comparison, the author shows ideas or things in the same way. If authors want to show the similarities between football and baseball, then they can list the equipment and rules for each game. Think about the similarities as they appear in the passage and take note of any differences.

Careful thinking about ideas and conclusions can seem like a difficult task. You can make this task easy by understanding the basic parts of ideas and writing skills. Looking at the way that ideas link to others is a good way for you to begin. Sometimes authors will write about two ideas that are against each other. Other times, an author will support a topic, and another author will argue against the topic. The review of these rival ideas is known as **contrast**. In contrast, all ideas should be presented clearly. If the author does favor a side, you need to read carefully to find where the author shows or hides this favoritism. Also, as you read the passage, you should write out how one side views the other.

> **Review Video: Compare and Contrast**
> Visit mometrix.com/academy and enter code: 798319

CONTEXT

Learning new words is an important part of **comprehending** and **integrating** unfamiliar information. When a reader encounters a new word, he can stop and find it in the dictionary or the glossary of terms, but sometimes those reference tools aren't readily available or using them at the moment is impractical (e.g., during a test). Furthermore, most readers are usually not willing to take the time. Another way to determine the meaning of a word is by considering the **context** in which it is being used. These indirect learning hints are called **context clues**. They include definitions, descriptions, examples, and restatements. Because most words are learned by listening to conversations, people use this tool all the time even if they do it unconsciously. But to be effective in written text, context clues must be used judiciously because the unfamiliar word may have several subtle variations, and therefore the context clues could be misinterpreted.

Context refers to how a word is **used in a sentence**. Identifying context can help determine the definition of unknown words. There are different contextual clues such as definition, description, example, comparison, and contrast. The following are examples:

- **Definition**: the unknown word is clearly defined by the previous words. – "When he was painting, his instrument was a __." (paintbrush)
- **Description**: the unknown word is described by the previous words. – "I was hot, tired, and thirsty; I was __." (dehydrated)
- **Example**: the unknown word is part of a series of examples. – "Water, soda, and __ were the offered beverages." (coffee)
- **Comparison**: the unknown word is compared to another word. – "Barney is agreeable and happy like his __ parents." (positive)
- **Contrast**: the unknown word is contrasted with another word. – "I prefer cold weather to __ conditions." (hot)

> **Review Video: Context Clues**
> Visit mometrix.com/academy and enter code: 613660

On standardized tests, as well as in everyday life, you may be faced with words that you are not familiar with. In most cases, the definition of an unknown word can be derived from context clues. The term "context clues" refers to the ways or manner in which a word is used. When reading a passage, students should carefully examine the unfamiliar word and the words and sentences that surround it. The writer may have provided a **definition** in parentheses following the word, or the writer may have provided a **synonym**. Synonyms are useful because they offer a common substitute for the unfamiliar word. Also, the author may have provided an antonym, or opposite, for the unfamiliar word. Finally, a context clue might be found in the prior or later **restatement** of the idea that contained the word, and sometimes the writer may have even provided a detailed **explanation** of the unfamiliar word.

LITERAL COMPREHENSION

A reader should always be drawing conclusions from the text. Sometimes conclusions are implied from written information, and other times the information is **stated directly** within the passage. One should always aim to draw conclusions from information stated within a passage, rather than to draw them from mere **implications**. At times an author may provide some information and then describe a counterargument. Readers should be alert for direct statements that are subsequently rejected or weakened by the author. Furthermore, you should always read through the entire passage before drawing conclusions. Many readers are trained to expect the author's conclusions at either the beginning or the end of the passage, but many texts do not adhere to this format.

INFERENTIAL COMPREHENSION

Drawing conclusions from information implied within a passage requires confidence on the part of the reader. **Implications** are things that the author does not state directly, but readers can assume based on what the author does say. Consider the following passage: *I stepped outside and opened my umbrella. By the time I got to work, the cuffs of my pants were soaked.* The author never states that it is raining, but this fact is clearly implied. **Conclusions** based on implication must be well supported by the text. In order to draw a solid conclusion, readers should have multiple pieces of evidence. If readers have only one piece, they must be assured that there is no other possible explanation than their conclusion. A good reader will be able to draw many conclusions from information implied by the text, which will be a great help in the exam.

Readers are often required to understand a text that claims and suggests ideas without stating them directly. An **inference** is a piece of information that is implied but not written outright by the author. For instance, consider the following sentence: *After the final out of the inning, the fans were filled with joy and rushed the field.* From this sentence, a reader can infer that the fans were watching a baseball game and their team won the game. Readers should take great care to avoid using information beyond the provided passage before making inferences. As you practice drawing inferences, you will find that they require concentration and attention.

> **Review Video: Inference**
> Visit mometrix.com/academy and enter code: 379203

One of the most important skills in reading comprehension is the identification of **topics** and **main ideas.** There is a subtle difference between these two features. The topic is the **subject** of a text (i.e., what the text is all about). The main idea, on the other hand, is the **most important point** being made by the author. The topic is usually expressed in a few words at the most while the main idea often needs a full sentence to be completely defined. As an example, a short passage might have the topic of penguins and the main idea could be written as *Penguins are different from other birds in many ways.* In most nonfiction writing, the topic and the main idea will be stated directly and often appear in a sentence at the very beginning or end of the text. When being tested on an understanding of the author's topic, you may be able to skim the passage for the general idea, by reading only the first sentence of each paragraph. A body paragraph's first sentence is often—but not always—the main topic sentence which gives you a summary of the content in the paragraph.

However, there are cases in which the reader must figure out an **unstated** topic or main idea. In these instances, you must read every sentence of the text and try to come up with an overarching idea that is supported by each of those sentences.

Note: A **thesis statement** should not be confused with the main idea of the passage. While the main idea gives a brief, general summary of a text, the thesis statement provides a specific perspective on an issue that the author supports with evidence.

> **Review Video: Topics and Main Ideas**
> Visit mometrix.com/academy and enter code: 407801

Supporting details provide evidence and backing for the main point. In order to show that a main idea is correct, or valid, authors add details that prove their point. All texts contain details, but they are only classified as supporting details when they serve to reinforce some **larger point**. Supporting details are most commonly found in informative and persuasive texts. In some cases, they will be clearly indicated with terms like *for example* or *for instance*, or they will be enumerated with terms like *first, second,* and *last.* However, you need to be prepared for texts that do not contain those indicators. As a reader, you should consider whether the author's supporting details really back up his or her main point. Supporting details can be factual and correct, yet they may not be relevant to the author's point. Conversely, supporting details can seem pertinent, but they can be ineffective because they are based on opinion or assertions that cannot be proven.

> **Review Video: Supporting Details**
> Visit mometrix.com/academy and enter code: 396297

An example of a **main idea** is: *Giraffes live in the Serengeti of Africa*. A **supporting detail** about giraffes could be: *A giraffe in this region benefits from a long neck by reaching twigs and leaves on tall trees.* The main idea expresses that the text is about giraffes in general. The supporting detail gives a specific fact about how the giraffes eat.

Readers must often **draw conclusions** about the information they have read. When asked for a *conclusion* that may be drawn, look for critical "hedge" phrases, such as *likely, may, can, will often*, among many others. When you are being tested on this knowledge, remember the question that writers insert into these hedge phrases to cover every possibility. Often an answer will be wrong simply because there is no room for exception. Extreme positive or negative answers (such as always or never) are usually not correct. The reader should not use any outside knowledge that is not gathered from the passage to answer the related questions. Correct answers can be derived straight from the passage.

Text evidence is the information that supports a main argument or minor argument. This evidence, or proof, can lead you to a conclusion. Information used as text evidence is clear, descriptive, and full of facts. Supporting details give evidence to back-up an argument.

For example, a passage may state that winter occurs during opposite months in the Northern hemisphere (i.e., north of the equator) and Southern hemisphere (i.e., south of the equator). Text evidence for this claim may include a list of countries where winter occurs in opposite months. Also, you may be given reasons that winter occurs at different times of the year in these hemispheres (e.g., the tilt of the earth as it rotates around the sun).

> **Review Video: Textual Evidence**
> Visit mometrix.com/academy and enter code: 486236

INDUCTIVE AND DEDUCTIVE REASONING

Inductive reasoning is a method of logic that uses particulars to draw a **general** conclusion. The inductive reasoning process starts with **data**. For example, if someone observes for several months that zebras have stripes, then they may conclude that all zebras in existence have stripes. This individual's conclusion (e.g., that all zebras in existence have stripes) is not considered definite since every zebra in existence has not been observed. Unless every piece of data is examined, conclusions are based on probabilities. As another example, inductive reasoning is used to make **inferences** about the universe. The entire universe has not been examined, but inferences can be made based on observations about what has been examined from the universe. These inferences may be proven false when more data is available, but they are valid at the time they are made from observable data.

Deductive reasoning involves the use of general facts or premises to come to a **specific** conclusion. For example: *Susan is a sophomore in high school*, and *all sophomores take geometry*. Thus, one can infer that *Susan takes geometry*. The word *all* does not allow for exceptions. If all sophomores take geometry, then the assertion that Susan has a geometry class is a logical

25

conclusion. As an intelligent reader, you need to recognize inductive and deductive reasoning so you can follow the line of an argument and determine if the inference or conclusion is valid.

> **Review Video: Inductive and Deductive Reasoning**
> Visit mometrix.com/academy and enter code: 507014

LOGICAL FALLACIES

A logical fallacy is a failure of reasoning. As a reader, you want to recognize logical fallacies because they diminish the value of the author's message. The four most common logical fallacies in writing are the false analogy, circular reasoning, false dichotomy, and overgeneralization.

In a **false analogy**, the author suggests that two things are similar when they are **different**. This fallacy is committed when the author is attempting to convince readers that something unknown is like something relatively familiar. The author takes advantage of the reader's ignorance to make this false comparison. One example might be the following statement: *Failing to tip a waitress is like stealing money out of somebody's wallet.* To compare stingy diners with thieves is a false analogy. While failing to tip is considered very rude, people are not arrested for their failure to tip as they would be for stealing money from someone's wallet.

Circular reasoning is a difficult logical fallacy to identify because the fallacy is typically hidden behind dense language and complicated sentences. Reasoning is described as circular when the argument offers no support for assertions other than **restating** them in different words. Put another way, a circular argument refers to itself as evidence of truth. A simple example of a circular argument is when a person uses a word to define itself, such as: *Niceness is the state of being nice.* If you do not know what *nice* means, then this definition will not be very useful. In a text, circular reasoning is more complex. For instance, an author may write: *Poverty is a problem for society because poverty creates trouble for people throughout the community.* Do you notice the redundancy within the statement that poverty is a problem because it creates trouble? When authors engage in circular reasoning, they either have not given sufficient thought to the argument, or they have not come up with any legitimate justifications for the argument.

A common logical fallacy is the **false dichotomy**. With this logical fallacy, the author creates an artificial sense that there are **only two possible options** in a situation. This fallacy is common when the author has an agenda and wants to give the impression that his or her view is the only sensible one. A false dichotomy has the effect of limiting the reader's options and imagination. An example of a false dichotomy: *You need to go to the party with me, otherwise you'll just be bored at home.* The speaker suggests that the only other possibility besides being at the party is being bored at home. Of course, this is not a true statement, since, one is able to be entertained at home or to go somewhere other than the party. When authors limit alternatives, you are always wise to ask whether they are being valid.

Overgeneralization is a logical fallacy where the author makes a **broad claim** that cannot be proved or disproved. In most cases, overgeneralization occurs when authors want to create an illusion of authority, or when they are using sensational language to sway the opinion of the reader. For example: *Everybody knows that she is a terrible teacher.* In this sentence, the author makes an assumption that cannot be true. This kind of statement is made when the author wants to create the illusion of consensus when none exists. Perhaps most people have a negative view of the teacher but to say that *everybody* feels that way is an exaggeration. When you spot overgeneralization, you

should become skeptical about the author's argument because the author may hide a weak or unsupported assertion behind authoritative language.

Review Video: Logical Fallacies
Visit mometrix.com/academy and enter code: 644845

When considering problems and solutions, the full range of possible options should be mentioned before recommending one solution above others. It is unfair to say that there are only two options, when there can be more options. When you are faced with a choice between a preferred option and a clearly inferior one, the author is committing the "either...or" fallacy. All reasonable alternatives should be included in the possible solutions.

Assumptions are claims that are taken to be true without **proof**. If a claim is controversial, proof should be provided to verify the assumption. So, any assumption that is subject to debate and cannot be accepted without supporting evidence is suspect.

PURPOSES FOR WRITING

In order to be an effective reader, one must pay attention to the author's **position** and **purpose**. Even those texts that seem objective and impartial, like textbooks, have a position and bias. Readers need to take these positions into account when considering the author's message. When an author uses emotional language or clearly favors one side of an argument, his or her **position** is clear. However, the author's position may be evident not only in what he or she writes, but also in what he or she doesn't write. In a normal setting, a reader would want to review some other texts on the same topic in order to develop a view of the author's position. If this was not possible, then you would want to acquire some background about the author. However, since you are in the middle of an exam and the only source of information is the text, you should look for language and argumentation that seems to indicate a particular stance on the subject.

Review Video: Author's Position
Visit mometrix.com/academy and enter code: 827954

Usually, identifying the **purpose** of an author is easier than identifying his or her position. In most cases, the author has no interest in hiding his or her purpose. A text that is meant to entertain, for instance, should be written to please the reader. Most narratives, or stories, are written to **entertain**, though they may also inform or persuade. **Informative** texts are easy to identify, while the most difficult purpose of a text to identify is **persuasion** because the author has an interest in making this purpose hard to detect. When a reader discovers that the author is trying to persuade, he or she should be skeptical of the argument. For this reason, persuasive texts often try to establish an entertaining tone and hope to amuse the reader into agreement. On the other hand, an informative tone may be implemented to create an appearance of authority and objectivity.

An author's purpose is evident often in the **organization** of the text (e.g., section headings in bold font points to an informative text). However, you may not have such organization available to you in your exam. Instead, if the author makes his or her main idea clear from the beginning, then the likely purpose of the text is to inform. If the author begins by making a claim and provides various arguments to support that claim, then the purpose is probably to persuade. If the author tells a story or seems to want the attention of the reader more than to push a particular point or deliver information, then his or her purpose is most likely to entertain. As a reader, you must judge authors on how well they **accomplish their purpose**. In other words, you need to consider the type of passage (e.g., technical, persuasive, etc.) that the author has written and whether the author has followed the requirements of the passage type.

Review Video: **Understanding the Author's Intent**
Visit mometrix.com/academy and enter code: 511819

The author's purpose for writing will affect his or her writing style and the response of the reader. In a **persuasive essay**, the author is attempting to change the reader's mind or convince him or her of something that he or she did not believe previously. There are several identifying characteristics of persuasive writing. One is *opinion presented as fact*. When authors attempt to persuade readers, they often present their opinions as if they were fact. Readers must be on guard for statements that sound factual but which cannot be subjected to research, observation, or experiment. Another characteristic of persuasive writing is *emotional language*. An author will often try to play on the emotions of readers by appealing to their sympathy or sense of morality. When an author uses colorful or evocative language with the intent of arousing the reader's passions, then the author may be attempting to persuade. Finally, in many cases, a persuasive text will give an *unfair explanation of opposing positions*, if these positions are mentioned at all.

An **informative text** is written to educate and enlighten readers. Informative texts are almost always nonfiction and are rarely structured as a story. The intention of an informative text is to deliver information in the most comprehensible way. So, look for the structure of the text to be very clear. In an informative text, the thesis statement is one or two sentences that normally appears at the end of the first paragraph. The author may use some colorful language, but he or she is likely to put more emphasis on clarity and precision. Informative essays do not typically appeal to the emotions. They often contain facts and figures and rarely include the opinion of the author; however, readers should remain aware of the possibility for a bias as those facts are presented. Sometimes a persuasive essay can resemble an informative essay, especially if the author maintains an even tone and presents his or her views as if they were established fact.

The success or failure of an author's intent to **entertain** is determined by those who read the author's work. Entertaining texts may be either fiction or nonfiction, and they may describe real or imagined people, places, and events. Entertaining texts are often narratives or poems. A text that is written to entertain is likely to contain colorful language that engages the imagination and the emotions. Such writing often features a great deal of figurative language, which typically enlivens the subject matter with images and analogies.

Though an entertaining text is not usually written to persuade or inform, authors may accomplish both of these tasks in their work. An entertaining text may appeal to the reader's emotions and cause him or her to think differently about a particular subject. In any case, entertaining texts tend to showcase the personality of the author more than other types of writing.

When an author intends to **express feelings,** he or she may use expressive and bold language. An author may write with emotion for any number of reasons. Sometimes, authors will express feelings because they are describing a personal situation of great pain or happiness. In other situations, authors will attempt to persuade the reader and will use emotion to stir up the passions. This kind of expression is easy to identify when the writer uses phrases like *I felt* and *I sense*. However, readers may find that the author will simply describe feelings without introducing them. As a reader, you must know the importance of recognizing when an author is expressing emotion and not to become overwhelmed by sympathy or passion. Readers should maintain some detachment so that they can still evaluate the strength of the author's argument or the quality of the writing.

In a sense, almost all writing is descriptive, insofar as an author seeks to describe events, ideas, or people to the reader. Some texts, however, are primarily concerned with **description**. A descriptive text focuses on a particular subject and attempts to depict the subject in a way that will be clear to readers. Descriptive texts contain many adjectives and adverbs (i.e., words that give shades of meaning and create a more detailed mental picture for the reader). A descriptive text fails when it is unclear to the reader. A descriptive text will certainly be informative and may be persuasive and entertaining as well.

As opposed to a main idea, themes are seldom expressed directly in a text and can be difficult to identify. A **theme** is an issue, an idea, or a question raised by the text. For instance, a theme of *Cinderella* (the Charles Perrault version) is perseverance as the title character serves her step-sisters and step-mother, and the prince seeks to find the girl with the missing slipper. A passage may have many themes, and a dedicated reader must take care to identify only themes that you are asked to find. One common characteristic of themes is that they raise more questions than they answer. In a good piece of fiction, authors are trying to elevate the reader's perspective and encourage him or her to consider the themes in a deeper way. In the process of reading, one can identify themes by constantly asking about the general issues that the text is addressing. A good way to evaluate an author's approach to a theme is to begin reading with a question in mind (e.g., How does this text approach the theme of love?) and to look for evidence in the text that addresses that question.

> **Review Video: Themes in Literature**
> Visit mometrix.com/academy and enter code: 732074

OPINIONS, FACTS, AND PREDICTIONS

Critical thinking skills are mastered through understanding various **types** of writing and the different **purposes** of authors in writing their passages. Every author writes for a purpose. When you understand their purpose and how they accomplish their goal, you will be able to analyze their writing and determine whether or not you agree with their conclusions.

Readers must always be conscious of the distinction between fact and opinion. A **fact** can be subjected to analysis and can be either proved or disproved. An **opinion**, on the other hand, is the author's personal thoughts or feelings which may not be alterable by research or evidence. If the author writes that the distance from New York to Boston is about two hundred miles, then he or she is stating a fact. If an author writes that New York is too crowded, then he or she is giving an opinion because there is no objective standard for overpopulation. An opinion may be indicated by words like *believe*, *think*, or *feel*. Readers must be aware that an *opinion may be supported by facts*. For instance, the author might give the population density of New York as a reason for an overcrowded population. An opinion supported by fact tends to be more convincing. On the other hand, when authors support their opinions with other opinions, readers should not be persuaded by the argument to any degree.

When you have an **argumentative passage**, you need to be sure that facts are presented to the reader from **reliable sources**. An opinion is what the author thinks about a given topic. An opinion is not common knowledge or proven by expert sources, instead the information is the personal beliefs and thoughts of the author. To distinguish between fact and opinion, a reader needs to consider the type of source that is presenting information, the information that backs up a claim, and the author's motivation to have a certain point-of-view on a given topic. For example, if a panel of scientists has conducted multiple studies on the effectiveness of taking a certain vitamin, then the results are more likely to be factual than a company that is selling a vitamin and claims that taking the vitamin can produce positive effects. The company is motivated to sell their product, and the scientists are using the scientific method to prove a theory. Remember: if you find sentences that contain phrases such as "I think…", then the statement is an opinion.

Review Video: <u>Fact or Opinion</u>
Visit mometrix.com/academy and enter code: 870899

In their attempts to **persuade**, writers often make mistakes in their thinking patterns and writing choices. These patterns and choices are important to understand so you can make an informed decision. Every author has a point-of-view, but authors demonstrate a **bias** when they ignore reasonable counterarguments or distort opposing viewpoints. A bias is evident whenever the author is unfair or inaccurate in his or her presentation. Bias may be intentional or unintentional, and readers should be skeptical of the author's argument. Remember that a biased author may still be correct; however, the author will be correct in spite of his or her bias, not because of the bias. A **stereotype** is like a bias, yet a stereotype is applied specifically to a group or place. Stereotyping is considered to be particularly abhorrent because the practice promotes negative generalizations about people. Readers should be very cautious of authors who stereotype in their writing. These faulty assumptions typically reveal the author's ignorance and lack of curiosity.

Review Video: <u>Bias and Stereotype</u>
Visit mometrix.com/academy and enter code: 644829

When reading a good passage, readers are moved to engage actively in the text. One part of being an active reader involves making predictions. A **prediction** is a guess about what will happen next. Readers constantly make predictions based on what they have read and what they already know. Consider the following sentence: *Staring at the computer screen in shock, Kim blindly reached over for the brimming glass of water on the shelf to her side.* The sentence suggests that Kim is agitated, and that she is not looking at the glass that she is going to pick up. So, a reader might predict that Kim is going to knock over the glass. Of course, not every prediction will be accurate: perhaps Kim will pick the glass up cleanly. Nevertheless, the author has certainly created the expectation that the water might be spilled. Predictions are always subject to revision as the reader acquires more information.

Review Video: <u>Predictive Reading</u>
Visit mometrix.com/academy and enter code: 437248

Test-taking tip: To respond to questions requiring future predictions, your answers should be based on evidence of past or present behavior.

EVALUATING A PASSAGE

When you read informational passages, you need to make a conclusion from the author's writing. You can **identify a logical conclusion** (i.e., find a conclusion that makes sense) to know whether you agree or disagree with an author. Coming to this conclusion is like making an inference. You combine the information from the passage with what you already know. From the passage's information and your knowledge, you can come to a conclusion that makes sense. One way to have a conclusion that makes sense is to take notes of all the author's points. When the notes are organized, they may point to the logical conclusion. Another way to reach conclusions is to ask if the author's passage raises any helpful questions. Sometimes you will be able to draw many conclusions from a passage. Yet, some of these may be conclusions that were never imagined by the author. Therefore, find reasons in the passage for the conclusions that you make.

Review Video: How to Support a Conclusion
Visit mometrix.com/academy and enter code: 281653

A text is **credible**, or believable, when the author is both knowledgeable and objective. When evaluating the credibility of a text, it is important to look at the author of the text. The author's motive should be the dissemination of information. When an author writes a persuasive text, his motive is to persuade the reader to do or believe something. If a text is being written by an author with a specific agenda (e.g., a business owner seeking more profit), that text is going to be biased in a particular direction. The author's motivations for writing the text play a critical role in determining the credibility of the text and must be evaluated when assessing that credibility.

Literary Text

LITERARY GENRES

A literary genre is used to put different pieces of passages into the basic groups of poetry, drama, fiction, and nonfiction. These basic groups can be broken down further into subgroups. Novels, novellas, and short stories are subgroups of fiction. Drama may also be divided into the main subgroups of comedy and tragedy. Subgroups of nonfiction are journals, textbooks, biographies, and journalism (e.g., newspapers). The differences between genres can be difficult to see. Some examples combine groups like the *nonfiction novel* and *poetic novel*.

Review Video: Types of Literary Genre
Visit mometrix.com/academy and enter code: 587617

Most fiction, nonfiction, and drama are written in prose. Prose is ordinary spoken language compared to poetry (i.e., language with metric patterns). This everyday, normal communication is known as prose. Prose can be found in textbooks, essays, reports, articles, short stories, and novels. Prose is put together with sentences. Also, there should be smooth connections among sentences. The sentences and paragraphs that you are reading right now are written in prose.

Fiction is a general term for any type of narrative that is invented or imagined. Your exam will have a passage that was written for your test. Or, a passage may be taken from a published work. During your exam, you may recognize a passage that you have read. In this case, you still need to follow the rule of reading the passage once. Then, go to the test questions. This rule applies to the other genres as well. Now, let's start with fiction.

Fiction has many subgroups, but the genre can be put into three main subgroups:

- **Short stories**: a fictional passage that has fewer than 20,000 words. Short stories have only a few characters and normally have one important event. The short story began in magazines in the late 1800s.
- **Novels**: longer works of fiction that may have many characters and a far-reaching plot. The attention may be on an event, action, social problem, or an experience. Note: novels may be written like poetry.
- **Novellas**: a work of fiction that is longer than a short story, but shorter than a novel. Novellas may also be called short novels or novelettes. They come from the German tradition and have increased in popularity across the world.

Many elements influence a work of fiction. Some important ones are:

- **Speech and dialogue**: Dialogue is the communication among characters. These characters may speak for themselves. Or, the narrator may share what a character has spoken. This speech or dialogue may seem realistic or obviously imaginary. The choice depends on the author's purpose.
- **External and internal conflict**: External conflict is the action and events that are around the character. Internal conflict is the thoughts and feelings that bother a character. This conflict that happens inside a character is used to develop the plot. Or, the internal conflict can be used to show the growth or lack of growth in a character.
- **Dramatic involvement**: Some narrators want readers to join with the events of the story (e.g., Thornton Wilder's *Our Town*). Other authors try to separate themselves from readers with figurative language.

- **Action**: The events that continue the plot, such as interactions between characters and physical movement and conflict.
- **Duration**: The amount of time that passes in the passage may be long or short. If the author gives an amount of time (e.g., three days later), then that information is important to remember.
- **Setting and description**: Is the setting (i.e., time and place within the passage) important to the plot or characters? How are the action scenes described?
- **Themes**: This is any point of view or topic that is given constant attention.
- **Symbolism**: Authors may share what they mean through imagery and other figurative devices. For example, smoke can be a symbol of danger, and doves are often symbols of peace.

Read slowly and carefully through passages of fiction. The story can become so interesting that the language of the passage (i.e., the author's choice of vocabulary) is forgotten. A reward of careful reading is to see how the author uses different language to describe familiar objects, events, or feelings. Some passages have you focus on an author's unusual use of language. Other passages may make the characters or storyline important. The events of a story are not always the most important parts in a passage. You may find that reading carefully is difficult at first. However, the rewards are greater than the early struggle.

Plot lines are one way to show the information given in a story. Every plot line has the same stages. You can find each of these stages in every story that you read. These stages include the introduction, rising action, conflict, climax, falling action, and resolution. The introduction tells you the point of the story and sets up the plot. The rising action is the events that lead up to the conflict (i.e., an internal or external problem) with the climax at the peak. The falling action is the events that come after the climax of the conflict. The resolution is the conclusion and may have the final solution to the problem in the conflict. A plot line looks like this:

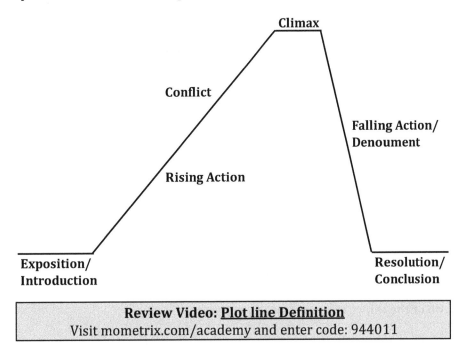

Review Video: Plot line Definition
Visit mometrix.com/academy and enter code: 944011

Most passages put events in chronological order. However, some authors may use an unusual order to have a particular influence on readers. For example, many of the Greek epics begin *in medias res*

33

(i.e., in the middle of things). The passage begins with an introduction to the climax. Then, the author goes to the beginning and shares how events came to that climax. This order is found in many mystery novels. First, a crime is committed. Then, a detective must go back and piece together the events that led to the crime. As you read, try to keep in mind the cause-and-effect relationships that shape the story. A cause must come before an effect. So, use an outline of the different causes and effects in a passage. Be sure that this outline will show the correct chronological order. Remember that the order of events in a story is not always the order that they happened.

The **narrator** can give insight about the purpose of the work and the main themes and ideas. There are important questions to ask about understanding the voice and role of the narrator:

- Who is the narrator of the passage? What is the narrator's perspective: first person or third person? Is the narrator involved in the plot? Are there changes in narrators?
- Does the narrator explain things in the passage? Or, are things explained with the plot and events? Does the narrator give special description to one character or event and not to others? A narrator may express approval or disapproval about a character or events in the work.
- Tone is the attitude of a character through his or her words. If the narrator is involved in the story, how is the narrator addressing others? Is the tone casual or formal? Close or distant? Does the narrator's vocabulary give any information about the narrator?

> **Review Video: The Narrator**
> Visit mometrix.com/academy and enter code: 742528

A **character** is someone or something that is connected closely with the plot and growth of the passage. As characters grow in a story, they move along the plot line. Characters can be named as flat or round and static or dynamic. Flat characters are simple individuals that are known for one or two things. Often, they are supporting characters to round characters. Minor flat characters are stock characters that fill out the story without influencing the outcome. Round characters, usually protagonists, are crucial to the story. They are explored widely and explained in much detail. If characters change or develop, they can be known as static or dynamic. Static characters either do not change or change very little in a passage. In other words, who they are at the beginning is who they are at the end. However, dynamic characters change over the course of a passage. In other words, who they are at the beginning is not at all who they are at the end.

> **Review Video: What is the Definition of a Character in a Story**
> Visit mometrix.com/academy and enter code: 429493

A **drama** is a play that is meant to be performed by a group. As you read drama, you should use your imagination to re-create the play with characters and settings. Fiction can be read in the same way. However, you will not have the same amount of information about the setting and characters in drama. For a drama, the information comes from the dialogue or speeches. You can help your understanding of the passage with imagination. Many dramas have some dialogue and several scenes of action. In these passages, try to imagine the events taking place. **Action** can be the events that characters do or the things that are done to a character.

There are other devices that authors use in the growth of the plot and characters. Be sure to read carefully to know which characters are speaking to others. **Asides** are moments where no characters or not every character knows that another is speaking. This may be a way of explaining the plot in a quiet way. **Soliloquies** are when the character shares thoughts and opinions out loud when they are alone or with others. So, this device gives insight to a character's motives, feelings, and emotions. Careful review of these devices provides you with many ideas on the major themes and plot of the passage.

Conversations in drama can be difficult to understand. So, your review of speech and dialogue is important as you read the passages. Authors may use speeches to develop their characters. Some characters may have a special way of speaking which highlights aspects of the drama. The placement of stresses in a dramatic dialogue can help you know how to understand a character's lines. Changes in stress are one way to shape a statement in drama. For example, "You *are coming* with me to dinner." The italicized words might mean that the speaker wants a person to come whether the person wants to or not.

You can try to add stress to understand a passage. However, be sure that you are using the surrounding context as a guide. Remember that your attempt may not be the correct one. So, be open to other possibilities. As you begin to understand the characters and situations, you will pick up on the stress of some characters. Other pieces that add to the understanding of dialogue are setting, possible reactions of the characters to a speech, and gestures of the actors.

> **Review Video: Dramas**
> Visit mometrix.com/academy and enter code: 216060

WRITING DEVICES

Style is the manner in which a writer uses language in prose or poetry. Style is affected by:

- Diction or word choices
- Sentence structure and syntax
- Types and extent of use of figurative language
- Patterns of rhythm or sound
- Conventional or creative use of punctuation

Tone is the attitude of the writer or narrator towards the theme of, subject of, or characters in a work. Sometimes the attitude is stated, but it is most often implied through word choices. Examples of tone are serious, humorous, satiric, stoic, cynical, flippant, and surprised.

Authors will use different writing devices to make their message clear for readers. One of those devices is comparison and contrast. As you read already, when authors show how two things are alike, they are **comparing** them. When authors describe how two things are different, they are **contrasting** them. The compare and contrast passage is a common part of nonfiction. Comparisons are known by certain words or phrases: *both, same, like, too,* and *as well.* Yet, contrasts may have words or phrases like *but, however, on the other hand, instead,* and *yet.* Of course, comparisons and contrasts may be understood without using those words or phrases. A single sentence may compare and contrast. Think about the sentence *Brian and Sheila love ice cream, but Brian loves vanilla and Sheila loves strawberry.* In one sentence, the author has described both a similarity (e.g., love of ice cream) and a difference (e.g., favorite flavor).

> **Review Video: Compare and Contrast**
> Visit mometrix.com/academy and enter code: 171799

Another regular writing device is **cause and effect**. A cause is an act or event that makes something happen. An effect is what comes from the cause. A cause and effect relationship is not always easy to find. So, there are some words and phrases that show causes: *since, because,* and *due to.* Words and phrases that show effects include *consequently, therefore, this lead(s) to, as a result.* For example, *Because the sky was clear, Ron did not bring an umbrella.* The cause is the clear sky, and the effect is that Ron did not bring an umbrella. Readers may find that the cause and effect relationship is not clear. For example, *He was late and missed the meeting.* This does not have any words that show cause or effect. Yet, the sentence still has a cause (e.g., he was late) and an effect (e.g., he missed the meeting).

Remember the chance for a single cause to have many effects (e.g., *Single cause*: Because you left your homework on the table, your dog eats the homework. *Many effects*: (1) As a result, you fail your homework. (2) Your parents do not let you see your friends. (3) You miss out on the new movie. (4) You miss holding the hand of an important person.).

Also, the chance of a single effect to have many causes (e.g.. *Single effect*: Alan has a fever. *Many causes*: (1) An unexpected cold front came through the area, and (2) Alan forgot to take his multi-vitamin.)

Now, an effect can become the cause of another effect. This is known as a cause and effect chain. (e.g., As a result of her hatred for not doing work, Lynn got ready for her exam. This led to her passing her test with high marks. Hence, her resume was accepted, and her application was accepted.)

Often, authors use analogies to add meaning to their passages. An **analogy** is a comparison of two things. The words in the analogy are connected by a relationship. Look at this analogy: *moo is to cow as quack is to duck.* This analogy compares the sound that a cow makes with the sound that a duck makes. What could you do if the word *quack* was not given? Well, you could finish the analogy if you know the connection between *moo* and *cow*. Relationships for analogies include synonyms, antonyms, part to whole, definition, and actor to action.

Point of view has an important influence on a passage. A passage's point of view is how the author or a character sees or thinks about things. A point of view influences the events of a passage, the meetings among characters, and the ending to the story. For example, two characters watch a child ride a bike. Character one watches outside. Character two watches from inside a house. Both see the same event, yet they are around different noises, sights, and smells. Character one may see different things that happen outside that character two cannot see from inside. Also, point of view can be influenced by past events and beliefs. For example, if character one loves bikes, then she will remember how proud she is of the child. If character two is afraid of riding bikes, then he may not remember the event or fear for the child's safety.

In fiction, the two main points of view are first person and third person. The narrator is the person who tells a story's events. The protagonist is the main character of a story. If the narrator is the protagonist in a story, then the story is written in first-person. In first person, the author writes from the view of *I*. Third-person point of view is the most common among stories. With third person, authors refer to each character by using *he* or *she* and the narrator is not involved in the story. In third-person omniscient, the narrator is not a character in the story and tells the story of all of the characters at the same time.

Transitional words and phrases are devices that guide readers through a passage. You may know the common transitions. Though you may not have thought about how they are used. Some transitional phrases (*after, before, during, in the middle of*) give information about time. Some hint that an example is about to be given (*for example, in fact, for instance*). Writers use transitions to compare (*also, likewise*) and contrast (*however, but, yet*). Transitional words and phrases can point

36

to addition (*and, also, furthermore, moreover*) and understood relationships (*if, then, therefore, as a result, since*). Finally, transitional words and phrases can separate the chronological steps (*first, second, last*).

> **Review Video: What are Transition Words?**
> Visit mometrix.com/academy and enter code: 707563

HISTORY AND CULTURE IN LITERATURE

History has an important influence on passages. The events, information, and thoughts of an author's time impact every part of his or her work. Sometimes, authors use language that would be inappropriate or wrong in a modern setting. However, those ideas were acceptable in the author's time. Think about how an event had an influence on a passage. Then, think about how today's opinions and ideas shape the way that you read passages from the past.

For example: In most societies of the past, women were treated as second-class people. Some authors who wrote in 18th-century England could be considered feminists in their time. However, you may think that they sound hateful toward women. The incorrect assumptions and prejudices of the past should not be excused or forgotten. Instead, they should be thought of as a result of their time and culture.

Studying world literature shows that writers from very different cultures write on similar themes. Dramas like the *Odyssey* and *Hamlet* focus on someone's battle for self-control and independence. In most cultures, authors write about themes of personal growth and the struggle for maturity. Another example is the conflict between the person and society. Works that are as different as *Native Son*, the *Aeneid*, and *1984* show how people try to keep their identity in large (sometimes) abusive groups. Also, many cultures have passages of the hero's or heroine's journey. For this journey, the character must overcome difficulties to gain more knowledge, power, and perspective. Some famous works of this journey are the *Epic of Gilgamesh*, Dante's *Divine Comedy*, and Cervantes' *Don Quixote*.

Authors from different genres and cultures may look at similar themes. Yet, they show these themes in different ways. For example, poets may write on a topic with images and allusions. In a play, the author may show themes with characters that are expressing different points of view. In a passage, the author does not need to write about themes directly. They can be shown with events and actions. Different movements and styles become popular in different regions. For example, in Greece and England, authors tend to use more irony. In the 1950s Latin American authors popularized the use of unusual and surreal events to show themes about real life in the genre of magical realism. Japanese authors use the well-established poetic form of the haiku to organize their treatment of common themes.

FIGURATIVE LANGUAGE

When authors want to share their message in a creative way, they use figurative language devices. Learning these devices will help you understand what you read. **Figurative language** is communication that goes beyond the actual meaning of a word or phrase. **Descriptive language** that awakens imagery in the reader's mind is one type of figurative language. Exaggeration is another type of figurative language. Also, when you compare two things, you are using figurative language. Similes and metaphors are the two main ways of comparing things. An example of a simile: *The child howled like a coyote when her mother told her to pick up the toys.* In this example, the child's howling is compared to a coyote. This helps the reader understand the sound being made by the child.

A **figure of speech** is a word or phrase that is not a part of straightforward, everyday language. Figures of speech are used for emphasis, fresh expression, or clearness. However, clearness of a passage may be incomplete with the use of these devices. For example: *I am going to crown you.*

The author may mean:

1. I am going to place a real crown on your head.
2. I am going to make you king or queen of this area.
3. I am going to punch you in the head with my fist.
4. I am going to put a second checker's piece on top of your checker piece to show that it has become a king.

> **Review Video: Figures of Speech**
> Visit mometrix.com/academy and enter code: 111295

An **allusion** is a comparison of someone or something to a person or event in history or literature. Allusions that point to people or events that are a part of today's culture are called topical allusions. Those that name a specific person are known as personal allusions. For example, *His desire for power was his Achilles' heel*. This example points to Achilles: a notable hero in Greek mythology who was thought to be invincible (i.e., cannot be hurt) except for his heels. Today, the term *Achilles' heel* points to an individual's weakness.

> **Review Video: Allusions**
> Visit mometrix.com/academy and enter code: 294065

Alliteration uses a string of words which begin with the same sound or letter. Alliteration is common in prose, yet the device finds more use in poetry. An example, *We thrashed through the thick forest with our blades*. In this sentence, a *th* sound is an example of alliteration. You may hear how the phrase shows the difficulty of moving through tall grass. Now, think about the description of eyes as *glassy globes of glitter*. This is alliteration since the *gl* sound is used three times. Related to alliteration is **assonance**, the repetition of vowel sounds. For example: *Low and slow, he rolled the coal*. Assonance is used in the same way as alliteration. Remember that vowels are *a, e, i, o, u,* and *y*. **Consonance** is the repetition of consonant sounds.

> **Review Video: Alliterations Are All Around**
> Visit mometrix.com/academy and enter code: 462837

A **metaphor** is the comparison of one thing with a different thing. For example: *The bird was an arrow flying across the sky*. In this sentence, the arrow is compared to a bird. The metaphor asks you to think about the bird in another way. Let's continue with this metaphor for a bird. You are asked to view the bird's flight as the flight of an arrow. So, you may imagine the flight to be quick and purposeful. Metaphors allow the author to describe a thing without being direct. Remember that the thing being described will not always be mentioned directly by the author. Think about a forest in winter: *Swaying skeletons reached for the sky and groaned as the wind blew through them.* In this sentence, the author uses *skeletons* as a metaphor for trees without leaves.

> **Review Video: Metaphors in Writing**
> Visit mometrix.com/academy and enter code: 133295

Metonymy is naming one thing with words or phrases of a closely related thing. This is similar to metaphor. However, the comparison has a close connection, unlike metaphor. An example of

38

metonymy is to call the news media *the press*. Of course, *the press* is the machine that prints newspapers. Metonymy is a way of naming something without using the same name constantly.

Synecdoche points to the whole by naming one of the parts. An example of synecdoche would be calling a construction worker a *hard hat*. Like metonymy, synecdoche is an easy way of naming something without having to overuse a name. The device allows writers to highlight pieces of the thing being described. For example, referring to businessmen as *suits* suggests professionalism and unity.

Hyperbole is overstatement or exaggeration. For example: *He jumped ten feet in the air when he heard the good news*. Obviously, no person can jump ten feet in the air without help. The author exaggerates because the hyperbole shares a lot of feeling. Let's say that the author shared: *He jumped when he heard the good news*. With this information, you might think that the character is not feeling very excited. Hyperbole can be dangerous if the author does not exaggerate enough. For example: *He jumped two feet in the air when he heard the good news*. You may think that the author is writing a fact. Be careful with confusing hyperboles. Some test questions may have a hyperbole and a fact listed in the answer choices.

Understatement is the opposite of hyperbole. This device discounts or downplays something. Think about someone who climbs Mount Everest. Then, they say that the journey was *a little stroll*. As with other types of figurative language, understatement has a range of uses. The device may show self-defeat or modesty as in the Mount Everest example. However, some may think of understatement as false modesty (i.e., an attempt to bring attention to you or a situation). For example, a woman is praised on her diamond engagement ring. The woman says, *Oh, this little thing?* Her understatement might be heard as stuck-up or unfeeling.

> **Review Video: Hyperbole and Understatement**
> Visit mometrix.com/academy and enter code: 308470

A **simile** is a comparison that needs the separation words *like* or *as*. Some examples: *The Sun was like an orange, eager as a beaver*, and *quick as a mountain goat*. Because a simile includes *like* or *as*, the comparison uses a different tone than a simple description of something. For example: *the house was like a shoebox*. The tone is different than the author saying that the house *was* a shoebox.

> **Review Video: Similes**
> Visit mometrix.com/academy and enter code: 642949

Personification is the explanation of a nonhuman thing with human attributes. The basic purpose of personification is to describe something in a way that readers will understand. An author says that a tree *groans* in the wind. The author does not mean that the tree is giving a low, pained sound from a mouth. However, the author means that the tree is making a noise like a human groan. Of course, this personification creates a tone of sadness or suffering. A different tone would be made if the author said that the tree *sways* or *dances*.

> **Review Video: Personification**
> Visit mometrix.com/academy and enter code: 260066

Irony is a statement that hints at the opposite of what you expect. In other words, the device is used when an author or character says one thing but means another. For example, imagine a man who is covered in mud and dressed in tattered clothes. He walks in his front door to meet his wife. Then, his wife asks him, "How was your day?" He says, "Great!" The man's response to his wife is an

39

example of irony. There is a difference between irony and sarcasm. Sarcasm is similar to irony. However, sarcasm is hurtful for the person receiving the sarcastic statement. A sarcastic statement points to the foolishness of a person to believe that a false statement is true.

> **Review Video: <u>What is the Definition of Irony?</u>**
> Visit mometrix.com/academy and enter code: 374204

As you read, you will see more words in the context of a sentence. This will strengthen your vocabulary. Be sure to read on a regular basis. This practice will increase the number of ways that you have seen a word in context. Based on experience, a person can remember how a word was used in the past and use that knowledge for a new context. For example, a person may have seen the word *gull* used to mean a bird that is found near the seashore. However, a *gull* can be a person who is tricked easily. If the word in context is used for a person, you will see the insult. After all, gulls are not thought to be very smart. Use your knowledge of a word to find comparisons. This knowledge can be used to learn a new use of a word.

Vocabulary

The **denotative** meaning of a word is the literal meaning. The **connotative** meaning goes beyond the denotative meaning to include the emotional reaction that a word may invoke. The connotative meaning often takes the denotative meaning a step further due to associations which the reader makes with the denotative meaning. Readers can differentiate between the denotative and connotative meanings by first recognizing how authors use each meaning. Most nonfiction, for example, is fact-based, and nonfiction authors rarely use flowery, figurative language. The reader can assume that the writer is using the denotative meaning of words. In fiction, the author may use the connotative meaning. Readers can determine whether the author is using the denotative or connotative meaning of a word by implementing context clues.

> **Review Video: <u>Connotation and Denotation</u>**
> Visit mometrix.com/academy and enter code: 310092

Readers can use **contrasts** to define an unfamiliar word in context. In many sentences, the author will not describe the unfamiliar word directly; instead, he or she will describe the opposite of the unfamiliar word. Thus, you are provided with some information that will bring you closer to defining the word. Consider the following example: *Despite his intelligence, Hector's low brow and bad posture made him look obtuse.* The author writes that Hector's appearance does not convey intelligence. Therefore, *obtuse* must mean unintelligent. Here is another example: *Despite the horrible weather, we were beatific about our trip to Alaska.* The word *despite* indicates that the speaker's feelings were at odds with the weather. Since the weather is described as *horrible*, then *beatific* must mean something positive.

In some cases, there will be very few contextual clues to help a reader define the meaning of an unfamiliar word. When this happens, one strategy that readers may employ is **substitution**. A good reader will brainstorm some possible synonyms for the given word, and he or she will substitute these words into the sentence. If the sentence and the surrounding passage continue to make sense, then the substitution has revealed at least some information about the unfamiliar word. Consider the sentence: *Frank's admonition rang in her ears as she climbed the mountain.* A reader unfamiliar with *admonition* might come up with some substitutions like *vow, promise, advice, complaint*, or *compliment*. All of these words make general sense of the sentence though their meanings are diverse. The process has suggested; however, that an admonition is some sort of message. The substitution strategy is rarely able to pinpoint a precise definition, but this process can be effective as a last resort.

Occasionally, you will be able to define an unfamiliar word by looking at the **descriptive words** in the context. Consider the following sentence: *Fred dragged the recalcitrant boy kicking and screaming up the stairs.* The words *dragged*, *kicking*, and *screaming* all suggest that the boy does not want to go up the stairs. The reader may assume that *recalcitrant* means something like unwilling or protesting. In this example, an unfamiliar adjective was identified.

Additionally, using **description** to define an unfamiliar noun is a common practice compared to unfamiliar adjectives, as in this sentence: *Don's wrinkled frown and constantly shaking fist identified him as a curmudgeon of the first order.* Don is described as having a *wrinkled frown and constantly shaking fist* suggesting that a *curmudgeon* must be a grumpy person. Contrasts do not always provide detailed information about the unfamiliar word, but they at least give the reader some clues.

When a word has **more than one meaning**, readers can have difficulty with determining how the word is being used in a given sentence. For instance, the verb *cleave*, can mean either *join* or *separate*. When readers come upon this word, they will have to select the definition that makes the most sense. Consider the following sentence: *Hermione's knife cleaved the bread cleanly.* Since, a knife cannot join bread together, the word must indicate separation. A slightly more difficult example would be the sentence: *The birds cleaved together as they flew from the oak tree.* Immediately, the presence of the word *together* should suggest that in this sentence *cleave* is being used to mean *join*. Discovering the intent of a word with multiple meanings requires the same tricks as defining an unknown word: look for contextual clues and evaluate the substituted words.

Language Test

Foundations of Grammar

THE EIGHT PARTS OF SPEECH

NOUNS

When you talk about a person, place, thing, or idea, you are talking about **nouns**. The two main types of nouns are **common** and **proper** nouns. Also, nouns can be abstract (i.e., general) or concrete (i.e., specific).

Common nouns are the class or group of people, places, and things (Note: Do not capitalize common nouns). Examples of common nouns:

> *People*: boy, girl, worker, manager

> *Places*: school, bank, library, home

> *Things*: dog, cat, truck, car

Proper nouns are the names of a specific person, place, or thing (Note: Capitalize all proper nouns). Examples of proper nouns:

> *People*: Abraham Lincoln, George Washington, Martin Luther King, Jr.

> *Places*: Los Angeles, California / New York / Asia

> *Things*: Statue of Liberty, Earth*, Lincoln Memorial

> *Note: When you talk about the planet that we live on, you capitalize *Earth*. When you mean the dirt, rocks, or land, you lowercase *earth*.

General nouns are the names of conditions or ideas. **Specific nouns** name people, places, and things that are understood by using your senses.

General nouns:

> *Condition*: beauty, strength

> *Idea*: truth, peace

Specific nouns:

> *People*: baby, friend, father

> *Places*: town, park, city hall

> *Things*: rainbow, cough, apple, silk, gasoline

Collective nouns are the names for a person, place, or thing that may act as a whole. The following are examples of collective nouns: *class, company, dozen, group, herd, team,* and *public.*

42

PRONOUNS

Pronouns are words that are used to stand in for a noun. A pronoun may be classified as personal, intensive, relative, interrogative, demonstrative, indefinite, and reciprocal.

Personal: *Nominative* is the case for nouns and pronouns that are the subject of a sentence. *Objective* is the case for nouns and pronouns that are an object in a sentence. *Possessive* is the case for nouns and pronouns that show possession or ownership.

SINGULAR

	Nominative	Objective	Possessive
First Person	I	me	my, mine
Second Person	you	you	your, yours
Third Person	he, she, it	him, her, it	his, her, hers, its

PLURAL

	Nominative	Objective	Possessive
First Person	we	us	our, ours
Second Person	you	you	your, yours
Third Person	they	them	their, theirs

Intensive: I myself, you yourself, he himself, she herself, the (thing) itself, we ourselves, you yourselves, they themselves

Relative: which, who, whom, whose

Interrogative: what, which, who, whom, whose

Demonstrative: this, that, these, those

Indefinite: all, any, each, everyone, either/neither, one, some, several

Reciprocal: each other, one another

> **Review Video: Nouns and Pronouns**
> Visit mometrix.com/academy and enter code: 312073

VERBS

If you want to write a sentence, then you need a verb in your sentence. Without a verb, you have no sentence. The verb of a sentence explains action or being. In other words, the verb shows the subject's movement or the movement that has been done to the subject.

TRANSITIVE AND INTRANSITIVE VERBS

A transitive verb is a verb whose action (e.g., drive, run, jump) points to a receiver (e.g., car, dog, kangaroo). Intransitive verbs do not point to a receiver of an action. In other words, the action of the verb does not point to a subject or object.

Transitive: He plays the piano. | The piano was played by him.

Intransitive: He plays. | John writes well.

A dictionary will let you know whether a verb is transitive or intransitive. Some verbs can be transitive and intransitive.

ACTION VERBS AND LINKING VERBS

An action verb is a verb that shows what the subject is doing in a sentence. In other words, an action verb shows action. A sentence can be complete with one word: an action verb. Linking verbs are intransitive verbs that show a condition (i.e., the subject is described but does no action).

Linking verbs link the subject of a sentence to a noun or pronoun, or they link a subject with an adjective. You always need a verb if you want a complete sentence. However, linking verbs are not able to complete a sentence.

Common linking verbs include *appear, be, become, feel, grow, look, seem, smell, sound,* and *taste.* However, any verb that shows a condition and has a noun, pronoun, or adjective that describes the subject of a sentence is a linking verb.

Action: He sings. | Run! | Go! | I talk with him every day. | She reads.

Linking:

Incorrect: I am.

Correct: I am John. | I smell roses. | I feel tired.

Note: Some verbs are followed by words that look like prepositions, but they are a part of the verb and a part of the verb's meaning. These are known as phrasal verbs and examples include *call off, look up,* and *drop off.*

VOICE

Transitive verbs come in active or passive voice. If the subject does an action or receives the action of the verb, then you will know whether a verb is active or passive. When the subject of the sentence is doing the action, the verb is **active voice**. When the subject receives the action, the verb is **passive voice**.

Active: Jon drew the picture. (The subject *Jon* is doing the action of *drawing a picture.*)

Passive: The picture is drawn by Jon. (The subject *picture* is receiving the action from Jon.)

VERB TENSES

A verb tense shows the different form of a verb to point to the time of an action. The present and past tense are shown by changing the verb's form. An action in the present *I talk* can change form for the past: *I talked.* However, for the other tenses, an auxiliary (i.e., helping) verb is needed to show the change in form. These helping verbs include *am, are, is | have, has, had | was, were, will* (or *shall*).

Present: I talk	Present perfect: I have talked
Past: I talked	Past perfect: I had talked
Future: I will talk	Future perfect: I will have talked

Present: The action happens at the current time.

Example: He *walks* to the store every morning.

To show that something is happening right now, use the progressive present tense: I *am walking.*

Past: The action happened in the past.

> Example: He *walked* to the store an hour ago.

Future: The action is going to happen later.

> Example: I *will walk* to the store tomorrow.

Present perfect: The action started in the past and continues into the present.

> Example: I *have walked* to the store three times today.

Past perfect: The second action happened in the past. The first action came before the second.

> Example: Before I walked to the store (Action 2), I *had walked* to the library (Action 1).

Future perfect: An action that uses the past and the future. In other words, the action is complete before a future moment.

> Example: When she comes for the supplies (future moment), I *will have walked* to the store (action completed in the past).

> Review Video: **Present Perfect, Past Perfect, and Future Perfect Verb Tenses**
> Visit mometrix.com/academy and enter code: 269472

CONJUGATING VERBS

When you need to change the form of a verb, you are **conjugating** a verb. The key parts of a verb are first person singular, present tense (dream); first person singular, past tense (dreamed); and the past participle (dreamed). Note: the past participle needs a helping verb to make a verb tense. For example, I *have dreamed* of this day. | I *am dreaming* of this day.

Present Tense: Active Voice

	Singular	Plural
First Person	I dream	We dream
Second Person	You dream	You dream
Third Person	He, she, it dreams	They dream

MOOD

There are three moods in English: the indicative, the imperative, and the subjunctive.

The **indicative mood** is used for facts, opinions, and questions.

> Fact: You can do this.

> Opinion: I think that you can do this.

> Question: Do you know that you can do this?

The **imperative** is used for orders or requests.

> Order: You are going to do this!

> Request: Will you do this for me?

The **subjunctive mood** is for wishes and statements that go against fact.

> Wish: I wish that I were going to do this.

> Statement against fact: If I were you, I would do this. (This goes against fact because I am not you. You have the chance to do this, and I do not have the chance.)

The mood that causes trouble for most people is the subjunctive mood. If you have trouble with any of the moods, then be sure to practice.

ADJECTIVES

An adjective is a word that is used to modify a noun or pronoun. An adjective answers a question: *Which one? What kind of?* or *How many?* Usually, adjectives come before the words that they modify, but they may also come after a linking verb.

> Which one? The *third* suit is my favorite.

> What kind? This suit is *navy blue*.

> How many? Can I look over the *four* neckties for the suit?

ARTICLES

Articles are adjectives that are used to mark nouns. There are only three: the **definite** (i.e., limited or fixed amount) article *the*, and the **indefinite** (i.e., no limit or fixed amount) articles *a* and *an*. Note: *An* comes before words that start with a vowel sound (i.e., vowels include *a, e, i, o, u,* and *y*). For example, "Are you going to get an **umbrella**?"

> **Definite**: I lost *the* bottle that belongs to me.

> **Indefinite**: Does anyone have *a* bottle to share?

COMPARISON WITH ADJECTIVES

Some adjectives are relative and other adjectives are absolute. Adjectives that are **relative** can show the comparison between things. Adjectives that are **absolute** can show comparison. However, they show comparison in a different way. Let's say that you are reading two books. You think that one book is perfect, and the other book is not exactly perfect. It is not possible for the book to be more perfect than the other. Either you think that the book is perfect, or you think that the book is not perfect.

The adjectives that are relative will show the different **degrees** of something or someone to something else or someone else. The three degrees of adjectives include positive, comparative, and superlative.

The **positive** degree is the normal form of an adjective.

> Example: This work is *difficult*. | She is *smart*.

The **comparative** degree compares one person or thing to another person or thing.

Example: This work is *more difficult* than your work. | She is *smarter* than me.

The **superlative** degree compares more than two people or things.

Example: This is the *most difficult* work of my life. | She is the *smartest* lady in school.

> **Review Video: What is an Adjective?**
> Visit mometrix.com/academy and enter code: 470154

ADVERBS

An adverb is a word that is used to **modify** a verb, adjective, or another adverb. Usually, adverbs answer one of these questions: *When?*, *Where?*, *How?*, and *Why?*. The negatives *not* and *never* are known as adverbs. Adverbs that modify adjectives or other adverbs **strengthen** or **weaken** the words that they modify.

Examples:

He walks quickly through the crowd.

The water flows smoothly on the rocks.

Note: While many adverbs end in *-ly*, you need to remember that not all adverbs end in *-ly*. Also, some words that end in *-ly* are adjectives, not adverbs. Some examples include: *early, friendly, holy, lonely, silly*, and *ugly*. To know if a word that ends in *-ly* is an adjective or adverb, you need to check your dictionary.

Examples:

He is *never* angry.

You talk *too* loudly.

COMPARISON WITH ADVERBS

The rules for comparing adverbs are the same as the rules for adjectives.

The **positive** degree is the standard form of an adverb.

Example: He arrives soon. | She speaks softly to her friends.

The **comparative** degree compares one person or thing to another person or thing.

Example: He arrives sooner than Sarah. | She speaks more softly than him.

The **superlative** degree compares more than two people or things.

Example: He arrives soonest of the group. | She speaks most softly of any of her friends.

> **Review Video: What is an Adverb?**
> Visit mometrix.com/academy and enter code: 713951

47

PREPOSITIONS

A preposition is a word placed before a noun or pronoun that shows the relationship between an object and another word in the sentence.

Common prepositions:

about	before	during	on	under
after	beneath	for	over	until
against	between	from	past	up
among	beyond	in	through	with
around	by	of	to	within
at	down	off	toward	without

Examples:

The napkin is *in* the drawer.

The Earth rotates *around* the Sun.

The needle is *beneath* the haystack.

Can you find me *among* the words?

> **Review Video: Prepositions**
> Visit mometrix.com/academy and enter code: 946763

CONJUNCTIONS

Conjunctions join words, phrases, or clauses, and they show the connection between the joined pieces. **Coordinating** conjunctions connect equal parts of sentences. **Correlative** conjunctions show the connection between pairs. **Subordinating** conjunctions join subordinate (i.e., dependent) clauses with independent clauses.

COORDINATING CONJUNCTIONS

The coordinating conjunctions include: *and, but, yet, or, nor, for,* and *so*

Examples:

The rock was small, but it was heavy.

She drove in the night, and he drove in the day.

CORRELATIVE CONJUNCTIONS

The correlative conjunctions are: *either...or* | *neither...nor* | *not only...but also*

Examples:

Either you are coming *or* you are staying.

He ran *not only* three miles *but also* swam 200 yards.

> **Review Video: Coordinating and Correlative Conjunctions**
> Visit mometrix.com/academy and enter code: 390329

SUBORDINATING CONJUNCTIONS

Common subordinating conjunctions include:

after	since	whenever
although	so that	where
because	unless	wherever
before	until	whether
in order that	when	while

Examples:

> I am hungry *because* I did not eat breakfast.

> He went home *when* everyone left.

> **Review Video: Subordinating Conjunctions**
> Visit mometrix.com/academy and enter code: 958913

INTERJECTIONS

An interjection is a word for **exclamation** (i.e., great amount of feeling) that is used alone or as a piece to a sentence. Often, they are used at the beginning of a sentence for an **introduction**. Sometimes, they can be used in the middle of a sentence to show a **change** in thought or attitude.

Common Interjections: Hey! | Oh, | Ouch! | Please! | Wow!

Agreement and Sentence Structure

SUBJECTS AND PREDICATES
SUBJECTS

Every sentence has two things: a subject and a verb. The **subject** of a sentence names who or what the sentence is all about. The subject may be directly stated in a sentence, or the subject may be the implied *you*.

The **complete subject** includes the simple subject and all of its modifiers. To find the complete subject, ask *Who* or *What* and insert the verb to complete the question. The answer is the complete subject. To find the **simple subject**, remove all of the modifiers (adjectives, prepositional phrases, etc.) in the complete subject. Being able to locate the subject of a sentence helps with many problems, such as those involving sentence fragments and subject-verb agreement.

Examples:

The small red car is the one that he wants for Christmas.

(The complete subject is *the small red car*.)

The young artist is coming over for dinner.

(The complete subject is *the young artist*.)

> **Review Video: Subjects in English**
> Visit mometrix.com/academy and enter code: 444771

In **imperative** sentences, the verb's subject is understood (e.g., [You] Run to the store), but not actually present in the sentence. Normally, the subject comes before the verb. However, the subject comes after the verb in sentences that begin with *There are* or *There was*.

Direct:

John knows the way to the park.

(Who knows the way to the park? Answer: John)

The cookies need ten more minutes.

(What needs ten minutes? Answer: The cookies)

By five o' clock, Bill will need to leave.

(Who needs to leave? Answer: Bill)

Remember: The subject can come after the verb.

There are five letters on the table for him.

(What is on the table? Answer: Five letters)

There were coffee and doughnuts in the house.

(What was in the house? Answer: Coffee and doughnuts)

Implied:

> Go to the post office for me.

> (Who is going to the post office? Answer: You are.)

> Come and sit with me, please?

> (Who needs to come and sit? Answer: You do.)

PREDICATES

In a sentence, you always have a predicate and a subject. The subject tells what the sentence is about, and the **predicate** explains or describes the subject.

Think about the sentence: *He sings*. In this sentence, we have a subject (He) and a predicate (sings). This is all that is needed for a sentence to be complete. Would we like more information? Of course, we would like to know more. However, if this all the information that you are given, you have a complete sentence.

Now, let's look at another sentence:

> *John and Jane sing on Tuesday nights at the dance hall.*

What is the subject of this sentence?

> **Answer**: John and Jane.

What is the predicate of this sentence?

> **Answer**: Everything else in the sentence (sing on Tuesday nights at the dance hall).

SUBJECT-VERB AGREEMENT

Verbs **agree** with their subjects in number. In other words, *singular* subjects need *singular* verbs. *Plural* subjects need *plural* verbs. Singular is for one person, place, or thing. Plural is for more than one person, place, or thing. Subjects and verbs must also agree in person: first, second, or third. The present tense ending *-s* is used on a verb if its subject is third person singular; otherwise, the verb takes no ending.

> **Review Video: Subject-Verb Agreement**
> Visit mometrix.com/academy and enter code: 479190

NUMBER AGREEMENT EXAMPLES:

> Single Subject and Verb: *Dan calls home.*

> (Dan is one person. So, the singular verb *calls* is needed.)

> Plural Subject and Verb: *Dan and Bob call home.*

> (More than one person needs the plural verb *call*.)

PERSON AGREEMENT EXAMPLES:

First Person: I *am* walking.

Second Person: You *are* walking.

Third Person: He *is* walking.

COMPLICATIONS WITH SUBJECT-VERB AGREEMENT

WORDS BETWEEN SUBJECT AND VERB

Words that come between the simple subject and the verb may serve as an effective distraction, but they have no bearing on subject-verb agreement.

Examples:

The joy of my life returns home tonight.

(**Singular Subject**: joy. **Singular Verb**: returns)

The phrase *of my life* does not influence the verb *returns*.

The question that still remains unanswered is "Who are you?"

(**Singular Subject**: question. **Singular Verb**: is)

Don't let the phrase "*that still remains...*" trouble you. The subject *question* goes with *is*.

COMPOUND SUBJECTS

A compound subject is formed when two or more nouns joined by *and*, *or*, or *nor* jointly act as the subject of the sentence.

JOINED BY AND

When a compound subject is joined by *and*, it is treated as a plural subject and requires a plural verb.

Examples:

You and Jon are invited to come to my house.

(**Plural Subject**: You and Jon. **Plural Verb**: are)

The pencil and paper belong to me.

(**Plural Subject**: pencil and paper. **Plural Verb**: belong)

JOINED BY OR/NOR

For a compound subject joined by *or* or *nor*, the verb must agree in number with the part of the subject that is closest to the verb (italicized in the examples below).

Examples:

Today or *tomorrow is* the day.

(**Subject**: Today / tomorrow. **Verb**: is)

52

Stan or *Phil wants* to read the book.

(**Subject**: Stan / Phil. **Verb**: wants)

Neither the books nor the *pen is* on the desk.

(**Subject**: Books / Pen. **Verb**: is)

Either the blanket or *pillows arrive* this afternoon.

(**Subject**: Blanket / Pillows. **Verb**: arrive)

INDEFINITE PRONOUNS AS SUBJECT

An indefinite pronoun is a pronoun that does not refer to a specific noun. Indefinite pronouns may be only singular, be only plural, or change depending on how they are used.

ALWAYS SINGULAR

Pronouns such as *each*, *either*, *everybody*, *anybody*, *somebody*, and *nobody* are always singular.

Examples:

Each of the runners *has* a different bib number.

(**Singular Subject**: Each. **Singular Verb**: has)

Is either of you ready for the game?

(**Singular Subject**: Either. **Singular Verb**: is)

Note: The words *each* and *either* can also be used as adjectives (e.g., *each* person is unique). When one of these adjectives modifies the subject of a sentence, it is always a singular subject.

Everybody grows a day older every day.

(**Singular Subject**: Everybody. **Singular Verb**: grows)

Anybody is welcome to bring a tent.

(**Singular Subject**: Anybody. **Singular Verb**: is)

ALWAYS PLURAL

Pronouns such as *both*, *several*, and *many* are always plural.

Examples:

Both of the siblings *were* too tired to argue.

(**Plural Subject**: Both. **Plural Verb**: were)

Many have tried, but none have succeeded.

(**Plural Subject**: Many. **Plural Verb**: have tried)

DEPEND ON CONTEXT

Pronouns such as *some*, *any*, *all*, *none*, *more*, and *most* can be either singular or plural depending on what they are representing in the context of the sentence.

Examples:

All of my dog's food *was* still there in his bowl

(**Singular Subject**: All. **Singular Verb**: was)

By the end of the night, *all* of my guests *were* already excited about coming to my next party.

(**Plural Subject**: All. **Plural Verb**: were)

OTHER CASES INVOLVING PLURAL OR IRREGULAR FORM

Some nouns are **singular in meaning but plural in form**: news, mathematics, physics, and economics.

The *news is* coming on now.

Mathematics is my favorite class.

Some nouns are plural in form and meaning, and have **no singular equivalent**: scissors and pants.

Do these *pants come* with a shirt?

The *scissors are* for my project.

Mathematical operations are **irregular** in their construction, but are normally considered to be **singular in meaning**.

One plus one is two.

Three times three is nine.

Note: Look to your **dictionary** for help when you aren't sure whether a noun with a plural form has a singular or plural meaning.

COMPLEMENTS

A complement is a noun, pronoun, or adjective that is used to give more information about the subject or verb in the sentence.

DIRECT OBJECTS

A direct object is a noun or pronoun that takes or receives the **action** of a verb. (Remember: a complete sentence does not need a direct object, so not all sentences will have them. A sentence needs only a subject and a verb.) When you are looking for a direct object, find the verb and ask *who* or *what*.

Examples:

> I took the blanket. (Who or what did I take? *The blanket*)
>
> Jane read books. (Who or what does Jane read? *Books*)

INDIRECT OBJECTS

An indirect object is a word or group of words that show how an action had an **influence** on someone or something. If there is an indirect object in a sentence, then you always have a direct object in the sentence. When you are looking for the indirect object, find the verb and ask *to/for whom or what*.

Examples:

> We taught the old dog a new trick.
>
> (To/For Whom or What was taught? *The old dog*)
>
> I gave them a math lesson.
>
> (To/For Whom or What was given? *Them*)

PREDICATE NOMINATIVES AND PREDICATE ADJECTIVES

As we looked at previously, verbs may be classified as either action verbs or linking verbs. A linking verb is so named because it links the subject to words in the predicate that describe or define the subject. These words are called predicate nominatives (if nouns or pronouns) or predicate adjectives (if adjectives).

Examples:

> My father is a *lawyer*.
>
> (Father is the **subject**. Lawyer is the **predicate nominative**.)
>
> Your mother is *patient*.
>
> (Mother is the **subject**. Patient is the **predicate adjective**.)

PRONOUN USAGE

The **antecedent** is the noun that has been replaced by a pronoun. A pronoun and its antecedent **agree** when they have the same number (singular or plural) and gender (male, female, or neuter).

Examples:

> **Singular agreement**: *John* came into town, and *he* played for us.
>
> (The word *he* replaces *John*.)
>
> **Plural agreement**: *John and Rick* came into town, and *they* played for us.
>
> (The word *they* replaces *John and Rick*.)

To determine which is the correct pronoun to use in a compound subject or object, try each pronoun **alone** in place of the compound in the sentence. Your knowledge of pronouns will tell you which one is correct.

Example:

Bob and (I, me) will be going.

Test: (1) *I will be going* or (2) *Me will be going*. The second choice cannot be correct because *me* cannot be used as the subject of a sentence. Instead, *me* is used as an object.

Answer: Bob and I will be going.

When a pronoun is used with a noun immediately following (as in "we boys"), try the sentence **without the added noun**.

Example:

(We/Us) boys played football last year.

Test: (1) *We played football last year* or (2) *Us played football last year*. Again, the second choice cannot be correct because *us* cannot be used as a subject of a sentence. Instead, *us* is used as an object.

Answer: We boys played football last year.

> **Review Video: Pronoun Usage**
> Visit mometrix.com/academy and enter code: 666500
>
> **Review Video: What is Pronoun-Antecedent Agreement?**
> Visit mometrix.com/academy and enter code: 919704

A pronoun should point clearly to the **antecedent**. Here is how a pronoun reference can be unhelpful if it is not directly stated or puzzling.

Unhelpful: Ron and Jim went to the store, and *he* bought soda.

(Who bought soda? Ron or Jim?)

Helpful: Jim went to the store, and *he* bought soda.

(The sentence is clear. Jim bought the soda.)

Some pronouns change their form by their placement in a sentence. A pronoun that is a subject in a sentence comes in the **subjective case**. Pronouns that serve as objects appear in the **objective case**. Finally, the pronouns that are used as possessives appear in the **possessive case**.

Examples:

Subjective case: *He* is coming to the show.

(The pronoun *He* is the subject of the sentence.)

Objective case: Josh drove *him* to the airport.

(The pronoun *him* is the object of the sentence.)

Possessive case: The flowers are *mine*.

(The pronoun *mine* shows ownership of the flowers.)

The word *who* is a subjective-case pronoun that can be used as a **subject**. The word *whom* is an objective-case pronoun that can be used as an **object**. The words *who* and *whom* are common in subordinate clauses or in questions.

Examples:

Subject: He knows who wants to come.

(*Who* is the subject of the verb *wants*.)

Object: He knows the man whom we want at the party.

(*Whom* is the object of *we want*.)

CLAUSES

A clause is a group of words that contains both a subject and a predicate (verb). There are two types of clauses: independent and dependent. An **independent clause** contains a complete thought, while a **dependent (or subordinate) clause** does not. A dependent clause includes a subject and a verb, and may also contain objects or complements, but it cannot stand as a complete thought without being joined to an independent clause. Dependent clauses function within sentences as adjectives, adverbs, or nouns.

Example:

Independent Clause: I am running

Dependent Clause: because I want to stay in shape

The clause *I am running* is an independent clause: it has a subject and a verb, and it gives a complete thought. The clause *because I want to stay in shape* is a dependent clause: it has a subject and a verb, but it does not express a complete thought. It adds detail to the independent clause to which it is attached.

Combined: I am running because I want to stay in shape.

Review Video: <u>What is a Clause?</u>
Visit mometrix.com/academy and enter code: 940170

Review Video: <u>Independent and Dependent Clause Examples</u>
Visit mometrix.com/academy and enter code: 556903

TYPES OF DEPENDENT CLAUSES

ADJECTIVE CLAUSES

An **adjective clause** is a dependent clause that modifies a noun or a pronoun. Adjective clauses begin with a relative pronoun (*who, whose, whom, which*, and *that*) or a relative adverb (*where, when*, and *why*).

Also, adjective clauses come after the noun that the clause needs to explain or rename. This is done to have a clear connection to the independent clause.

Examples:

I learned the reason *why I won the award.*

This is the place *where I started my first job.*

An adjective clause can be an essential or nonessential clause. An essential clause is very important to the sentence. **Essential clauses** explain or define a person or thing. **Nonessential clauses** give more information about a person or thing but are not necessary to define them. Nonessential clauses are set off with commas while essential clauses are not.

Examples:

Essential: A person *who works hard at first* can often rest later in life.

Nonessential: Neil Armstrong, *who walked on the moon*, is my hero.

> **Review Video: Adjective Clauses and Phrases**
> Visit mometrix.com/academy and enter code: 520888

ADVERB CLAUSES

An **adverb clause** is a dependent clause that modifies a verb, adjective, or adverb. In sentences with multiple dependent clauses, adverb clauses are usually placed immediately before or after the independent clause. An adverb clause is introduced with words such as *after, although, as, before, because, if, since, so, unless, when, where*, and *while*.

Examples:

When you walked outside, I called the manager.

I will go with you *unless you want to stay.*

NOUN CLAUSES

A **noun clause** is a dependent clause that can be used as a subject, object, or complement. Noun clauses begin with words such as *how, that, what, whether, which, who*, and *why*. These words can also come with an adjective clause. Unless the noun clause is being used as the subject of the sentence, it should come after the verb of the independent clause.

Examples:

The real mystery is *how you avoided serious injury.*

What you learn from each other depends on your honesty with others.

SUBORDINATION

When two related ideas are not of equal importance, the ideal way to combine them is to make the more important idea an independent clause, and the less important idea a dependent or subordinate clause. This is called **subordination**.

Example:

Separate ideas: The team had a perfect regular season. The team lost the championship.

Subordinated: Despite having a perfect regular season, *the team lost the championship.*

PHRASES

A phrase is a group of words that functions as a single part of speech, usually a noun, adjective, or adverb. A phrase is not a complete thought, but it adds **detail** or **explanation** to a sentence, or **renames** something within the sentence.

PREPOSITIONAL PHRASES

One of the most common types of phrases is the prepositional phrase. A **prepositional phrase** begins with a preposition and ends with a noun or pronoun that is the object of the preposition. Normally, the prepositional phrase functions as an **adjective** or an **adverb** within the sentence.

Examples:

The picnic is *on the blanket.*

I am sick *with a fever* today.

Among the many flowers, John found a four-leaf clover.

VERBAL PHRASES

A verbal is a word or phrase that is formed from a verb but does not function as a verb. Depending on its particular form, it may be used as a noun, adjective, or adverb. A verbal does **not** replace a verb in a sentence.

Examples:

Correct: *Walk* a mile daily.

(*Walk* is the verb of this sentence. The subject is the implied *you.*)

Incorrect: *To walk* a mile.

(*To walk* is a type of verbal. This is not a sentence since there is no functional verb)

There are three types of verbals: **participles**, **gerunds**, and **infinitives**. Each type of verbal has a corresponding **phrase** that consists of the verbal itself along with any complements or modifiers.

PARTICIPLES

A **participle** is a type of verbal that always functions as an adjective. The present participle always ends with *-ing*. Past participles end with *-d, -ed, -n,* or *-t.*

Examples: Verb: *dance* | Present Participle: *dancing* | Past Participle: *danced*

Participial phrases most often come right before or right after the noun or pronoun that they modify.

Examples:

Shipwrecked on an island, the boys started to fish for food.

Having been seated for five hours, we got out of the car to stretch our legs.

Praised for their work, the group accepted the first-place trophy.

GERUNDS

A **gerund** is a type of verbal that always functions as a noun. Like present participles, gerunds always end with *-ing*, but they can be easily distinguished from one another by the part of speech they represent (participles always function as adjectives). Since a gerund or gerund phrase always functions as a noun, it can be used as the subject of a sentence, the predicate nominative, or the object of a verb or preposition.

Examples:

We want to be known for *teaching the poor*. (Object of preposition)

Coaching this team is the best job of my life. (Subject)

We like *practicing our songs* in the basement. (Object of verb)

INFINITIVES

An **infinitive** is a type of verbal that can function as a noun, an adjective, or an adverb. An infinitive is made of the word *to* + the basic form of the verb. As with all other types of verbal phrases, an infinitive phrase includes the verbal itself and all of its complements or modifiers.

Examples:

To join the team is my goal in life. (Noun)

The animals have enough food *to eat for the night*. (Adjective)

People lift weights *to exercise their muscles*. (Adverb)

APPOSITIVE PHRASES

An **appositive** is a word or phrase that is used to explain or rename nouns or pronouns. Noun phrases, gerund phrases, and infinitive phrases can all be used as appositives.

Examples:

Terriers, *hunters at heart*, have been dressed up to look like lap dogs.

(The noun phrase *hunters at heart* renames the noun *terriers*.)

His plan, *to save and invest his money*, was proven as a safe approach.

(The infinitive phrase explains what the plan is.)

Appositive phrases can be **essential** or **nonessential**. An appositive phrase is essential if the person, place, or thing being described or renamed is too general for its meaning to be understood without the appositive.

Examples:

Essential: Two Founding Fathers George Washington and Thomas Jefferson served as presidents.

Nonessential: George Washington and Thomas Jefferson, two Founding Fathers, served as presidents.

ABSOLUTE PHRASES

An absolute phrase is a phrase that consists of **a noun followed by a participle**. An absolute phrase provides **context** to what is being described in the sentence, but it does not modify or explain any particular word; it is essentially independent.

Examples:

The alarm ringing, he pushed the snooze button.

The music paused, she continued to dance through the crowd.

Note: Absolute phrases can be confusing, so don't be discouraged if you have a difficult time with them.

PARALLELISM

When multiple items or ideas are presented in a sentence in series, such as in a list, the items or ideas must be stated in grammatically equivalent ways. In other words, if one idea is stated in gerund form, the second cannot be stated in infinitive form. For example, to write, *I enjoy reading and to study* would be incorrect. An infinitive and a gerund are not equivalent. Instead, you should write *I enjoy reading and studying*. In lists of more than two, it can be harder to keep straight, but all items in a list must be parallel.

Example:

Incorrect: He stopped at the office, grocery store, and the pharmacy before heading home.

The first and third items in the list of places include the article *the*, so the second item needs it as well.

Correct: He stopped at the office, *the* grocery store, and the pharmacy before heading home.

Example:

Incorrect: While vacationing in Europe, she went biking, skiing, and climbed mountains.

The first and second items in the list are gerunds, so the third item must be as well.

Correct: While vacationing in Europe, she went biking, skiing, and *mountain climbing*.

61

SENTENCE PURPOSE

There are four types of sentences: declarative, imperative, interrogative, and exclamatory.

A **declarative** sentence states a fact and ends with a period.

> Example: *The football game starts at seven o'clock.*

An **imperative** sentence tells someone to do something and generally ends with a period. (An urgent command might end with an exclamation point instead.)

> Example: *Don't forget to buy your ticket.*

An **interrogative** sentence asks a question and ends with a question mark.

> Example: *Are you going to the game on Friday?*

An **exclamatory** sentence shows strong emotion and ends with an exclamation point.

> Example: *I can't believe we won the game!*

SENTENCE STRUCTURE

Sentences are classified by structure based on the type and number of clauses present. The four classifications of sentence structure are the following:

Simple: A simple sentence has one independent clause with no dependent clauses. A simple sentence may have **compound elements** (i.e., compound subject or verb).

Examples:

> Judy *watered* the lawn. (single subject, single *verb*)

> Judy and Alan *watered* the lawn. (compound subject, single *verb*)

> Judy *watered* the lawn and *pulled* weeds. (single subject, compound *verb*)

> Judy and Alan *watered* the lawn and *pulled* weeds. (compound subject, compound *verb*)

Compound: A compound sentence has two or more independent clauses with no dependent clauses. Usually, the independent clauses are joined with a comma and a coordinating conjunction or with a semicolon.

Examples:

> The time has come, and we are ready.

> I woke up at dawn; the sun was just coming up.

Complex: A complex sentence has one independent clause and at least one *dependent clause*.

Examples:

> *Although he had the flu*, Harry went to work.

> Marcia got married *after she finished college.*

Compound-Complex: A compound-complex sentence has at least two <u>independent clauses</u> and at least one *dependent clause*.

Examples:

<u>John is my friend</u> *who went to India*, and <u>he brought back souvenirs</u>.

<u>You may not realize this</u>, but <u>we heard the music</u> *that you played last night*.

> **Review Video: <u>Sentence Structure</u>**
> Visit mometrix.com/academy and enter code: 700478

SENTENCE FRAGMENTS

Usually when the term *sentence fragment* comes up, it is because you have to decide whether or not a group of words is a complete sentence, and if it's not a complete sentence, you're about to have to fix it. Recall that a group of words must contain at least one **independent clause** in order to be considered a sentence. If it doesn't contain even one independent clause, it would be called a **sentence fragment**. (If it contains two or more independent clauses that are not joined correctly, it would be called a run-on sentence.)

The process to use for **repairing** a sentence fragment depends on what type of fragment it is. If the fragment is a dependent clause, it can sometimes be as simple as removing a subordinating word (e.g., when, because, if) from the beginning of the fragment. Alternatively, a dependent clause can be incorporated into a closely related neighboring sentence. If the fragment is missing some required part, like a subject or a verb, the fix might be as simple as adding it in.

Examples:

Fragment: Because he wanted to sail the Mediterranean.

Removed subordinating word: He wanted to sail the Mediterranean.

Combined with another sentence: Because he wanted to sail the Mediterranean, he booked a Greek island cruise.

RUN-ON SENTENCES

Run-on sentences consist of multiple independent clauses that have not been joined together properly. Run-on sentences can be corrected in several different ways:

Join clauses properly: This can be done with a comma and coordinating conjunction, with a semicolon, or with a colon or dash if the second clause is explaining something in the first.

Example:

Incorrect: I went on the trip, we visited lots of castles.

Corrected: I went on the trip, and we visited lots of castles.

Split into separate sentences: This correction is most effective when the independent clauses are very long or when they are not closely related.

Example:

Incorrect: The drive to New York takes ten hours, my uncle lives in Boston.

Corrected: The drive to New York takes ten hours. My uncle lives in Boston.

Make one clause dependent: This is the easiest way to make the sentence correct and more interesting at the same time. It's often as simple as adding a subordinating word between the two clauses.

Example:

Incorrect: I finally made it to the store and I bought some eggs.

Corrected: When I finally made it to the store, I bought some eggs.

Reduce to one clause with a compound verb: If both clauses have the same subject, remove the subject from the second clause, and you now have just one clause with a compound verb.

Example:

Incorrect: The drive to New York takes ten hours, it makes me very tired.

Corrected: The drive to New York takes ten hours and makes me very tired.

Note: While these are the simplest ways to correct a run-on sentence, often the best way is to completely reorganize the thoughts in the sentence and rewrite it.

> **Review Video: Fragments and Run-on Sentences**
> Visit mometrix.com/academy and enter code: 541989

DANGLING AND MISPLACED MODIFIERS
DANGLING MODIFIERS

A dangling modifier is a dependent clause or verbal phrase that does not have a **clear logical connection** to a word in the sentence.

Example:

Dangling: *Reading each magazine article*, the stories caught my attention.

The word *stories* cannot be modified by *Reading each magazine article*. People can read, but stories cannot read. Therefore, the subject of the sentence must be a person.

Corrected: Reading each magazine article, *I* was entertained by the stories.

Example:

Dangling: Ever since childhood, my grandparents have visited me for Christmas.

The speaker in this sentence can't have been visited by her grandparents when *they* were children, since she wouldn't have been born yet. Either the modifier should be **clarified** or the sentence should be **rearranged** to specify whose childhood is being referenced.

Clarified: Ever since I was a child, my grandparents have visited for Christmas.

Rearranged: Ever since childhood, I have enjoyed my grandparents visiting for Christmas.

MISPLACED MODIFIERS

Because modifiers are grammatically versatile, they can be put in many different places within the structure of a sentence. The danger of this versatility is that a modifier can accidentally be placed where it is modifying the wrong word or where it is not clear which word it is modifying.

Example:

Misplaced: She read the book to a crowd *that was filled with beautiful pictures*.

The book was filled with beautiful pictures, not the crowd.

Corrected: She read the book *that was filled with beautiful pictures* to a crowd.

Example:

Ambiguous: Derek saw a bus nearly hit a man *on his way to work*.

Was Derek on his way to work? Or was the other man?

Derek: *On his way to work*, Derek saw a bus nearly hit a man.

The other man: Derek saw a bus nearly hit a man *who was on his way to work*.

SPLIT INFINITIVES

A split infinitive occurs when a modifying word comes between the word *to* and the verb that pairs with *to*.

Example: To *clearly* explain vs. *To explain* clearly | To *softly* sing vs. *To sing* softly

Though considered improper by some, split infinitives may provide better clarity and simplicity in some cases than the alternatives. As such, avoiding them should not be considered a universal rule.

DOUBLE NEGATIVES

Standard English allows **two negatives** only when a **positive** meaning is intended. For example, *The team was not displeased with their performance*. Double negatives to emphasize negation are not used in standard English.

Negative modifiers (e.g., never, no, and not) should not be paired with other negative modifiers or negative words (e.g., none, nobody, nothing, or neither). The modifiers *hardly, barely*, and *scarcely* are considered negatives in standard English, so they should not be used with other negatives.

Punctuation

END PUNCTUATION

PERIODS

Use a period to end all sentences except direct questions, exclamations.

DECLARATIVE SENTENCE

A declarative sentence gives information or makes a statement.

Examples: I can fly a kite. | The plane left two hours ago.

IMPERATIVE SENTENCE

An imperative sentence gives an order or command.

Examples: You are coming with me. | Bring me that note.

PERIODS FOR ABBREVIATIONS

Examples: 3 P.M. | 2 A.M. | Mr. Jones | Mrs. Stevens | Dr. Smith | Bill Jr. | Pennsylvania Ave.

Note: an abbreviation is a shortened form of a word or phrase.

QUESTION MARKS

Question marks should be used following a direct question. A polite request can be followed by a period instead of a question mark.

Direct Question: What is for lunch today? | How are you? | Why is that the answer?

Polite Requests: Can you please send me the item tomorrow. | Will you please walk with me on the track.

> **Review Video: When to Use a Question Mark**
> Visit mometrix.com/academy and enter code: 118471

EXCLAMATION MARKS

Exclamation marks are used after a word group or sentence that shows much feeling or has special importance. Exclamation marks should not be overused. They are saved for proper **exclamatory interjections**.

Example: We're going to the finals! | You have a beautiful car! | That's crazy!

> **Review Video: What Does an Exclamation Point Mean?**
> Visit mometrix.com/academy and enter code: 199367

COMMAS

The comma is a punctuation mark that can help you understand connections in a sentence. Not every sentence needs a comma. However, if a sentence needs a comma, you need to put it in the right place. A comma in the wrong place (or an absent comma) will make a sentence's meaning unclear. These are some of the rules for commas:

1. Use a comma **before a coordinating conjunction** joining independent clauses
   Example: Bob caught three fish, and I caught two fish.

2. Use a comma after an introductory phrase or an adverbial clause

   Examples:

   > *After the final out,* we went to a restaurant to celebrate.
   > *Studying the stars,* I was surprised at the beauty of the sky.

3. Use a comma between items in a series.

   Example: I will bring the turkey, the pie, and the coffee.

4. Use a comma **between coordinate adjectives** not joined with *and*

   Incorrect: The kind, brown dog followed me home.
   Correct: The *kind, loyal* dog followed me home.
   Not all adjectives are **coordinate** (i.e., equal or parallel). There are two simple ways to know if your adjectives are coordinate. One, you can join the adjectives with *and*: *The kind and loyal dog.* Two, you can change the order of the adjectives: *The loyal, kind dog.*

5. Use commas for **interjections** and **after *yes* and *no*** responses

   Examples:

   > **Interjection**: Oh, I had no idea. | Wow, you know how to play this game.
   > **Yes and No**: *Yes,* I heard you. | *No,* I cannot come tomorrow.

6. Use commas to separate nonessential modifiers and nonessential appositives

   Examples:

   > **Nonessential Modifier**: John Frank, who is coaching the team, was promoted today.
   > **Nonessential Appositive**: Thomas Edison, an American inventor, was born in Ohio.

7. Use commas to set off nouns of direct address, interrogative tags, and contrast

   Examples:

   > **Direct Address**: You, *John,* are my only hope in this moment.
   > **Interrogative Tag**: This is the last time, *correct*?
   > **Contrast**: You are my friend, *not my enemy.*

8. Use commas with dates, addresses, geographical names, and titles

   Examples:

   > **Date**: *July 4, 1776,* is an important date to remember.
   > **Address**: He is meeting me at *456 Delaware Avenue, Washington, D.C.,* tomorrow morning.
   > **Geographical Name**: *Paris, France,* is my favorite city.
   > **Title**: John Smith, *Ph. D.,* will be visiting your class today.

9. Use commas to **separate expressions like *he said*** and ***she said*** if they come between a sentence of a quote

   Examples:

   > "I want you to know," he began, "that I always wanted the best for you."
   > "You can start," Jane said, "with an apology."

> **Review Video: When To Use a Comma**
> Visit mometrix.com/academy and enter code: 786797

SEMICOLONS

The semicolon is used to connect major sentence pieces of equal value. Some rules for semicolons include:

1. Use a semicolon **between closely connected independent clauses** that are not connected with a coordinating conjunction.

   Examples:

   > She is outside; we are inside.
   > You are right; we should go with your plan.

2. Use a semicolon **between independent clauses linked with a transitional word.**

   Examples:

   > I think that we can agree on this; *however,* I am not sure about my friends.
   > You are looking in the wrong places; *therefore,* you will not find what you need.

3. Use a semicolon **between items in a series that has internal punctuation.**

   Example: I have visited New York, New York; Augusta, Maine; and Baltimore, Maryland.

> **Review Video: How to Use Semicolons**
> Visit mometrix.com/academy and enter code: 370605

COLONS

The colon is used to call attention to the words that follow it. A colon must come after a **complete independent clause**. The rules for colons are as follows:

1. Use a colon after an independent clause to **make a list.**

   Example: I want to learn many languages: Spanish, German, and Italian.

2. Use a colon for **explanations** or to **give a quote.**

   Examples:

   > **Quote**: He started with an idea: "We are able to do more than we imagine."
   > **Explanation**: There is one thing that stands out on your resume: responsibility.

3. Use a colon **after the greeting in a formal letter**, to **show hours and minutes**, and to **separate a title and subtitle.**

   Examples:

   > **Greeting in a formal letter**: Dear Sir: | To Whom It May Concern:
   > **Time**: It is 3:14 P.M.
   > **Title**: The essay is titled "America: A Short Introduction to a Modern Country"

> **Review Video: What is a Colon?**
> Visit mometrix.com/academy and enter code: 868673

PARENTHESES

Parentheses are used for additional information. Also, they can be used to put labels for letters or numbers in a series. Parentheses should be not be used very often. If they are overused, parentheses can be a distraction instead of a help.

Examples:

Extra Information: The rattlesnake (see Image 2) is a dangerous snake of North and South America.

Series: Include in the email (1) your name, (2) your address, and (3) your question for the author.

> **Review Video: When to Use Parentheses**
> Visit mometrix.com/academy and enter code: 947743

QUOTATION MARKS

Use quotation marks to close off **direct quotations** of a person's spoken or written words. Do not use quotation marks around indirect quotations. An indirect quotation gives someone's message without using the person's exact words. Use **single quotation marks** to close off a quotation inside a quotation.

Direct Quote: Nancy said, "I am waiting for Henry to arrive."

Indirect Quote: Henry said that he is going to be late to the meeting.

Quote inside a Quote: The teacher asked, "Has everyone read 'The Gift of the Magi'?"

Quotation marks should be used around the titles of **short works**: newspaper and magazine articles, poems, short stories, songs, television episodes, radio programs, and subdivisions of books or web sites.

Examples:

"Rip van Winkle" (short story by Washington Irving)

"O Captain! My Captain!" (poem by Walt Whitman)

Although it is not standard usage, quotation marks are sometimes used to highlight **irony**, or the use of words to mean something other than their dictionary definition. This type of usage should be employed sparingly, if at all.

Examples:

The boss warned Frank that he was walking on "thin ice."

(Frank is not walking on real ice. Instead, Frank is being warned to avoid mistakes.)

The teacher thanked the young man for his "honesty."

(In this example, the quotation marks around *honesty* show that the teacher does not believe the young man's explanation.)

> **Review Video: Quotation Marks**
> Visit mometrix.com/academy and enter code: 884918

Periods and commas are put **inside** quotation marks. Colons and semicolons are put **outside** the quotation marks. Question marks and exclamation points are placed inside quotation marks when

69

they are part of a quote. When the question or exclamation mark goes with the whole sentence, the mark is left outside of the quotation marks.

Examples:

> *Period and comma*: We read "The Gift of the Magi," "The Skylight Room," and "The Cactus."

> *Semicolon*: They watched "The Nutcracker"; then, they went home.

> *Exclamation mark that is a part of a quote*: The crowd cheered, "Victory!"

> *Question mark that goes with the whole sentence*: Is your favorite short story "The Tell-Tale Heart"?

APOSTROPHES

An apostrophe is used to show **possession** or the **deletion of letters in contractions**. An apostrophe is not needed with the possessive pronouns *his, hers, its, ours, theirs, whose*, and *yours*.

> **Singular Nouns**: David's car | a book's theme | my brother's board game

> **Plural Nouns with -*s***: the scissors' handle | boys' basketball

> **Plural Nouns without -*s***: Men's department | the people's adventure

> **Review Video: <u>When to Use an Apostrophe</u>**
> Visit mometrix.com/academy and enter code: 213068
>
> **Review Video: <u>Punctuation Errors in Possessive Pronouns</u>**
> Visit mometrix.com/academy and enter code: 221438

HYPHENS

Hyphens are used to **separate compound words**. Use hyphens in the following cases:

1. **Compound numbers** between 21 and 99 when written out in words
   Example: This team needs *twenty-five* points to win the game.

2. **Written-out fractions** that are used as **adjectives**
   Correct: The recipe says that we need a *three-fourths* cup of butter.
   Incorrect: *One-fourth* of the road is under construction.

3. Compound words used as **adjectives that come before a noun**
   Correct: The *well-fed* dog took a nap.
   Incorrect: The dog was *well-fed* for his nap.

4. Compound words that would be **hard to read** or **easily confused with other words**
   Examples: Semi-irresponsible | Anti-itch | Re-sort

Note: This is not a complete set of the rules for hyphens. A dictionary is the best tool for knowing if a compound word needs a hyphen.

> **Review Video: <u>Hyphens</u>**
> Visit mometrix.com/academy and enter code: 981632

DASHES

Dashes are used to show a **break** or a **change in thought** in a sentence or to act as parentheses in a sentence. When typing, use two hyphens to make a dash. Do not put a space before or after the dash. The following are the rules for dashes:

1. To set off **parenthetical statements** or an **appositive with internal punctuation**

   Example: The three trees—oak, pine, and magnolia—are coming on a truck tomorrow.

2. To show a **break or change in tone or thought**

   Example: The first question—how silly of me—does not have a correct answer.

ELLIPSIS MARKS

The ellipsis mark has three periods (...) to show when **words have been removed** from a quotation. If a full sentence or more is removed from a quoted passage, you need to use four periods to show the removed text and the end punctuation mark. The ellipsis mark should not be used at the beginning of a quotation. The ellipsis mark should also not be used at the end of a quotation unless some words have been deleted from the end of the final sentence.

Example:

   "Then he picked up the groceries...paid for them...later he went home."

BRACKETS

There are two main reasons to use brackets:

1. When **placing parentheses inside of parentheses**

   Example: The hero of this story, Paul Revere (a silversmith and industrialist [see Ch. 4]), rode through towns of Massachusetts to warn of advancing British troops.

2. When adding **clarification or detail** to a quotation that is **not part of the quotation**
   Example:

   The father explained, "My children are planning to attend my alma mater [State University]."

> **Review Video: <u>Using Brackets in Sentences</u>**
> Visit mometrix.com/academy and enter code: 727546

Spelling

SPELLING RULES
WORDS ENDING WITH A CONSONANT

Usually the final consonant is **doubled** on a word before adding a suffix. This is the rule for single syllable words, words ending with one consonant, and multi-syllable words with the last syllable accented. The following are examples:

- *beg* becomes *begging* (single syllable)
- *shop* becomes *shopped* (single syllable)
- *add* becomes *adding* (already ends in double consonant, do not add another *d*)
- *deter* becomes *deterring* (multi-syllable, accent on last syllable)
- *regret* becomes *regrettable* (multi-syllable, accent on last syllable)
- *compost* becomes *composting* (do not add another *t* because the accent is on the first syllable)

WORDS ENDING WITH Y OR C

The general rule for words ending in *y* is to **keep the *y*** when adding a suffix if the *y* is preceded by a vowel. If the word ends in a consonant and *y* the *y* is changed to an *i* before the suffix is added (unless the suffix itself begins with *i*). The following are examples:

- *pay* becomes *paying* (keep the *y*)
- *bully* becomes *bullied* (change to *i*)
- *bully* becomes *bullying* (keep the *y* because the suffix is –*ing*)

If a word ends with *c* and the suffix begins with an *e, i,* or *y*, the **letter *k*** is usually added to the end of the word. The following are examples:

- panic becomes panicky
- mimic becomes mimicking

WORDS CONTAINING IE OR EI, AND/OR ENDING WITH E

Most words are spelled with an *i* before *e*, except when they follow the letter *c,* **or** sound like *a*. For example, the following words are spelled correctly according to these rules:

- piece, friend, believe (*i* before *e*)
- receive, ceiling, conceited (except after *c*)
- weight, neighborhood, veil (sounds like *a*)

To add a suffix to words ending with the letter *e*, first determine if the ***e* is silent**. If it is, the *e* will be kept if the added suffix begins with a consonant. If the suffix begins with a vowel, the *e* is dropped. The following are examples:

- *age* becomes *ageless* (keep the *e*)
- *age* becomes *aging* (drop the *e*)

An exception to this rule occurs when the word ends in *ce* or *ge* and the suffix *able* or *ous* is added; these words will retain the letter *e*. The following are examples:

- courage becomes courageous
- notice becomes noticeable

WORDS ENDING WITH ISE OR IZE

A small number of words end with *ise*. Most of the words in the English language with the same sound end in *ize*. The following are examples:

- advertise, advise, arise, chastise, circumcise, and comprise
- compromise, demise, despise, devise, disguise, enterprise, excise, and exercise
- franchise, improvise, incise, merchandise, premise, reprise, and revise
- supervise, surmise, surprise, and televise

Words that end with *ize* include the following:

- accessorize, agonize, authorize, and brutalize
- capitalize, caramelize, categorize, civilize, and demonize
- downsize, empathize, euthanize, idolize, and immunize
- legalize, metabolize, mobilize, organize, and ostracize
- plagiarize, privatize, utilize, and visualize

(Note that some words may technically be spelled with *ise*, especially in British English, but it is more common to use *ize*. Examples include *symbolize/symbolise*, and *baptize/baptise*.)

WORDS ENDING WITH CEED, SEDE, OR CEDE

There are only three words in the English language that end with *ceed*: *exceed, proceed,* and *succeed*. There is only one word in the English language that ends with *sede*: *supersede*. Most other words that sound like *sede* or *ceed* end with *cede*. The following are examples:

concede, recede, and precede

WORDS ENDING IN ABLE OR IBLE

For words ending in *able* or *ible*, there are no hard and fast rules. The following are examples:

- adjustable, unbeatable, collectable, deliverable, and likeable
- edible, compatible, feasible, sensible, and credible

There are more words ending in *able* than *ible*; this is useful to know if guessing is necessary.

WORDS ENDING IN ANCE OR ENCE

The suffixes *ence, ency,* and *ent* are used in the following cases:

- the suffix is preceded by the letter *c* but sounds like *s* – *innocence*
- the suffix is preceded by the letter *g* but sounds like *j* – *intelligence, negligence*

The suffixes *ance, ancy,* and *ant* are used in the following cases:

- the suffix is preceded by the letter *c* but sounds like *k* – *significant, vacant*
- the suffix is preceded by the letter *g* with a hard sound – *elegant, extravagance*

If the suffix is preceded by other letters, there are no clear rules. For example: *finance, abundance,* and *assistance* use the letter *a*, while *decadence, competence,* and *excellence* use the letter *e*.

WORDS ENDING IN TION, SION, OR CIAN

Words ending in *tion, sion,* or *cian* all sound like *shun* or *zhun*. There are no rules for which ending is used for words. The following are examples:

- action, agitation, caution, fiction, nation, and motion
- admission, expression, mansion, permission, and television
- electrician, magician, musician, optician, and physician (note that these words tend to describe occupations)

WORDS WITH THE AI OR IA COMBINATION

When deciding if *ai* or *ia* is correct, the combination of *ai* usually sounds like one vowel sound, as in *Britain*, while the vowels in *ia* are pronounced separately, as in *guardian*. The following are examples:

- captain, certain, faint, hair, malaise, and praise (*ai* makes one sound)
- bacteria, beneficiary, diamond, humiliation, and nuptial (*ia* makes two sounds)

PLURAL FORMS OF NOUNS

NOUNS ENDING IN CH, SH, S, X, OR Z

When a noun ends in the letters *ch, sh, s, x,* or *z*, **an es instead of a singular s** is added to the end of the word to make it plural. The following are examples:

- church becomes churches
- bush becomes bushes
- bass becomes basses
- mix becomes mixes
- buzz becomes buzzes

This is the rule with proper names as well; the Ross family would become the Rosses.

NOUNS ENDING IN Y OR AY/EY/IY/OY/UY

If a noun ends with a consonant and y, the plural is formed by **replacing the y with ies**. For example, *fly* becomes *flies* and *puppy* becomes *puppies*. If a noun ends with a vowel and y, the plural is formed by adding an s. For example, *alley* becomes *alleys* and *boy* becomes *boys*.

NOUNS ENDING IN F OR FE

Most nouns ending in *f* or *fe* are pluralized by **replacing the f with v and adding es**. The following are examples:

knife becomes knives; self becomes selves; wolf becomes wolves.

An exception to this rule is the word *roof; roof* becomes *roofs*.

NOUNS ENDING IN O

Most nouns ending with a consonant and *o* are pluralized by **adding es**. The following are examples:

hero becomes *heroes; tornado* becomes *tornadoes; potato* becomes *potatoes*

Most nouns ending with a vowel and *o* are pluralized by **adding *s***. The following are examples:

portfolio becomes *portfolios*; *radio* becomes *radios*; *cameo* becomes *cameos*.

An exception to these rules is seen with musical terms ending in *o*. These words are pluralized by adding *s* even if they end in a consonant and *o*. The following are examples: *soprano* becomes *sopranos*; *banjo* becomes *banjos*; *piano* becomes *pianos*.

EXCEPTIONS TO THE RULES OF PLURALS

Some words do not fall into any specific category for making the singular form plural. They are **irregular**. Certain words become plural by changing the vowels within the word. The following are examples:

woman becomes *women*; *goose* becomes *geese*; *foot* becomes *feet*

Some words change in unusual ways in the plural form. The following are examples:

mouse becomes *mice*; *ox* becomes *oxen*; *person* becomes *people*

Some words are the same in both the singular and plural forms. The following are examples:

Salmon, *deer*, and *moose* are the same whether singular or plural.

PLURAL FORMS OF LETTERS, NUMBERS, SYMBOLS, AND COMPOUND NOUNS WITH HYPHENS

Letters and numbers become plural by adding **an apostrophe and *s***. The following are examples:

- The *L's* are the people whose names begin with the letter *L*.
- They broke the teams down into groups of *3's*.
- The sorority girls were all *KD's*.

A **compound noun** is a noun that is made up of two or more words; they can be written with **hyphens**. For example, *mother-in-law* or *court-martial* are compound nouns. To make them plural, an *s* or *es* is added to the noun portion of the word. The following are examples: *mother-in-law* becomes *mothers-in-law*; *court-martial* becomes *courts-martial*.

COMMONLY MISSPELLED WORDS

accidentally	accommodate	accompanied
accompany	achieved	acknowledgment
across	address	aggravate
aisle	ancient	anxiety
apparently	appearance	arctic
argument	arrangement	attendance
auxiliary	awkward	bachelor
barbarian	beggar	beneficiary
biscuit	brilliant	business
cafeteria	calendar	campaign
candidate	ceiling	cemetery
changeable	changing	characteristic
chauffeur	colonel	column
commit	committee	comparative

compel	competent	competition
conceive	congratulations	conqueror
conscious	coolly	correspondent
courtesy	curiosity	cylinder
deceive	deference	deferred
definite	describe	desirable
desperate	develop	diphtheria
disappear	disappoint	disastrous
discipline	discussion	disease
dissatisfied	dissipate	drudgery
ecstasy	efficient	eighth
eligible	embarrass	emphasize
especially	exaggerate	exceed
exhaust	exhilaration	existence
explanation	extraordinary	familiar
fascinate	February	fiery
finally	forehead	foreign
foreigner	foremost	forfeit
ghost	glamorous	government
grammar	grateful	grief
grievous	handkerchief	harass
height	hoping	hurriedly
hygiene	hypocrisy	imminent
incidentally	incredible	independent
indigestible	inevitable	innocence
intelligible	intentionally	intercede
interest	irresistible	judgment
legitimate	liable	library
likelihood	literature	maintenance
maneuver	manual	mathematics
mattress	miniature	mischievous
misspell	momentous	mortgage
neither	nickel	niece
ninety	noticeable	notoriety
obedience	obstacle	occasion
occurrence	omitted	operate
optimistic	organization	outrageous
pageant	pamphlet	parallel
parliament	permissible	perseverance
persuade	physically	physician
possess	possibly	practically
prairie	preceding	prejudice
prevalent	professor	pronunciation

pronouncement	propeller	protein
psychiatrist	psychology	quantity
questionnaire	rally	recede
receive	recognize	recommend
referral	referred	relieve
religious	resistance	restaurant
rhetoric	rhythm	ridiculous
sacrilegious	salary	scarcely
schedule	secretary	sentinel
separate	severely	sheriff
shriek	similar	soliloquy
sophomore	species	strenuous
studying	suffrage	supersede
suppress	surprise	symmetry
temperament	temperature	tendency
tournament	tragedy	transferred
truly	twelfth	tyranny
unanimous	unpleasant	usage
vacuum	valuable	vein
vengeance	vigilance	villain
Wednesday	weird	wholly

Paragraph Development

LEVEL OF FORMALITY

The relationship between writer and reader is important in choosing a **level of formality** as most writing requires some degree of formality. **Formal writing** is for addressing a superior in a school or work environment. Business letters, textbooks, and newspapers use a moderate to high level of formality. **Informal writing** is appropriate for private letters, personal e-mails, and business correspondence between close associates.

For your exam, you will want to be aware of informal and formal writing. One way that this can be accomplished is to watch for shifts in **point of view** in the essay. For example, unless writers are using a personal example, they will rarely refer to themselves (e.g., "*I* think that *my* point is very clear.") to avoid being informal when they need to be formal. Also, be mindful of an author who addresses his or her audience directly in their writing (e.g., "Readers, *like you*, will understand this argument.") as this can be a sign of informal writing. Good writers understand the need to be **consistent** with their level of formality. Shifts in levels of formality or point of view can confuse readers and discount the message of an author's writing.

CLICHÉS

Clichés are phrases that have been **overused** to the point that the phrase has no importance or has lost the original meaning. The phrases have no originality and add very little to a passage. Therefore, most writers will **avoid** the use of clichés. Another option is to make changes to a cliché so that it is not predictable and empty of meaning.

EXAMPLES

When life gives you lemons, make lemonade.

Every cloud has a silver lining.

JARGON

Jargon is a **specialized vocabulary** that is used among members of a trade or profession. Since jargon is understood by a small audience, writers tend to leave them to passages where certain readers will understand the vocabulary. Jargon includes exaggerated language that tries to impress rather than inform. Sentences filled with jargon are not precise and difficult to understand.

EXAMPLES

"He is going to *toenail* these frames for us." (Toenail is construction jargon for nailing at an angle.)

"They brought in a *kip* of material today." (Kip refers to 1000 pounds in architecture and engineering.)

SLANG

Slang is an **informal** and sometimes private language that is understood by some individuals. Slang has some usefulness, but the language can have a small audience. So, most formal writing will **not** include this kind of language.

EXAMPLES

"Yes, the event was a blast!" (In this sentence, *blast* means that the event was a great experience.)

"That attempt was an epic fail." (By *epic fail*, the speaker means that his or her attempt was not a success.)

COLLOQUIALISM

A colloquialism is a word or phrase that is found in **informal writing**. Unlike slang, colloquial language will be familiar to a greater range of people. Colloquial language can include some slang, but these are limited to contractions for the most part.

EXAMPLES

"Can *y'all* come back another time?" (Y'all is contraction of "you all" which has become a colloquialism.)

"Will you stop him from building this *castle in the air*?" (A "castle in the air" is an improbable or unlikely event.)

POINT OF VIEW

Point of view is the **perspective** from which writing occurs. There are several possibilities:

- *First person* is written so that the *I* of the story is a participant or observer.
- *Second person* is written directly to the reader. It is a device to draw the reader in more closely. In second person, "you" the reader, are the one taking action in a sentence.
- *Third person*, the most traditional form of point of view, is the omniscient narrator, in which the narrative voice, presumed to be the writer's, is presumed to know everything about the characters, plot, and action. Most novels use this point of view.
- A *multiple point of view* is narration delivered from the perspective of several characters.

> **Review Video: Point of View**
> Visit mometrix.com/academy and enter code: 383336

PRACTICE MAKES PREPARED WRITERS

Writing is a skill that continues to need development throughout a person's life. For some people, writing seems to be a natural gift. They rarely struggle with writer's block. When you read their papers, you likely find their ideas persuasive. For others, writing is an intimidating task that they endure. As you prepare for the test, believe that you can improve your skills and be better prepared for reviewing several types of writing.

A traditional way to prepare for the English and Language Usage Section is to **read**. When you read newspapers, magazines, and books, you learn about new ideas. You can read newspapers and magazines to become informed about issues that affect many people. As you think about those issues and ideas, you can take a position and form opinions. Try to develop these ideas and your opinions by sharing them with friends. After you develop your opinions, try writing them down as if you were going to spread your ideas beyond your friends.

Remember that you are practicing for more than an exam. Two of the most valuable skills in life are the abilities to **read critically** and to **write clearly**. When you work on evaluating the arguments of a passage and explain your thoughts well, you are developing skills that you will use for a lifetime.

BRAINSTORMING

Brainstorming is a technique that is used to find a creative approach to a subject. This can be accomplished by simple free-association with a topic. For example, with paper and pen, you write every thought that you have about the topic in a word or phrase. This is done without critical thinking. Everything that comes to your mind about the topic, you should put on your scratch

79

paper. Then, you need to read the list over a few times. Next, you look for patterns, repetitions, and clusters of ideas. This allows a variety of fresh ideas to come as you think about the topic.

FREE WRITING

Free writing is a more structured form of brainstorming. The method involves a limited amount of time (e.g., 2 to 3 minutes) and writing everything that comes to mind about the topic in complete sentences. When time expires, you need to review everything that has been written down. Many of your sentences may make little or no sense, but the insights and observations that can come from free writing make this method a valuable approach. Usually, free writing results in a fuller expression of ideas than brainstorming because thoughts and associations are written in complete sentences. However, both techniques can be used to complement each other.

REVISIONS

A writer's choice of words is a signature of their **style**. Careful thought about the use of words can improve a piece of writing. A passage can be an exciting piece to read when attention is given to the use of **specific nouns** rather than general ones.

Example:

General: His kindness will never be forgotten.

Specific: His thoughtful gifts and bear hugs will never be forgotten.

Attention should also be given to the kind of verbs that are used in sentences. **Active verbs** (e.g., run, swim) should be about an action. Whenever possible, an active verb should replace a linking verb to provide clear examples for arguments and to strengthen a passage overall.

Example:

Passive: The winners were called to the stage by the judges.

Active: The judges called the winners to the stage.

Revising sentences is done to make writing more effective. **Editing** sentences is done to correct any errors. Sentences are the building blocks of writing, and they can be changed in regards to sentence length, sentence structure, and sentence openings. You should add **variety** to sentence length, structure, and openings so that the essay does not seem boring or repetitive. A careful analysis of a piece of writing will expose these stylistic problems, and they can be corrected before you finish your essay. Changing up your sentence structure and sentence length can make your essay more inviting and appealing to readers.

RECURSIVE WRITING PROCESS

However you approach writing, you may find comfort in knowing that the revision process can occur in any order. The **recursive writing process** is not as difficult as the phrase may make it seem. Simply put, the recursive writing process means that the steps in the writing process occur in **no particular order**. For example, planning, drafting, and revising (all a part of the writing process) can all take place at about the same time and you may not notice that all three happen so close together. Truly, the writing process is a series of moving back and forth between planning,

80

drafting, and revising followed by more planning, more drafting, and more revising until the writing is complete.

TRANSITIONS

Transitions are **bridges** between what has been read and what is about to be read. Transitions smooth the reader's path between sentences and inform the reader of major connections to new ideas forthcoming in the text. **Transitional phrases** should be used with care, selecting the appropriate phrase for a transition. **Tone** is another important consideration in using transitional phrases, and a good writer varies tone for different audiences. For example, in a scholarly essay, *in summary* would be preferable to the more informal *in short*.

When working with transitional words and phrases, writers usually find a natural **flow** that indicates when a transition is needed. In reading a draft of the text, it should become apparent where the flow is uneven or rough. At this point, the writer can add transitional elements during the revision process. Revising can also afford an opportunity to delete transitional devices that seem heavy handed or unnecessary.

Transitional words and phrases are used to transition **between** paragraphs and also to transition **within** a single paragraph. Transitions assist the flow of ideas and help to unify an essay. A writer can use certain words to indicate that an example or summary is being presented. The following phrases, among others, can be used as this type of transition: *as a result, as I have said, for example, for instance, in any case, in any event, in brief, in conclusion, in fact, in other words, in short, on the whole,* and *to sum it up*.

TRANSITIONAL WORDS
LINK SIMILAR IDEAS

When a writer links ideas that are similar in nature, there are a variety of words and phrases he or she can choose, including but not limited to: *also, and, another, besides, equally important, further, furthermore, in addition, likewise, too, similarly, nor, of course,* and *for instance*.

LINK DISSIMILAR OR CONTRADICTORY IDEAS

Writers can link contradictory ideas in an essay by using, among others, the following words and phrases: *although, and yet, even if, conversely, but, however, otherwise, still, yet, instead, in spite of, nevertheless, on the contrary,* and *on the other hand*.

INDICATE CAUSE, PURPOSE, OR RESULT

Writers may need to indicate that one thing is the cause, purpose, or result of another thing. To show this relationship, writers can use, among others, the following linking words and phrases: *as, as a result, because, consequently, hence, for, for this reason, since, so, then, thus,* and *therefore*.

INDICATE TIME OR POSITION

Certain words can be used to indicate the time and position of one thing in relation to another. Writers can use, for example, the following terms to create a timeline of events in an essay: *above, across, afterward, before, beyond, eventually, meanwhile, next, presently, around, at once, at the present time, finally, first, here, second, thereafter,* and *upon*. These words can show the order or placement of items or ideas in an essay.

PARAGRAPHS

After the introduction of a passage, a series of **body paragraphs** will carry a message through to the conclusion. A paragraph should be unified around a **main point**. Normally, a good topic sentence summarizes the paragraph's main point. A **topic sentence** is a general sentence that gives an introduction to the paragraph. The sentences that follow are a support to the topic sentence. However, the topic sentence can come as the final sentence to the paragraph if the earlier sentences give a clear explanation of the topic sentence. Overall, the paragraphs need to stay true to the main point. This means that any unnecessary sentences that do not advance the main point should be removed.

The main point of a paragraph requires adequate **development** (i.e., a substantial paragraph that covers the main point). A paragraph of two or three sentences does not cover a main point. This is true when the main point of the paragraph gives strong support to the argument of the thesis. An occasional short paragraph is fine as a transitional device. However, a well-developed argument will have paragraphs with more than a few sentences.

METHODS OF DEVELOPING PARAGRAPHS

A common method of development with paragraphs can be done with **examples**. These examples are the supporting details to the main idea of a paragraph or a passage. When authors write about something that their audience may not understand, they can provide an example to show their point. When authors write about something that is not easily accepted, they can give examples to prove their point.

Illustrations are extended examples that require several sentences. Well selected illustrations can be a great way for authors to develop a point that may not be familiar to their audience.

Analogies make comparisons between items that appear to have nothing in common. Analogies are employed by writers to provoke fresh thoughts about a subject. These comparisons may be used to explain the unfamiliar, to clarify an abstract point, or to argue a point. Although analogies are effective literary devices, they should be used carefully in arguments. Two things may be alike in some respects but completely different in others.

Cause and effect is an excellent device used when the cause and effect are accepted as true. One way that authors can use cause and effect is to state the effect in the topic sentence of a paragraph and add the causes in the body of the paragraph. With this method, an author's paragraphs can have structure which always strengthens writing.

TYPES OF PARAGRAPHS

A **paragraph of narration** tells a story or a part of a story. Normally, the sentences are arranged in chronological order (i.e., the order that the events happened). However, flashbacks (i.e., beginning the story at an earlier time) can be included.

A **descriptive paragraph** makes a verbal portrait of a person, place, or thing. When specific details are used that appeal to one or more of the senses (i.e., sight, sound, smell, taste, and touch), authors give readers a sense of being present in the moment.

A **process paragraph** is related to time order (i.e., First, you open the bottle. Second, you pour the liquid, etc.). Usually, this describes a process or teaches readers how to perform a process.

82

Comparing two things draws attention to their similarities and indicates a number of differences. When authors contrast, they focus only on differences. Both comparisons and contrasts may be used point-by-point or in following paragraphs.

Reasons for **starting a new paragraph** include:

1. To mark off the introduction and concluding paragraphs
2. To signal a shift to a new idea or topic
3. To indicate an important shift in time or place
4. To explain a point in additional detail
5. To highlight a comparison, contrast, or cause and effect relationship

PARAGRAPH LENGTH

Most readers find that their comfort level for a paragraph is between **100 and 200 words**. Shorter paragraphs cause too much starting and stopping, and give a choppy effect. Paragraphs that are too long often test the attention span of readers. Two notable exceptions to this rule exist. In scientific or scholarly papers, longer paragraphs suggest seriousness and depth. In journalistic writing, constraints are placed on paragraph size by the narrow columns in a newspaper format.

The first and last paragraphs of a text will usually be the **introduction** and **conclusion**. These special-purpose paragraphs are likely to be shorter than paragraphs in the body of the work. Paragraphs in the body of the essay follow the subject's outline; one paragraph per point in short essays and a group of paragraphs per point in longer works. Some ideas require more development than others, so it is good for a writer to remain flexible. A paragraph of excessive length may be divided, and shorter ones may be combined.

COHERENT PARAGRAPHS

A smooth flow of sentences and paragraphs without gaps, shifts, or bumps will lead to **paragraph coherence**. Ties between old and new information can be smoothed by several methods:

- **Linking ideas clearly**, from the topic sentence to the body of the paragraph, is essential for a smooth transition. The topic sentence states the main point, and this should be followed by specific details, examples, and illustrations that support the topic sentence. The support may be direct or indirect. In indirect support, the illustrations and examples may support a sentence that in turn supports the topic directly.
- The **repetition of key words** adds coherence to a paragraph. To avoid dull language, variations of the key words may be used.
- **Parallel structures** are often used within sentences to emphasize the similarity of ideas and connect sentences giving similar information.
- Maintaining a **consistent verb tense** throughout the paragraph helps. Shifting tenses affects the smooth flow of words and can disrupt the coherence of the paragraph.

Mathematics Test

Numbers and Numeration

CLASSIFICATIONS OF NUMBERS

Numbers are the basic building blocks of mathematics. Specific features of numbers are identified by the following terms:

Integer – any positive or negative whole number, including zero. Integers do not include fractions $\left(\frac{1}{3}\right)$, decimals (0.56), or mixed numbers $\left(7\frac{3}{4}\right)$.

Prime number – any whole number greater than 1 that has only two factors, itself and 1; that is, a number that can be divided evenly only by 1 and itself.

Composite number – any whole number greater than 1 that has more than two different factors; in other words, any whole number that is not a prime number. For example: The composite number 8 has the factors of 1, 2, 4, and 8.

Even number – any integer that can be divided by 2 without leaving a remainder. For example: 2, 4, 6, 8, and so on.

Odd number – any integer that cannot be divided evenly by 2. For example: 3, 5, 7, 9, and so on.

Decimal number – any number that uses a decimal point to show the part of the number that is less than one. Example: 1.234.

Decimal point – a symbol used to separate the ones place from the tenths place in decimals or dollars from cents in currency.

Decimal place – the position of a number to the right of the decimal point. In the decimal 0.123, the 1 is in the first place to the right of the decimal point, indicating tenths; the 2 is in the second place, indicating hundredths; and the 3 is in the third place, indicating thousandths.

The **decimal**, or base 10, system is a number system that uses ten different digits (0, 1, 2, 3, 4, 5, 6, 7, 8, 9). An example of a number system that uses something other than ten digits is the **binary**, or base 2, number system, used by computers, which uses only the numbers 0 and 1. It is thought that the decimal system originated because people had only their 10 fingers for counting.

Rational numbers include all integers, decimals, and fractions. Any terminating or repeating decimal number is a rational number.

Irrational numbers cannot be written as fractions or decimals because the number of decimal places is infinite and there is no recurring pattern of digits within the number. For example, pi (π)

84

begins with 3.141592 and continues without terminating or repeating, so pi is an irrational number.

Real numbers are the set of all rational and irrational numbers.

> **Review Video and Practice: <u>Classification of Numbers</u>**
> Visit mometrix.com/academy and enter code: 461071
>
> **Review Video and Practice: <u>Rational and Irrational Numbers</u>**
> Visit mometrix.com/academy and enter code: 280645
>
> **Review Video and Practice: <u>Prime and Composite Numbers</u>**
> Visit mometrix.com/academy and enter code: 565581

THE NUMBER LINE

A number line is a graph to see the distance between numbers. Basically, this graph shows the relationship between numbers. So, a number line may have a point for zero and may show negative numbers on the left side of the line. Any positive numbers are placed on the right side of the line. For example, consider the points labeled on the following number line:

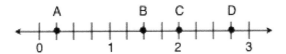

We can use the dashed lines on the number line to identify each point. Each dashed line between two whole numbers is $\frac{1}{4}$. The line halfway between two numbers is $\frac{1}{2}$.

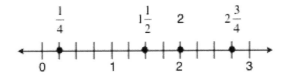

> **Review Video: <u>The Number Line</u>**
> Visit mometrix.com/academy and enter code: 816439

NUMBERS IN WORD FORM AND PLACE VALUE

When writing numbers out in word form or translating word form to numbers, it is essential to understand how a place value system works. In the decimal or base-10 system, each digit of a number represents how many of the corresponding place value – a specific factor of 10 – are contained in the number being represented. To make reading numbers easier, every three digits to the left of the decimal place is preceded by a comma. The following table demonstrates some of the place values:

Power of 10	10^3	10^2	10^1	10^0	10^{-1}	10^{-2}	10^{-3}
Value	1,000	100	10	1	0.1	0.01	0.001
Place	thousands	hundreds	tens	ones	tenths	hundredths	thousandths

For example, consider the number 4,546.09, which can be separated into each place value like this:

4: thousands
5: hundreds
4: tens
6: ones
0: tenths
9: hundredths

This number in word form would be *four thousand five hundred forty-six and nine hundredths.*

Review Video: Place Value
Visit mometrix.com/academy and enter code: 205433

ABSOLUTE VALUE

A precursor to working with negative numbers is understanding what **absolute values** are. A number's absolute value is simply the distance away from zero a number is on the number line. The absolute value of a number is always positive and is written $|x|$. For example, the absolute value of 3, written as $|3|$, is 3 because the distance between 0 and 3 on a number line is three units. Likewise, the absolute value of –3, written as $|-3|$, is 3 because the distance between 0 and –3 on a number line is three units. So, $|3| = |-3|$.

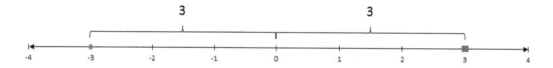

Review Video: Absolute Value
Visit mometrix.com/academy and enter code: 314669

PRACTICE

P1. Write the place value of each digit in 14,059.826

P2. Write out each of the following in words:

(a) 29
(b) 478
(c) 98,542
(d) 0.06
(e) 13.113

P3. Write each of the following in numbers:

(a) nine thousand four hundred thirty-five
(b) three hundred two thousand eight hundred seventy-six
(c) nine hundred one thousandths
(d) nineteen thousandths
(e) seven thousand one hundred forty-two and eighty-five hundredths

PRACTICE SOLUTIONS

P1. The place value for each digit would be as follows:

Digit	Place Value
1	ten-thousands
4	thousands
0	hundreds
5	tens
9	ones
8	tenths
2	hundredths
6	thousandths

P2. Each written out in words would be:

(a) twenty-nine
(b) four hundred seventy-eight
(c) ninety-eight thousand five hundred forty-two
(d) six hundredths
(e) thirteen and one hundred thirteen thousandths

P3. Each in numeric form would be:

(a) 9,435
(b) 302,876
(c) 0.901
(d) 0.019
(e) 7,142.85

OPERATIONS

An **operation** is simply a mathematical process that takes some value(s) as input(s) and produces an output. Elementary operations are often written in the following form: *value operation value*. For instance, in the expression $1 + 2$ the values are 1 and 2 and the operation is addition. Performing the operation gives the output of 3. In this way we can say that $1 + 2$ and 3 are equal, or $1 + 2 = 3$.

ADDITION

Addition increases the value of one quantity by the value of another quantity (both called **addends**). For example, $2 + 4 = 6$; $8 + 9 = 17$. The result is called the **sum**. With addition, the order does not matter, $4 + 2 = 2 + 4$.

When adding signed numbers, if the signs are the same simply add the absolute values of the addends and apply the original sign to the sum. For example, $(+4) + (+8) = +12$ and $(-4) + (-8) = -12$. When the original signs are different, take the absolute values of the addends and subtract the smaller value from the larger value, then apply the original sign of the larger value to the difference. For instance, $(+4) + (-8) = -4$ and $(-4) + (+8) = +4$.

SUBTRACTION

Subtraction is the opposite operation to addition; it decreases the value of one quantity (the **minuend**) by the value of another quantity (the **subtrahend**). For example, $6 - 4 = 2$; $17 - 8 = 9$. The result is called the **difference**. Note that with subtraction, the order does matter, $6 - 4 \neq 4 - 6$.

For subtracting signed numbers, change the sign of the subtrahend and then follow the same rules used for addition. For example, $(+4) - (+8) = (+4) + (-8) = -4$.

MULTIPLICATION

Multiplication can be thought of as repeated addition. One number (the **multiplier**) indicates how many times to add the other number (the **multiplicand**) to itself. For example, 3×2 (three times two) $= 2 + 2 + 2 = 6$. With multiplication, the order does not matter: $2 \times 3 = 3 \times 2$ or $3 + 3 = 2 + 2 + 2$, either way the result (the **product**) is the same.

If the signs are the same, the product is positive when multiplying signed numbers. For example, $(+4) \times (+8) = +32$ and $(-4) \times (-8) = +32$. If the signs are opposite, the product is negative. For example, $(+4) \times (-8) = -32$ and $(-4) \times (+8) = -32$. When more than two factors are multiplied together, the sign of the product is determined by how many negative factors are present. If there are an odd number of negative factors then the product is negative, whereas an even number of negative factors indicates a positive product. For instance, $(+4) \times (-8) \times (-2) = +64$ and $(-4) \times (-8) \times (-2) = -64$.

DIVISION

Division is the opposite operation to multiplication; one number (the **divisor**) tells us how many parts to divide the other number (the **dividend**) into. The result of division is called the **quotient**. For example, $20 \div 4 = 5$; if 20 is split into 4 equal parts, each part is 5. With division, the order of the numbers does matter, $20 \div 4 \neq 4 \div 20$.

The rules for dividing signed numbers are similar to multiplying signed numbers. If the dividend and divisor have the same sign, the quotient is positive. If the dividend and divisor have opposite signs, the quotient is negative. For example, $(-4) \div (+8) = -0.5$.

> **Review Video: Mathematical Operations**
> Visit mometrix.com/academy and enter code: 208095

PARENTHESES

Parentheses are used to designate which operations should be done first when there are multiple operations. Example: $4 - (2 + 1) = 1$; the parentheses tell us that we must add 2 and 1, and then subtract the sum from 4, rather than subtracting 2 from 4 and then adding 1 (this would give us an answer of 3).

> **Review Video: Mathematical Parentheses**
> Visit mometrix.com/academy and enter code: 978600

EXPONENTS

An **exponent** is a superscript number placed next to another number at the top right. It indicates how many times the base number is to be multiplied by itself. Exponents provide a shorthand way to write what would be a longer mathematical expression, for example: $2^4 = 2 \times 2 \times 2 \times 2$. A number with an exponent of 2 is said to be "squared," while a number with an exponent of 3 is said to be "cubed." The value of a number raised to an exponent is called its power. So, 8^4 is read as "8 to the 4th power," or "8 raised to the power of 4."

The properties of exponents are as follows:

Property	Description
$a^1 = a$	Any number to the power of 1 is equal to itself
$1^n = 1$	The number 1 raised to any power is equal to 1
$a^0 = 1$	Any number raised to the power of 0 is equal to 1
$a^n \times a^m = a^{n+m}$	Add exponents to multiply powers of the same base number
$a^n \div a^m = a^{n-m}$	Subtract exponents to divide powers of the same base number
$(a^n)^m = a^{n \times m}$	When a power is raised to a power, the exponents are multiplied
$(a \times b)^n = a^n \times b^n$ $(a \div b)^n = a^n \div b^n$	Multiplication and division operations inside parentheses can be raised to a power. This is the same as each term being raised to that power.
$a^{-n} = \dfrac{1}{a^n}$	A negative exponent is the same as the reciprocal of a positive exponent

Note that exponents do not have to be integers. Fractional or decimal exponents follow all the rules above as well. Example: $5^{\frac{1}{4}} \times 5^{\frac{3}{4}} = 5^{\frac{1}{4}+\frac{3}{4}} = 5^1 = 5$.

> **Review Video: What is an Exponent?**
> Visit mometrix.com/academy and enter code: 600998
>
> **Review Video: Properties of Exponents**
> Visit mometrix.com/academy and enter code: 532558

ROOTS

A **root**, such as a square root, is another way of writing a fractional exponent. Instead of using a superscript, roots use the radical symbol ($\sqrt{}$) to indicate the operation. A radical will have a number underneath the bar, and may sometimes have a number in the upper left: $\sqrt[n]{a}$, read as "the nth root of a." The relationship between radical notation and exponent notation can be described by this equation: $\sqrt[n]{a} = a^{\frac{1}{n}}$. The two special cases of $n = 2$ and $n = 3$ are called square roots and cube roots. If there is no number to the upper left, it is understood to be a square root ($n = 2$). Nearly all of the roots you encounter will be square roots. A square root is the same as a number raised to the one-half power. When we say that a is the square root of b ($a = \sqrt{b}$), we mean that a multiplied by itself equals b: ($a \times a = b$).

A **perfect square** is a number that has an integer for its square root. There are 10 perfect squares from 1 to 100: 1, 4, 9, 16, 25, 36, 49, 64, 81, 100 (the squares of integers 1 through 10).

> **Review Video: Roots**
> Visit mometrix.com/academy and enter code: 795655
>
> **Review Video: Square Root and Perfect Squares**
> Visit mometrix.com/academy and enter code: 648063

ORDER OF OPERATIONS

The **order of operations** is a set of rules that dictates the order in which we must perform each operation in an expression so that we will evaluate it accurately. If we have an expression that includes multiple different operations, the order of operations tells us which operations to do first. The most common mnemonic for the order of operations is **PEMDAS**, or "Please Excuse My Dear Aunt Sally." PEMDAS stands for parentheses, exponents, multiplication, division, addition, and subtraction. It is important to understand that multiplication and division have equal precedence, as do addition and subtraction, so those pairs of operations are simply worked from left to right in order.

For example, evaluating the expression $5 + 20 \div 4 \times (2 + 3) - 6$ using the correct order of operations would be done like this:

- **P:** Perform the operations inside the parentheses: $(2 + 3) = 5$
- **E:** Simplify the exponents.
  - The equation now looks like this: $5 + 20 \div 4 \times 5 - 6$
- **MD:** Perform multiplication and division from left to right: $20 \div 4 = 5$; then $5 \times 5 = 25$
  - The equation now looks like this: $5 + 25 - 6$
- **AS:** Perform addition and subtraction from left to right: $5 + 25 = 30$; then $30 - 6 = 24$

> **Review Video: Order of Operations**
> Visit mometrix.com/academy and enter code: 259675

SUBTRACTION WITH REGROUPING

A great way to make use of some of the features built into the decimal system would be regrouping when attempting longform subtraction operations. When subtracting within a place value, sometimes the minuend is smaller than the subtrahend, **regrouping** enables you to 'borrow' a unit from a place value to the left in order to get a positive difference. For example, consider subtracting 189 from 525 with regrouping.

> **Review Video: Subtracting Large Numbers**
> Visit mometrix.com/academy and enter code: 603350

First, set up the subtraction problem in vertical form:

```
   525
 - 189
```

Notice that the numbers in the ones and tens columns of 525 are smaller than the numbers in the ones and tens columns of 189. This means you will need to use regrouping to perform subtraction:

```
   5  2  5
 - 1  8  9
```

To subtract 9 from 5 in the ones column you will need to borrow from the 2 in the ten's columns:

```
   5  1  15
 - 1  8   9
          6
```

Next, to subtract 8 from 1 in the tens column you will need to borrow from the 5 in the hundred's column:

```
   4  11  15
 - 1   8   9
       3   6
```

90

Last, subtract the 1 from the 4 in the hundred's column:

	4	11	15
−	1	8	9
	3	3	6

PRACTICE

P1. Demonstrate how to subtract 477 from 620 using regrouping.

P2. Simplify the following expressions with exponents:

    (a) 37^0
    (b) 1^{30}
    (c) $2^3 \times 2^4 \times 2^x$
    (d) $(3^x)^3$
    (e) $(12 \div 3)^2$

PRACTICE SOLUTIONS

P1. First, set up the subtraction problem in vertical form:

	6	2	0
−	4	7	7

To subtract 7 from 0 in the ones column you will need to borrow from the 2 in the tens column:

	6	1	10
−	4	7	7
			3

Next, to subtract 7 from the 1 that's still in the tens column you will need to borrow from the 6 in the hundreds column:

	5	11	10
−	4	7	7
		4	3

Lastly, subtract 4 from the 5 remaining in the hundreds column:

	5	11	10
−	4	7	7
	1	4	3

P2. Using the properties of exponents and the proper order of operations:

    (a) Any number raised to the power of 0 is equal to 1: $37^0 = 1$
    (b) The number 1 raised to any power is equal to 1: $1^{30} = 1$
    (c) Add exponents to multiply powers of the same base: $2^3 \times 2^4 \times 2^x = 2^{(3+4+x)} = 2^{(7+x)}$
    (d) When a power is raised to a power, the exponents are multiplied: $(3^x)^3 = 3^{3x}$
    (e) Perform the operation inside the parentheses first: $(12 \div 3)^2 = 4^2 = 16$

FACTORS AND GREATEST COMMON FACTOR

Factors are numbers that are multiplied together to obtain a **product**. For example, in the equation $2 \times 3 = 6$, the numbers 2 and 3 are factors. A **prime number** has only two factors (1 and itself), but other numbers can have many factors.

A **common factor** is a number that divides exactly into two or more other numbers. For example, the factors of 12 are 1, 2, 3, 4, 6, and 12, while the factors of 15 are 1, 3, 5, and 15. The common factors of 12 and 15 are 1 and 3.

A **prime factor** is also a prime number. Therefore, the prime factors of 12 are 2 and 3. For 15, the prime factors are 3 and 5.

The **greatest common factor** (**GCF**) is the largest number that is a factor of two or more numbers. For example, the factors of 15 are 1, 3, 5, and 15; the factors of 35 are 1, 5, 7, and 35. Therefore, the greatest common factor of 15 and 35 is 5.

> **Review Video: Factors**
> Visit mometrix.com/academy and enter code: 920086
>
> **Review Video: Greatest Common Factor and Least Common Multiple**
> Visit mometrix.com/academy and enter code: 838699

MULTIPLES AND LEAST COMMON MULTIPLE

Often listed out in multiplication tables, **multiples** are integer increments of a given factor. In other words, dividing a multiple by the factor number will result in an integer. For example, the multiples of 7 include: $1 \times 7 = 7$, $2 \times 7 = 14$, $3 \times 7 = 21$, $4 \times 7 = 28$, $5 \times 7 = 35$. Dividing 7, 14, 21, 28, or 35 by 7 will result in the integers 1, 2, 3, 4, and 5, respectively.

The least common multiple (**LCM**) is the smallest number that is a multiple of two or more numbers. For example, the multiples of 3 include 3, 6, 9, 12, 15, etc.; the multiples of 5 include 5, 10, 15, 20, etc. Therefore, the least common multiple of 3 and 5 is 15.

> **Review Video: Multiples**
> Visit mometrix.com/academy and enter code: 626738

FRACTIONS

A **fraction** is a number that is expressed as one integer written above another integer, with a dividing line between them $\left(\frac{x}{y}\right)$. It represents the **quotient** of the two numbers "x divided by y." It can also be thought of as x out of y equal parts.

The top number of a fraction is called the **numerator**, and it represents the number of parts under consideration. The 1 in $\frac{1}{4}$ means that 1 part out of the whole is being considered in the calculation. The bottom number of a fraction is called the **denominator**, and it represents the total number of equal parts. The 4 in $\frac{1}{4}$ means that the whole consists of 4 equal parts. A fraction cannot have a denominator of zero; this is referred to as "*undefined*."

Fractions can be manipulated, without changing the value of the fraction, by multiplying or dividing (but not adding or subtracting) both the numerator and denominator by the same number. If you divide both numbers by a common factor, you are **reducing** or simplifying the fraction. Two fractions that have the same value but are expressed differently are known as **equivalent fractions**. For example, $\frac{2}{10}, \frac{3}{15}, \frac{4}{20}$, and $\frac{5}{25}$ are all equivalent fractions. They can also all be reduced or simplified to $\frac{1}{5}$.

When two fractions are manipulated so that they have the same denominator, this is known as finding a **common denominator**. The number chosen to be that common denominator should be the least common multiple of the two original denominators. Example: $\frac{3}{4}$ and $\frac{5}{6}$; the least common multiple of 4 and 6 is 12. Manipulating to achieve the common denominator: $\frac{3}{4} = \frac{9}{12}; \frac{5}{6} = \frac{10}{12}$.

PROPER FRACTIONS AND MIXED NUMBERS

A fraction whose denominator is greater than its numerator is known as a **proper fraction**, while a fraction whose numerator is greater than its denominator is known as an **improper fraction**. Proper fractions have values *less than one* and improper fractions have values *greater than one*.

A **mixed number** is a number that contains both an integer and a fraction. Any improper fraction can be rewritten as a mixed number. Example: $\frac{8}{3} = \frac{6}{3} + \frac{2}{3} = 2 + \frac{2}{3} = 2\frac{2}{3}$. Similarly, any mixed number can be rewritten as an improper fraction. Example: $1\frac{3}{5} = 1 + \frac{3}{5} = \frac{5}{5} + \frac{3}{5} = \frac{8}{5}$.

> **Review Video: Improper Fractions and Mixed Numbers**
> Visit mometrix.com/academy and enter code: 211077
>
> **Review Video: Overview of Fractions**
> Visit mometrix.com/academy and enter code: 262335

ADDING AND SUBTRACTING FRACTIONS

If two fractions have a common denominator, they can be added or subtracted simply by adding or subtracting the two numerators and retaining the same denominator. If the two fractions do not already have the same denominator, one or both of them must be manipulated to achieve a common denominator before they can be added or subtracted. Example: $\frac{1}{2} + \frac{1}{4} = \frac{2}{4} + \frac{1}{4} = \frac{3}{4}$.

> **Review Video: Adding and Subtracting Fractions**
> Visit mometrix.com/academy and enter code: 378080

MULTIPLYING FRACTIONS

Two fractions can be multiplied by multiplying the two numerators to find the new numerator and the two denominators to find the new denominator. Example: $\frac{1}{3} \times \frac{2}{3} = \frac{1 \times 2}{3 \times 3} = \frac{2}{9}$.

DIVIDING FRACTIONS

Two fractions can be divided by flipping the numerator and denominator of the second fraction and then proceeding as though it were a multiplication. Example: $\frac{2}{3} \div \frac{3}{4} = \frac{2}{3} \times \frac{4}{3} = \frac{8}{9}$.

> **Review Video: Multiplying and Dividing Fractions**
> Visit mometrix.com/academy and enter code: 473632

MULTIPLYING A MIXED NUMBER BY A WHOLE NUMBER OR A DECIMAL

When multiplying a mixed number by something, it is usually best to convert it to an improper fraction first. Additionally, if the multiplicand is a decimal, it is most often simplest to convert it to a fraction. For instance, to multiply $4\frac{3}{8}$ by 3.5, begin by rewriting each quantity as a whole number plus a proper fraction. Remember, a mixed number is a fraction added to a whole number and a decimal is a representation of the sum of fractions, specifically tenths, hundredths, thousandths, and so on:

$$4\frac{3}{8} \times 3.5 = \left(4 + \frac{3}{8}\right) \times \left(3 + \frac{1}{2}\right)$$

Next, the quantities being added need to be expressed with the same denominator. This is achieved by multiplying and dividing the whole number by the denominator of the fraction. Recall that a whole number is equivalent to that number divided by 1:

$$= \left(\frac{4}{1} \times \frac{8}{8} + \frac{3}{8}\right) \times \left(\frac{3}{1} \times \frac{2}{2} + \frac{1}{2}\right)$$

When multiplying fractions, remember to multiply the numerators and denominators separately:

$$= \left(\frac{4 \times 8}{1 \times 8} + \frac{3}{8}\right) \times \left(\frac{3 \times 2}{1 \times 2} + \frac{1}{2}\right)$$

$$= \left(\frac{32}{8} + \frac{3}{8}\right) \times \left(\frac{6}{2} + \frac{1}{2}\right)$$

Now that the fractions have the same denominators, they can be added:

$$= \frac{35}{8} \times \frac{7}{2}$$

Finally, perform the last multiplication and then simplify:

$$= \frac{35 \times 7}{8 \times 2} = \frac{245}{16} = \frac{240}{16} + \frac{5}{16} = 15\frac{5}{16}$$

DECIMALS

Decimals are one way to represent parts of a whole. Using the place value system, each digit to the right of a decimal point denotes the number of units of a corresponding *negative* power of ten. For example, consider the decimal 0.24. We can use a model to represent the decimal. Since a dime is worth one-tenth of a dollar and a penny is worth one-hundredth of a dollar, one possible model to represent this fraction is to have 2 dimes representing the 2 in the tenths place and 4 pennies representing the 4 in the hundredths place:

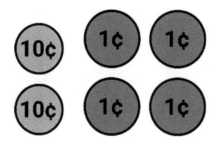

To write the decimal as a fraction, put the decimal in the numerator with 1 in the denominator. Multiply the numerator and denominator by tens until there are no more decimal places. Then simplify the fraction to lowest terms. For example, converting 0.24 to a fraction:

$$0.24 = \frac{0.24}{1} = \frac{0.24 \times 100}{1 \times 100} = \frac{24}{100} = \frac{6}{25}$$

> **Review Video: Decimals**
> Visit mometrix.com/academy and enter code: 837268

ADDING AND SUBTRACTING DECIMALS

When adding and subtracting decimals, the decimal points must always be aligned. Adding decimals is just like adding regular whole numbers. Example: $4.5 + 2.0 = 6.5$.

If the problem-solver does not properly align the decimal points, an incorrect answer of 4.7 may result. An easy way to add decimals is to align all of the decimal points in a vertical column visually. This will allow you to see exactly where the decimal should be placed in the final answer. Begin adding from right to left. Add each column in turn, making sure to carry the number to the left if a column adds up to more than 9. The same rules apply to the subtraction of decimals.

> **Review Video: Adding and Subtracting Decimals**
> Visit mometrix.com/academy and enter code: 381101

MULTIPLYING DECIMALS

A simple multiplication problem has two components: a **multiplicand** and a **multiplier**. When multiplying decimals, work as though the numbers were whole rather than decimals. Once the final product is calculated, count the number of places to the right of the decimal in both the multiplicand and the multiplier. Then, count that number of places from the right of the product and place the decimal in that position.

For example, 12.3×2.56 has a total of three places to the right of the respective decimals. Multiply 123×256 to get 31488. Now, beginning on the right, count three places to the left and insert the decimal. The final product will be 31.488.

> **Review Video: How to Multiply Decimals**
> Visit mometrix.com/academy and enter code: 731574

DIVIDING DECIMALS

Every division problem has a **divisor** and a **dividend**. The dividend is the number that is being divided. In the problem $14 \div 7$, 14 is the dividend and 7 is the divisor. In a division problem with decimals, the divisor must be converted into a whole number. Begin by moving the decimal in the divisor to the right until a whole number is created. Next, move the decimal in the dividend the same number of spaces to the right. For example, 4.9 into 24.5 would become 49 into 245. The decimal was moved one space to the right to create a whole number in the divisor, and then the same was done for the dividend. Once the whole numbers are created, the problem is carried out normally: $245 \div 49 = 5$.

> **Review Video: How to Divide Decimals**
> Visit mometrix.com/academy and enter code: 560690

PERCENTAGES

Percentages can be thought of as fractions that are based on a whole of 100; that is, one whole is equal to 100%. The word **percent** means "per hundred." Percentage problems are often presented in three main ways:

- Find what percentage of some number another number is.
  - Example: What percentage of 40 is 8?
- Find what number is some percentage of a given number.
  - Example: What number is 20% of 40?
- Find what number another number is a given percentage of.
  - Example: What number is 8 20% of?

There are three components in each of these cases: a **whole** (W), a **part** (P), and a **percentage** (%). These are related by the equation: $P = W \times \%$. This can easily be rearranged into other forms that may suit different questions better: $\% = \frac{P}{W}$ and $W = \frac{P}{\%}$. Percentage problems are often also word problems. As such, a large part of solving them is figuring out which quantities are what. For example, consider the following word problem:

In a school cafeteria, 7 students choose pizza, 9 choose hamburgers, and 4 choose tacos. What percentage of student choose tacos?

To find the whole, you must first add all of the parts: $7 + 9 + 4 = 20$. The percentage can then be found by dividing the part by the whole ($\% = \frac{P}{W}$): $\frac{4}{20} = \frac{20}{100} = 20\%$.

CONVERTING BETWEEN PERCENTAGES, FRACTIONS, AND DECIMALS

Converting decimals to percentages and percentages to decimals is as simple as moving the decimal point. To *convert from a decimal to a percentage*, move the decimal point **two places to the right**. To *convert from a percentage to a decimal*, move it **two places to the left**. It may be helpful to remember that the percentage number will always be larger than the equivalent decimal number. For example:

$$0.23 = 23\% \quad 5.34 = 534\% \quad 0.007 = 0.7\%$$
$$700\% = 7.00 \quad 86\% = 0.86 \quad 0.15\% = 0.0015$$

To convert a fraction to a decimal, simply divide the numerator by the denominator in the fraction. To convert a decimal to a fraction, put the decimal in the numerator with 1 in the denominator. Multiply the numerator and denominator by tens until there are no more decimal places. Then simplify the fraction to lowest terms. For example, converting 0.24 to a fraction:

$$0.24 = \frac{0.24}{1} = \frac{0.24 \times 100}{1 \times 100} = \frac{24}{100} = \frac{6}{25}$$

Fractions can be converted to a percentage by finding equivalent fractions with a denominator of 100. Example:

$$\frac{7}{10} = \frac{70}{100} = 70\% \quad \frac{1}{4} = \frac{25}{100} = 25\%$$

To convert a percentage to a fraction, divide the percentage number by 100 and reduce the fraction to its simplest possible terms. Example:

$$60\% = \frac{60}{100} = \frac{3}{5} \quad 96\% = \frac{96}{100} = \frac{24}{25}$$

> **Review Video: Converting Fractions to Percentages and Decimals**
> Visit mometrix.com/academy and enter code: 306233
>
> **Review Video: Converting Percentages to Decimals and Fractions**
> Visit mometrix.com/academy and enter code: 287297
>
> **Review Video: Converting Decimals to Fractions and Percentages**
> Visit mometrix.com/academy and enter code: 986765
>
> **Review Video: Converting Decimals, Improper Fractions, and Mixed Numbers**
> Visit mometrix.com/academy and enter code: 696924

RATIONAL NUMBERS

The term **rational** means that the number can be expressed as a ratio or fraction. That is, a number, r, is rational if and only if it can be represented by a fraction $\frac{a}{b}$ where a and b are integers and b does not equal 0. The set of rational numbers includes integers and decimals. If there is no finite way to represent a value with a fraction of integers, then the number is **irrational**. Common examples of irrational numbers include: $\sqrt{5}$, $(1 + \sqrt{2})$, and π.

> **Review Video: Rational and Irrational Numbers**
> Visit mometrix.com/academy and enter code: 280645
>
> **Review Video: Ordering Rational Numbers**
> Visit mometrix.com/academy and enter code: 419578

PRACTICE

P1. What is 30% of 120?

P2. What is 150% of 20?

P3. What is 14.5% of 96?

P4. Simplify the following expressions:

(a) $\left(\frac{2}{5}\right)/\left(\frac{4}{7}\right)$
(b) $\frac{7}{8} - \frac{8}{16}$
(c) $\frac{1}{2} + \left(3\left(\frac{3}{4}\right) - 2\right) + 4$
(d) $0.22 + 0.5 - (5.5 + 3.3 \div 3)$
(e) $\frac{3}{2} + (4(0.5) - 0.75) + 2$

P5. Convert the following to a fraction and to a decimal: **(a)** 15%; **(b)** 24.36%

P6. Convert the following to a decimal and to a percentage: **(a)** 4/5; **(b)** $3\frac{2}{5}$

P7. A woman's age is thirteen more than half of 60. How old is the woman?

P8. A patient was given pain medicine at a dosage of 0.22 grams. The patient's dosage was then increased to 0.80 grams. By how much was the patient's dosage increased?

P9. At a hotel, $\frac{3}{4}$ of the 100 rooms are occupied today. Yesterday, $\frac{4}{5}$ of the 100 rooms were occupied. On which day were more of the rooms occupied and by how much more?

P10. At a school, 40% of the teachers teach English. If 20 teachers teach English, how many teachers work at the school?

P11. A patient was given blood pressure medicine at a dosage of 2 grams. The patient's dosage was then decreased to 0.45 grams. By how much was the patient's dosage decreased?

P12. Two weeks ago, $\frac{2}{3}$ of the 60 customers at a skate shop were male. Last week, $\frac{3}{6}$ of the 80 customers were male. During which week were there more male customers?

P13. Jane ate lunch at a local restaurant. She ordered a \$4.99 appetizer, a \$12.50 entrée, and a \$1.25 soda. If she wants to tip her server 20%, how much money will she spend in all?

P14. According to a survey, about 82% of engineers were highly satisfied with their job. If 145 engineers were surveyed, how many reported that they were highly satisfied?

P15. A patient was given 40 mg of a certain medicine. Later, the patient's dosage was increased to 45 mg. What was the percent increase in his medication?

P16. Order the following rational numbers from least to greatest: 0.55, 17%, $\sqrt{25}$, $\frac{64}{4}$, $\frac{25}{50}$, 3

P17. Order the following rational numbers from greatest to least: 0.3, 27%, $\sqrt{100}$, $\frac{72}{9}$, $\frac{1}{9}$, 4.5

P18. Perform the following multiplication. Write each answer as a mixed number.

(a) $\left(1\frac{11}{16}\right) \times 4$

(b) $\left(12\frac{1}{3}\right) \times 1.1$

(c) $3.71 \times \left(6\frac{1}{5}\right)$

P19. Suppose you are making doughnuts and you want to triple the recipe you have. If the following list is the original amounts for the ingredients, what would be the amounts for the tripled recipe?

$1\,^3/_4$	cup	Flour
$1\,^1/_4$	tsp	Baking powder
$^3/_4$	tsp	Salt
$^3/_8$	cup	Sugar
$1\,^1/_2$	Tbsp	Butter
2	large	Eggs
$^3/_4$	tsp	Vanilla extract
$^3/_8$	cup	Sour cream

PRACTICE SOLUTIONS

P1. The word *of* indicates multiplication, so 30% of 120 is found by multiplying 120 by 30%. Change 30% to a decimal, then multiply: $120 \times 0.3 = 36$

P2. The word *of* indicates multiplication, so 150% of 20 is found by multiplying 20 by 150%. Change 150% to a decimal, then multiply: $20 \times 1.5 = 30$

P3. Change 14.5% to a decimal before multiplying. $0.145 \times 96 = 13.92$.

P4. Follow the order of operations and utilize properties of fractions to solve each:

(a) Rewrite the problem as a multiplication problem: $\frac{2}{5} \times \frac{7}{4} = \frac{2 \times 7}{5 \times 4} = \frac{14}{20}$. Make sure the fraction is reduced to lowest terms. Both 14 and 20 can be divided by 2.

$$\frac{14}{20} = \frac{14 \div 2}{20 \div 2} = \frac{7}{10}$$

(b) The denominators of $\frac{7}{8}$ and $\frac{8}{16}$ are 8 and 16, respectively. The lowest common denominator of 8 and 16 is 16 because 16 is the least common multiple of 8 and 16. Convert the first fraction to its equivalent with the newly found common denominator of 16: $\frac{7 \times 2}{8 \times 2} = \frac{14}{16}$. Now that the fractions have the same denominator, you can subtract them.

$$\frac{14}{16} - \frac{8}{16} = \frac{6}{16} = \frac{3}{8}$$

(c) When simplifying expressions, first perform operations within groups. Within the set of parentheses are multiplication and subtraction operations. Perform the multiplication first to get $\frac{1}{2} + \left(\frac{9}{4} - 2\right) + 4$. Then, subtract two to obtain $\frac{1}{2} + \frac{1}{4} + 4$. Finally, perform addition from left to right:

$$\frac{1}{2} + \frac{1}{4} + 4 = \frac{2}{4} + \frac{1}{4} + \frac{16}{4} = \frac{19}{4} = 4\frac{3}{4}$$

(d) First, evaluate the terms in the parentheses $(5.5 + 3.3 \div 3)$ using order of operations. $3.3 \div 3 = 1.1$, and $5.5 + 1.1 = 6.6$. Next, rewrite the problem: $0.22 + 0.5 - 6.6$. Finally, add and subtract from left to right: $0.22 + 0.5 = 0.72$; $0.72 - 6.6 = -5.88$. The answer is -5.88.

(e) First, simplify within the parentheses, then change the fraction to a decimal and perform addition from left to right:

$$\frac{3}{2} + (2 - 0.75) + 2 =$$
$$\frac{3}{2} + 1.25 + 2 =$$
$$1.5 + 1.25 + 2 = 4.75$$

P5. (a) 15% can be written as $\frac{15}{100}$. Both 15 and 100 can be divided by 5: $\frac{15 \div 5}{100 \div 5} = \frac{3}{20}$

When converting from a percentage to a decimal, drop the percent sign and move the decimal point two places to the left: $15\% = 0.15$

(b) 24.36% written as a fraction is $\frac{24.36}{100}$, or $\frac{2436}{10,000}$, which reduces to $\frac{609}{2500}$. 24.36% written as a decimal is 0.2436. Recall that dividing by 100 moves the decimal two places to the left.

P6. (a) Recall that in the decimal system the first decimal place is one tenth: $\frac{4 \times 2}{5 \times 2} = \frac{8}{10} = 0.8$

Percent means "per hundred." $\frac{4 \times 20}{5 \times 20} = \frac{80}{100} = 80\%$

(b) The mixed number $3\frac{2}{5}$ has a whole number and a fractional part. The fractional part $\frac{2}{5}$ can be written as a decimal by dividing 5 into 2, which gives 0.4. Adding the whole to the part gives 3.4.

To find the equivalent percentage, multiply the decimal by 100. $3.4(100) = 340\%$. Notice that this percentage is greater than 100%. This makes sense because the original mixed number $3\frac{2}{5}$ is greater than 1.

P7. "More than" indicates addition, and "of" indicates multiplication. The expression can be written as $\frac{1}{2}(60) + 13$. So, the woman's age is equal to $\frac{1}{2}(60) + 13 = 30 + 13 = 43$. The woman is 43 years old.

P8. The first step is to determine what operation (addition, subtraction, multiplication, or division) the problem requires. Notice the keywords and phrases "by how much" and "increased." "Increased" means that you go from a smaller amount to a larger amount. This change can be found by subtracting the smaller amount from the larger amount: 0.80 grams– 0.22 grams = 0.58 grams.

Remember to line up the decimal when subtracting:

$$
\begin{array}{r}
0.80 \\
- \ \ 0.22 \\
\hline
0.58
\end{array}
$$

P9. First, find the number of rooms occupied each day. To do so, multiply the fraction of rooms occupied by the number of rooms available:

$$\text{Number occupied} = \text{Fraction occupied} \times \text{Total number}$$
$$\text{Number of rooms occupied today} = \frac{3}{4} \times 100 = 75$$
$$\text{Number of rooms occupied} = \frac{4}{5} \times 100 = 80$$

The difference in the number of rooms occupied is: $80 - 75 = 5$ rooms

P10. To answer this problem, first think about the number of teachers that work at the school. Will it be more or less than the number of teachers who work in a specific department such as English? More teachers work at the school, so the number you find to answer this question will be greater than 20.

40% of the teachers are English teachers. "Of" indicates multiplication, and words like "is" and "are" indicate equivalence. Translating the problem into a mathematical sentence gives $40\% \times t = 20$, where t represents the total number of teachers. Solving for t gives $t = \frac{20}{40\%} = \frac{20}{0.40} = 50$. Fifty teachers work at the school.

P11. The decrease is represented by the difference between the two amounts:

$$2 \text{ grams} - 0.45 \text{ grams} = 1.55 \text{ grams.}$$

Remember to line up the decimal point before subtracting.

$$\begin{array}{r} 2.00 \\ -\ 0.45 \\ \hline 1.55 \end{array}$$

P12. First, you need to find the number of male customers that were in the skate shop each week. You are given this amount in terms of fractions. To find the actual number of male customers, multiply the fraction of male customers by the number of customers in the store.

$$\text{Actual number of male customers} = \text{fraction of male customers} \times \text{total customers}$$
$$\text{Number of male customers two weeks ago} = \frac{2}{3} \times 60 = \frac{120}{3} = 40$$
$$\text{Number of male customers last week} = \frac{3}{6} \times 80 = \frac{1}{2} \times 80 = \frac{80}{2} = 40$$

The number of male customers was the same both weeks.

P13. To find total amount, first find the sum of the items she ordered from the menu and then add 20% of this sum to the total.

$$\$4.99 + \$12.50 + \$1.25 = \$18.74$$

$$\$18.74 \times 20\% = (0.20)(\$18.74) = \$3.748 \approx \$3.75$$

$$\text{Total} = \$18.74 + \$3.75 = \$22.49$$

P14. 82% of 145 is 0.82 × 145 = 118.9. Because you can't have 0.9 of a person, we must round up to say that 119 engineers reported that they were highly satisfied with their jobs.

P15. To find the percent increase, first compare the original and increased amounts. The original amount was 40 mg, and the increased amount is 45 mg, so the dosage of medication was increased by 5 mg (45– 40 = 5). Note, however, that the question asks not by how much the dosage increased but by what percentage it increased.

$$\text{Percent increase} = \frac{\text{new amount} - \text{original amount}}{\text{original amount}} \times 100\%$$
$$= \frac{45 \text{ mg} - 40 \text{ mg}}{40 \text{ mg}} \times 100\% = \frac{5}{40} \times 100\% = 0.125 \times 100\% = 12.5\%$$

P16. Recall that the term rational simply means that the number can be expressed as a ratio or fraction. Notice that each of the numbers in the problem can be written as a decimal or integer:

$$17\% = 0.17$$
$$\sqrt{25} = 5$$
$$\frac{64}{4} = 16$$
$$\frac{25}{50} = \frac{1}{2} = 0.5$$

So, the answer is $17\%, \frac{25}{50}, 0.55, 3, \sqrt{25}, \frac{64}{4}$.

P17. Converting all the numbers to integers and decimals makes it easier to compare the values:

$$27\% = 0.27$$
$$\sqrt{100} = 10$$
$$\frac{72}{9} = 8$$
$$\frac{1}{9} \approx 0.11$$

So, the answer is $\sqrt{100}, \frac{72}{9}, 4.5, 0.3, 27\%, \frac{1}{9}$.

> **Review Video: Ordering Rational Numbers**
> Visit mometrix.com/academy and enter code: 419578

P18. For each, convert improper fractions, adjust to a common denominator, perform the operations, and then simplify:

(a) Sometimes, you can skip converting the denominator and just distribute the multiplication.

$$\left(1\frac{11}{16}\right) \times 4 = \left(1 + \frac{11}{16}\right) \times 4$$

$$= 1 \times 4 + \frac{11}{16} \times 4$$

$$= 4 + \frac{11}{16} \times \frac{4}{1}$$

$$= 4 + \frac{44}{16} = 4 + \frac{11}{4} = 4 + 2\frac{3}{4} = 6\frac{3}{4}$$

(b)

$$\left(12\frac{1}{3}\right) \times 1.1 = \left(12 + \frac{1}{3}\right) \times \left(1 + \frac{1}{10}\right)$$

$$= \left(\frac{12}{1} \times \frac{3}{3} + \frac{1}{3}\right) \times \left(\frac{10}{10} + \frac{1}{10}\right)$$

$$= \left(\frac{36}{3} + \frac{1}{3}\right) \times \frac{11}{10}$$

$$= \frac{37}{3} \times \frac{11}{10}$$

$$= \frac{407}{30} = \frac{390}{30} + \frac{17}{30} = 13\frac{17}{30}$$

(c)

$$3.71 \times \left(6\frac{1}{5}\right) = \left(3 + \frac{71}{100}\right) \times \left(6 + \frac{1}{5}\right)$$

$$= \left(\frac{300}{100} + \frac{71}{100}\right) \times \left(\frac{6}{1} \times \frac{5}{5} + \frac{1}{5}\right)$$

$$= \frac{371}{100} \times \left(\frac{30}{5} + \frac{1}{5}\right)$$

$$= \frac{371}{100} \times \frac{31}{5}$$

$$= \frac{11501}{500} = \frac{11500}{500} + \frac{1}{500} = 23\frac{1}{500}$$

P19. Fortunately, some of the amounts are duplicated, so we do not need to figure out every amount.

$$1\frac{3}{4} \times 3 = (1 \times 3) + \left(\frac{3}{4} \times 3\right)$$
$$= 3 + \frac{9}{4}$$
$$= 3 + 2\frac{1}{4}$$
$$= 5\frac{1}{4}$$

$$1\frac{1}{4} \times 3 = (1 \times 3) + \left(\frac{1}{4} \times 3\right)$$
$$= 3 + \frac{3}{4}$$
$$= 3\frac{3}{4}$$

$$\frac{3}{4} \times 3 = \frac{3}{4} \times 3$$
$$= \frac{9}{4}$$
$$= 2\frac{1}{4}$$

$$\frac{3}{8} \times 3 = \frac{3}{8} \times 3$$
$$= \frac{9}{8}$$
$$= 1\frac{1}{8}$$

$$1\frac{1}{2} \times 3 = 1 \times 3 + \frac{1}{2} \times 3$$
$$= 3 + \frac{3}{2}$$
$$= 3 + 1\frac{1}{2}$$
$$= 4\frac{1}{2}$$

$$2 \times 3 = 6$$

So, the result for the triple recipe is:

5 1/4	cup	Flour
3 3/4	tsp	Baking powder
2 1/4	tsp	Salt
1 1/8	cup	Sugar
4 1/2	Tbsp	Butter
6	large	Eggs
2 1/4	tsp	Vanilla extract
1 1/8	cup	Sour cream

PROPORTIONS

A proportion is a relationship between two quantities that dictates how one changes when the other changes. A **direct proportion** describes a relationship in which a quantity increases by a set amount for every increase in the other quantity, or decreases by that same amount for every decrease in the other quantity. Example: Assuming a constant driving speed, the time required for a car trip increases as the distance of the trip increases. The distance to be traveled and the time required to travel are directly proportional.

An **inverse proportion** is a relationship in which an increase in one quantity is accompanied by a decrease in the other, or vice versa. Example: the time required for a car trip decreases as the speed increases, and increases as the speed decreases, so the time required is inversely proportional to the speed of the car.

> **Review Video: Proportions**
> Visit mometrix.com/academy and enter code: 505355

RATIOS

A **ratio** is a comparison of two quantities in a particular order. Example: If there are 14 computers in a lab, and the class has 20 students, there is a student to computer ratio of 20 to 14, commonly written as 20:14. Ratios are normally reduced to their smallest whole number representation, so 20:14 would be reduced to 10:7 by dividing both sides by 2.

> **Review Video: Ratios**
> Visit mometrix.com/academy and enter code: 996914

CONSTANT OF PROPORTIONALITY

When two quantities have a proportional relationship, there exists a **constant of proportionality** between the quantities. The product of this constant and one of the quantities is equal to the other quantity. For example, if one lemon costs $0.25, two lemons cost $0.50, and three lemons cost $0.75, there is a proportional relationship between the total cost of lemons and the number of lemons purchased. The constant of proportionality is the **unit price**, namely $0.25/lemon. Notice that the total price of lemons, t, can be found by multiplying the unit price of lemons, p, and the number of lemons, n: $t = pn$.

WORK/UNIT RATE

Unit rate expresses a quantity of one thing in terms of one unit of another. For example, if you travel 30 miles every two hours, a unit rate expresses this comparison in terms of one hour: in one hour you travel 15 miles, so your unit rate is 15 miles per hour. Other examples are how much one ounce of food costs (price per ounce) or figuring out how much one egg costs out of the dozen (price per 1 egg, instead of price per 12 eggs). The denominator of a unit rate is always 1. Unit rates are used to compare different situations to solve problems. For example, to make sure you get the best deal when deciding which kind of soda to buy, you can find the unit rate of each. If soda #1 costs $1.50 for a 1-liter bottle, and soda #2 costs $2.75 for a 2-liter bottle, it would be a better deal to buy soda #2, because its unit rate is only $1.375 per 1-liter, which is cheaper than soda #1. Unit rates can also help determine the length of time a given event will take. For example, if you can paint 2 rooms in 4.5 hours, you can determine how long it will take you to paint 5 rooms by solving for the unit rate per room and then multiplying that by 5.

> **Review Video: Rates and Unit Rates**
> Visit mometrix.com/academy and enter code: 185363

SLOPE

On a graph with two points, (x_1, y_1) and (x_2, y_2), the **slope** is found with the formula $m = \frac{y_2 - y_1}{x_2 - x_1}$, where $x_1 \neq x_2$ and m stands for slope. If the value of the slope is **positive**, the line has an *upward direction* from left to right. If the value of the slope is **negative**, the line has a *downward direction* from left to right. Consider the following example:

A new book goes on sale in bookstores and online stores. In the first month, 5,000 copies of the book are sold. Over time, the book continues to grow in popularity. The data for the number of copies sold is in the table below.

# of Months on Sale	1	2	3	4	5
# of Copies Sold (In Thousands)	5	10	15	20	25

So, the number of copies that are sold and the time that the book is on sale is a proportional relationship. In this example, an equation can be used to show the data: $y = 5x$, where x is the number of months that the book is on sale, and y is the number of copies sold. So, the slope of the corresponding line is $\frac{\text{rise}}{\text{run}} = \frac{5}{1} = 5$.

> **Review Video: Finding the Slope of a Line**
> Visit mometrix.com/academy and enter code: 766664

FINDING AN UNKNOWN IN EQUIVALENT EXPRESSIONS

It is often necessary to apply information given about a rate or proportion to a new scenario. For example, if you know that Jedha can run a marathon (26 miles) in 3 hours, how long would it take her to run 10 miles at the same pace? Start by setting up equivalent expressions:

$$\frac{26 \text{ mi}}{3 \text{ hr}} = \frac{10 \text{ mi}}{x \text{ hr}}$$

Now, cross multiply and solve for x:

$$26x = 30$$
$$x = \frac{30}{26} = \frac{15}{13}$$
$$x \cong 1.15 \text{ hrs } or \text{ 1 hr 9 min}$$

So, at this pace, Jedha could run 10 miles in about 1.15 hours or about 1 hour and 9 minutes.

> **Review Video: Cross Multiplying Fractions**
> Visit mometrix.com/academy and enter code: 893904

PRACTICE

P1. Solve the following for x.

(a) $\frac{45}{12} = \frac{15}{x}$

(b) $\frac{0.50}{2} = \frac{1.50}{x}$

(c) $\frac{40}{8} = \frac{x}{24}$

P2. At a school, for every 20 female students there are 15 male students. This same student ratio happens to exist at another school. If there are 100 female students at the second school, how many male students are there?

P3. In a hospital emergency room, there are 4 nurses for every 12 patients. What is the ratio of nurses to patients? If the nurse-to-patient ratio remains constant, how many nurses must be present to care for 24 patients?

P4. In a bank, the banker-to-customer ratio is 1:2. If seven bankers are on duty, how many customers are currently in the bank?

P5. Janice made $40 during the first 5 hours she spent babysitting. She will continue to earn money at this rate until she finishes babysitting in 3 more hours. Find how much money Janice earns per hour and the total she earned babysitting.

P6. The McDonalds are taking a family road trip, driving 300 miles to their cabin. It took them 2 hours to drive the first 120 miles. They will drive at the same speed all the way to their cabin. Find the speed at which the McDonalds are driving and how much longer it will take them to get to their cabin.

P7. It takes Andy 10 minutes to read 6 pages of his book. He has already read 150 pages in his book that is 210 pages long. Find how long it takes Andy to read 1 page and also find how long it will take him to finish his book if he continues to read at the same speed.

PRACTICE SOLUTIONS

P1. Cross multiply, then solve for x:

(a) $45x = 12 \times 15$
$45x = 180$
$x = \frac{180}{45} = 4$

(b) $0.5x = 1.5 \times 2$
$0.5x = 3$
$x = \frac{3}{0.5} = 6$

(c) $8x = 40 \times 24$
$8x = 960$
$x = \frac{960}{8} = 120$

P2. One way to find the number of male students is to set up and solve a proportion.

$$\frac{\text{number of female students}}{\text{number of male students}} = \frac{20}{15} = \frac{100}{\text{number of male students}}$$

Represent the unknown number of male students as the variable x: $\frac{20}{15} = \frac{100}{x}$

Cross multiply and then solve for x:

$$20x = 15 \times 100$$
$$x = \frac{1500}{20}$$
$$x = 75$$

P3. The ratio of nurses to patients can be written as 4 to 12, 4:12, or $\frac{4}{12}$. Because four and twelve have a common factor of four, the ratio should be reduced to 1:3, which means that there is one nurse present for every three patients. If this ratio remains constant, there must be eight nurses present to care for 24 patients.

P4. Use proportional reasoning or set up a proportion to solve. Because there are twice as many customers as bankers, there must be fourteen customers when seven bankers are on duty. Setting up and solving a proportion gives the same result:

$$\frac{\text{number of bankers}}{\text{number of customers}} = \frac{1}{2} = \frac{7}{\text{number of customers}}$$

107

Represent the unknown number of customers as the variable x: $\frac{1}{2} = \frac{7}{x}$.

To solve for x, cross multiply: $1 \times x = 7 \times 2$, so $x = 14$.

P5. Janice earns \$8 per hour. This can be found by taking her initial amount earned, \$40, and dividing it by the number of hours worked, 5. Since $\frac{40}{5} = 8$, Janice makes \$8 in one hour. This can also be found by finding the unit rate, money earned per hour: $\frac{40}{5} = \frac{x}{1}$. Since cross multiplying yields $5x = 40$, and division by 5 shows that $x = 8$, Janice earns \$8 per hour.

Janice will earn \$64 babysitting in her 8 total hours (adding the first 5 hours to the remaining 3 gives the 8-hour total). Since Janice earns \$8 per hour and she worked 8 hours, $\frac{\$8}{\text{hr}} \times 8 \text{ hrs} = \$64$. This can also be found by setting up a proportion comparing money earned to babysitting hours. Since she earns \$40 for 5 hours and since the rate is constant, she will earn a proportional amount in 8 hours: $\frac{40}{5} = \frac{x}{8}$. Cross multiplying will yield $5x = 320$, and division by 5 shows that $x = 64$.

P6. The McDonalds are driving 60 miles per hour. This can be found by setting up a proportion to find the unit rate, the number of miles they drive per one hour: $\frac{120}{2} = \frac{x}{1}$. Cross multiplying yields $2x = 120$ and division by 2 shows that $x = 60$.

Since the McDonalds will drive this same speed for the remaining miles, it will take them another 3 hours to get to their cabin. This can be found by first finding how many miles the McDonalds have left to drive, which is $300 - 120 = 180$. The McDonalds are driving at 60 miles per hour, so a proportion can be set up to determine how many hours it will take them to drive 180 miles: $\frac{180}{x} = \frac{60}{1}$. Cross multiplying yields $60x = 180$, and division by 60 shows that $x = 3$. This can also be found by using the formula $D = r \times t$ (or distance = rate $\times$ time), where $180 = 60 \times t$, and division by 60 shows that $t = 3$.

P7. It takes Andy 10 minutes to read 6 pages, $\frac{10}{6} = 1\frac{2}{3}$ minutes, which is 1 minute and 40 seconds.

Next, determine how many pages Andy has left to read, $210 - 150 = 60$. Since it is now known that it takes him $1\frac{2}{3}$ minutes to read each page, that rate must be multiplied by however many pages he has left to read (60) to find the time he'll need: $60 \times 1\frac{2}{3} = 100$, so it will take him 100 minutes, or 1 hour and 40 minutes, to read the rest of his book.

Mømetrix

Measurements

METRIC MEASUREMENT PREFIXES

Giga-	One billion	1 *giga*watt is one billion watts
Mega-	One million	1 *mega*hertz is one million hertz
Kilo-	One thousand	1 *kilo*gram is one thousand grams
Deci-	One-tenth	1 *deci*meter is one-tenth of a meter
Centi-	One-hundredth	1 *centi*meter is one-hundredth of a meter
Milli-	One-thousandth	1 *milli*liter is one-thousandth of a liter
Micro-	One-millionth	1 *micro*gram is one-millionth of a gram

> **Review Video and Practice: Metric System Conversions**
> Visit mometrix.com/academy and enter code: 163709

MEASUREMENT CONVERSION

When converting between units, the goal is to maintain the same meaning but change the way it is displayed. In order to go from a larger unit to a smaller unit, multiply the number of the known amount by the equivalent amount. When going from a smaller unit to a larger unit, divide the number of the known amount by the equivalent amount.

For complicated conversions, it may be helpful to set up conversion fractions. In these fractions, one fraction is the **conversion factor**. The other fraction has the unknown amount in the numerator. So, the known value is placed in the denominator. Sometimes, the second fraction has the known value from the problem in the numerator and the unknown in the denominator. Multiply the two fractions to get the converted measurement. Note that since the numerator and the denominator of the factor are equivalent, the value of the fraction is 1. That is why we can say that the result in the new units is equal to the result in the old units even though they have different numbers.

It can often be necessary to chain known conversion factors together. As an example, consider converting 512 square inches to square meters. We know that there are 2.54 centimeters in an inch and 100 centimeters in a meter, and we know we will need to square each of these factors to achieve the conversion we are looking for.

$$\frac{512 \text{ in}^2}{1} \times \left(\frac{2.54 \text{ cm}}{1 \text{ in}}\right)^2 \times \left(\frac{1 \text{ m}}{100 \text{ cm}}\right)^2 = \frac{512 \text{ in}^2}{1} \times \left(\frac{6.4516 \text{ cm}^2}{1 \text{ in}^2}\right) \times \left(\frac{1 \text{ m}^2}{10000 \text{ cm}^2}\right) = 0.330 \text{ m}^2$$

> **Review Video and Practice: Measurement Conversions**
> Visit mometrix.com/academy and enter code: 316703

COMMON UNITS AND EQUIVALENTS
METRIC EQUIVALENTS

1000 µg (microgram)	1 mg
1000 mg (milligram)	1 g
1000 g (gram)	1 kg
1000 kg (kilogram)	1 metric ton
1000 mL (milliliter)	1 L
1000 µm (micrometer)	1 mm
1000 mm (millimeter)	1 m
100 cm (centimeter)	1 m
1000 m (meter)	1 km

DISTANCE AND AREA MEASUREMENT

Unit	Abbreviation	US equivalent	Metric equivalent
Inch	in	1 inch	2.54 centimeters
Foot	ft	12 inches	0.305 meters
Yard	yd	3 feet	0.914 meters
Mile	mi	5280 feet	1.609 kilometers
Acre	ac	4840 square yards	0.405 hectares
Square Mile	sq. mi. or mi.^{2}	640 acres	2.590 square kilometers

CAPACITY MEASUREMENTS

Unit	Abbreviation	US equivalent	Metric equivalent
Fluid Ounce	fl oz	8 fluid drams	29.573 milliliters
Cup	c	8 fluid ounces	0.237 liter
Pint	pt.	16 fluid ounces	0.473 liter
Quart	qt.	2 pints	0.946 liter
Gallon	gal.	4 quarts	3.785 liters
Teaspoon	t or tsp.	1 fluid dram	5 milliliters
Tablespoon	T or tbsp.	4 fluid drams	15 or 16 milliliters
Cubic Centimeter	cc or cm.^{3}	0.271 drams	1 milliliter

WEIGHT MEASUREMENTS

Unit	Abbreviation	US equivalent	Metric equivalent
Ounce	oz	16 drams	28.35 grams
Pound	lb	16 ounces	453.6 grams
Ton	tn.	2,000 pounds	907.2 kilograms

VOLUME AND WEIGHT MEASUREMENT CLARIFICATIONS

Always be careful when using ounces and fluid ounces. They are not equivalent.

1 pint = 16 fluid ounces	1 fluid ounce ≠ 1 ounce
1 pound = 16 ounces	1 pint ≠ 1 pound

Having one pint of something does not mean you have one pound of it. In the same way, just because something weighs one pound does not mean that its volume is one pint.

In the United States, the word "ton" by itself refers to a short ton or a net ton. Do not confuse this with a long ton (also called a gross ton) or a metric ton (also spelled *tonne*), which have different measurement equivalents.

$$1 \text{ US ton} = 2000 \text{ pounds} \quad \neq \quad 1 \text{ metric ton} = 1000 \text{ kilograms}$$

MILITARY TIME

The **24-hour clock** is a time system used by the military and on some digital clocks. On the 24-hour clock, minutes and seconds are the same as the standard 12-hour clock. However, time is expressed in 4 figures, and the hours run from 0000 hour (12 a.m.) to 2359 hours (11:59 p.m.).

To convert from 12-hour to 24-hour time, remove the colon and:

- for a.m. times, if the time has 3 digits, add a 0 to the beginning (e.g., 8:12 a.m. becomes 0812 hours). For times between 12 a.m. and 1 a. m., replace the 12 with a pair of zeros (e.g., 12:41 a.m. becomes 0041 hours).
- for p.m. times, add 12 to the hour number (e.g., 3:40 p.m. = 1540 hours), except for times between 12 p.m. and 1 p.m., which do not require any further change.

To convert from 24-hour to 12-hour time, add a colon between the second and third digits. If the first two digits are less than 12, the time is a.m.; otherwise, it is p.m. If the first two digits are zeros, the hour becomes 12 a.m. (e.g., 0020 becomes 12:20 a.m.) If only the first digit is zero, remove it (e.g., 0730 becomes 7:30 a.m.). If the first two digits are greater than 12, subtract 12 (e.g., 2325 becomes 11:25 p.m.).

TEMPERATURE CONVERSION

Converting between Fahrenheit (°F) and Celsius (°C) is slightly more involved than a direct proportion. From the following equations, we can see that a change of one degree Celsius is greater than a change of one degree Fahrenheit.

Conversion	Equation	Example
°F → °C	$°C = \dfrac{5}{9}(°F - 32)$	Convert 200.0 °F to °C $\dfrac{5}{9}(200.0 - 32) = \dfrac{5}{9}(168.0)$ $= 93.33 \, °C$
°C → °F	$°F = \dfrac{9}{5}(°C) + 32$	Convert 24.0 °C to °F $\dfrac{9}{5}(24.0) + 32 = 43.2 + 32$ $= 75.2 \, °F$

PRACTICE

P1. Perform the following conversions:

    (a) 1.4 meters to centimeters

    (b) 218 centimeters to meters

    (c) 42 inches to feet

    (d) 15 kilograms to pounds

    (e) 80 ounces to pounds

    (f) 2 miles to kilometers

    (g) 5 feet to centimeters

    (h) 15.14 liters to gallons

    (i) 8 quarts to liters

    (j) 13.2 pounds to grams

    (l) 0430 to 12-hour time

    (m) 3:50 p.m. to 24-hour time

    (n) 101.5 °F to °C

    (o) 140 °C to °F

PRACTICE SOLUTIONS

P1. (a) $\frac{100 \text{ cm}}{1 \text{ m}} = \frac{x \text{ cm}}{1.4 \text{ m}}$ Cross multiply to get $x = 140$

(b) $\frac{100 \text{ cm}}{1 \text{ m}} = \frac{218 \text{ cm}}{x \text{ m}}$ Cross multiply to get $100x = 218$, or $x = 2.18$

(c) $\frac{12 \text{ in}}{1 \text{ ft}} = \frac{42 \text{ in}}{x \text{ ft}}$ Cross multiply to get $12x = 42$, or $x = 3.5$

(d) 15 kilograms $\times \frac{2.2 \text{ pounds}}{1 \text{ kilogram}} = 33$ pounds

(e) 80 ounces $\times \frac{1 \text{ pound}}{16 \text{ ounces}} = 5$ pounds

(f) 2 miles $\times \frac{1.609 \text{ kilometers}}{1 \text{ mile}} = 3.218$ kilometers

(g) 5 feet $\times \frac{12 \text{ inches}}{1 \text{ foot}} \times \frac{2.54 \text{ centimeters}}{1 \text{ inch}} = 152.4$ centimeters

(h) 15.14 liters $\times \frac{1 \text{ gallon}}{3.785 \text{ liters}} = 4$ gallons

(i) 8 quarts $\times \frac{1 \text{ gallon}}{4 \text{ quarts}} \times \frac{3.785 \text{ liters}}{1 \text{ gallon}} = 7.57$ liters

(j) 13.2 pounds $\times \frac{1 \text{ kilogram}}{2.2 \text{ pounds}} \times \frac{1000 \text{ grams}}{1 \text{ kilogram}} = 6000$ grams

(l) Since 0430 is less than 1200 and begins with a single zero, drop the zero and use a.m.:

$$0430 = 4:30 \text{ a.m.}$$

(m) For p.m. times, drop the p.m. and add 1200:

$$3:50 \text{ p.m.} = 350 + 1200 = 1550$$

(n) For °F → °C, first subtract 32, then multiply by $\frac{5}{9}$:

$$101.5 - 32 = 69.5$$

$$69.5 \times \frac{5}{9} = 38.6 \text{ °C}$$

(o) For °C → °F, multiply by $\frac{9}{5}$, then add 32:

$$140 \times \frac{9}{5} = 252$$

$$252 + 32 = 284 \text{ °F}$$

Geometry

POINTS AND LINES

A **point** is a fixed location in space, has no size or dimensions, and is commonly represented by a dot. A **line** is a set of points that extends infinitely in two opposite directions. It has length, but no width or depth. A line can be defined by any two distinct points that it contains. A **line segment** is a portion of a line that has definite endpoints. A **ray** is a portion of a line that extends from a single point on that line in one direction along the line. It has a definite beginning, but no ending.

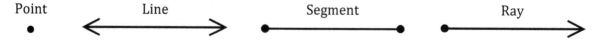

INTERACTIONS BETWEEN LINES

Intersecting lines are lines that have exactly one point in common. **Concurrent lines** are multiple lines that intersect at a single point. **Perpendicular lines** are lines that intersect at right angles. They are represented by the symbol ⊥. The shortest distance from a line to a point not on the line is a perpendicular segment from the point to the line. **Parallel lines** are lines in the same plane that have no points in common and never meet. It is possible for lines to be in different planes, have no points in common, and never meet, but they are not parallel because they are in different planes.

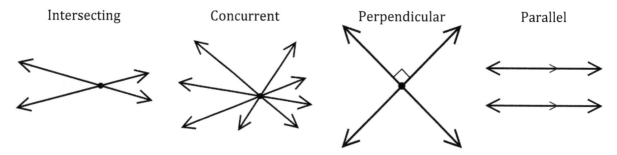

A **transversal** is a line that intersects at least two other lines, which may or may not be parallel to one another. A transversal that intersects parallel lines is a common occurrence in geometry. A **bisector** is a line or line segment that divides another line segment into two equal lengths. A **perpendicular bisector** of a line segment is composed of points that are equidistant from the endpoints of the segment it is dividing.

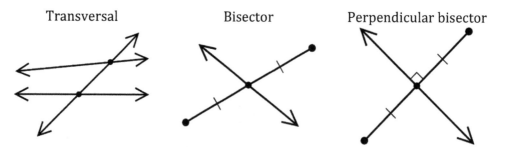

The **projection of a point on a line** is the point at which a perpendicular line drawn from the given point to the given line intersects the line. This is also the shortest distance from the given point to the line. The **projection of a segment on a line** is a segment whose endpoints are the points formed when perpendicular lines are drawn from the endpoints of the given segment to the given line. This is similar to the length a diagonal line appears to be when viewed from above.

Projection of a point on a line   Projection of a segment on a line

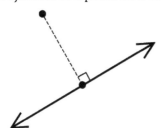 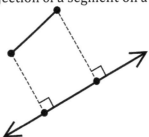

PLANES

A **plane** is a two-dimensional flat surface defined by three non-collinear points. A plane extends an infinite distance in all directions in those two dimensions. It contains an infinite number of points, parallel lines and segments, intersecting lines and segments, as well as parallel or intersecting rays. A plane will never contain a three-dimensional figure or skew lines, lines that don't intersect and are not parallel. Two given planes are either parallel or they intersect at a line. A plane may intersect a circular conic surface to form **conic sections**, such as a parabola, hyperbola, circle or ellipse.

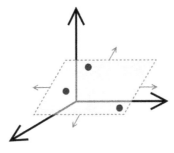

Review Video: Lines and Planes
Visit mometrix.com/academy and enter code: 554267

ANGLES AND VERTICES

An **angle** is formed when two lines or line segments meet at a common point. It may be a common starting point for a pair of segments or rays, or it may be the intersection of lines. Angles are represented by the symbol ∠.

The **vertex** is the point at which two segments or rays meet to form an angle. If the angle is formed by intersecting rays, lines, and/or line segments, the vertex is the point at which four angles are formed. The pairs of angles opposite one another are called vertical angles, and their measures are equal.

- An **acute** angle is an angle with a degree measure less than 90°.
- A **right** angle is an angle with a degree measure of exactly 90°.
- An **obtuse** angle is an angle with a degree measure greater than 90° but less than 180°.
- A **straight angle** is an angle with a degree measure of exactly 180°. This is also a semicircle.
- A **reflex angle** is an angle with a degree measure greater than 180° but less than 360°.

A **full angle** is an angle with a degree measure of exactly 360°. This is also a circle.

115

RELATIONSHIPS BETWEEN ANGLES

Two angles whose sum is exactly 90° are said to be **complementary**. The two angles may or may not be adjacent. In a right triangle, the two acute angles are complementary.

Two angles whose sum is exactly 180° are said to be **supplementary**. The two angles may or may not be adjacent. Two intersecting lines always form two pairs of supplementary angles. Adjacent supplementary angles will always form a straight line.

Two angles that have the same vertex and share a side are said to be **adjacent**. Vertical angles are not adjacent because they share a vertex but no common side.

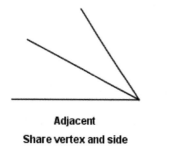

Adjacent	Not adjacent
Share vertex and side	Share part of side, but not vertex

When two parallel lines are cut by a transversal, the angles that are between the two parallel lines are **interior angles**. In the diagram below, angles 3, 4, 5, and 6 are interior angles.

When two parallel lines are cut by a transversal, the angles that are outside the parallel lines are **exterior angles**. In the diagram below, angles 1, 2, 7, and 8 are exterior angles.

When two parallel lines are cut by a transversal, the angles that are in the same position relative to the transversal and a parallel line are **corresponding angles**. The diagram below has four pairs of corresponding angles: angles 1 and 5, angles 2 and 6, angles 3 and 7, and angles 4 and 8. Corresponding angles formed by parallel lines are congruent.

When two parallel lines are cut by a transversal, the two interior angles that are on opposite sides of the transversal are called **alternate interior angles**. In the diagram below, there are two pairs of alternate interior angles: angles 3 and 6, and angles 4 and 5. Alternate interior angles formed by parallel lines are congruent.

When two parallel lines are cut by a transversal, the two exterior angles that are on opposite sides of the transversal are called **alternate exterior angles**.

> **Review Video: _Angles_**
> Visit mometrix.com/academy and enter code: 264624

In the diagram below, there are two pairs of alternate exterior angles: angles 1 and 8, and angles 2 and 7. Alternate exterior angles formed by parallel lines are congruent.

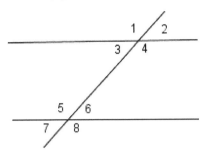

When two lines intersect, four angles are formed. The non-adjacent angles at this vertex are called vertical angles. Vertical angles are congruent. In the diagram, $\angle ABD \cong \angle CBE$ and $\angle ABC \cong \angle DBE$.

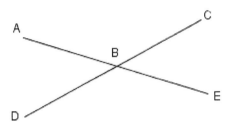

PRACTICE

P1. Find the measure of angles **(a)**, **(b)**, and **(c)** based on the figure with two parallel lines, two perpendicular lines and one transversal:

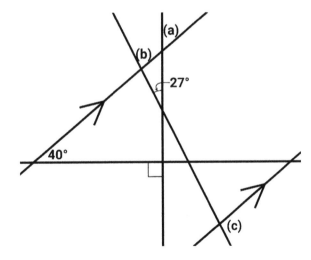

PRACTICE SOLUTIONS

P1. (a) The vertical angle paired with (a) is part of a right triangle with the 40° angle. Thus the measure can be found:

$$90° = 40° + a$$
$$a = 50°$$

(b) The triangle formed by the supplementary angle to (b) is part of a triangle with the vertical angle paired with (a) and the given angle of 27°. Since $a = 50°$:

$$180° = (180° - b) + 50° + 27°$$
$$103° = 180° - b$$
$$-77° = -b$$
$$77° = b$$

(c) As they are part of a transversal crossing parallel lines, angles (b) and (c) are supplementary. Thus $c = 103°$

$$V = \frac{1}{3}\pi r^2 h = \frac{1}{3}\pi(5 \text{ yd})^2(7 \text{ yd}) = \frac{35\pi}{3} \text{ yd}^3 \cong 36.65 \text{ yd}^3$$

POLYGONS

A **polygon** is a closed, two-dimensional figure with three or more straight line segments called **sides**. The point at which two sides of a polygon intersect is called the **vertex**. In a polygon, the number of sides is always equal to the number of vertices. A polygon with all sides congruent and all angles equal is called a **regular polygon**. Common polygons are:

Triangle = 3 sides
Quadrilateral = 4 sides
Pentagon = 5 sides
Hexagon = 6 sides
Heptagon = 7 sides
Octagon = 8 sides
Nonagon = 9 sides
Decagon = 10 sides
Dodecagon = 12 sides

More generally, an *n*-gon is a polygon that has *n* angles and *n* sides.

The sum of the interior angles of an *n*-sided polygon is $(n - 2) \times 180°$. For example, in a triangle $n = 3$. So the sum of the interior angles is $(3 - 2) \times 180° = 180°$. In a quadrilateral, $n = 4$, and the sum of the angles is $(4 - 2) \times 180° = 360°$.

> **Review Video: Intro to Polygons**
> Visit mometrix.com/academy and enter code: 271869
>
> **Review Video: Sum of Interior Angles**
> Visit mometrix.com/academy and enter code: 984991

APOTHEM AND RADIUS

A line segment from the center of a polygon that is perpendicular to a side of the polygon is called the **apothem**. A line segment from the center of a polygon to a vertex of the polygon is called a

radius. In a regular polygon, the apothem can be used to find the area of the polygon using the formula $A = \frac{1}{2}ap$, where a is the apothem, and p is the perimeter.

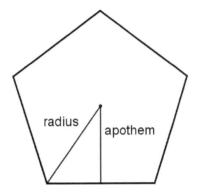

A **diagonal** is a line segment that joins two non-adjacent vertices of a polygon. The number of diagonals a polygon has can be found by using the formula:

$$\text{number of diagonals} = \frac{n(n-3)}{2}$$

Note that n is the number of sides in the polygon. This formula works for all polygons, not just regular polygons.

> **Review Video: <u>Diagonals of Parallelograms, Rectangles, and Rhombi</u>**
> Visit mometrix.com/academy and enter code: 320040

CONVEX AND CONCAVE POLYGONS

A **convex polygon** is a polygon whose diagonals all lie within the interior of the polygon. A **concave polygon** is a polygon with a least one diagonal that is outside the polygon. In the diagram below, quadrilateral *ABCD* is concave because diagonal $\overline{AC}$ lies outside the polygon and quadrilateral *EFGH* is convex because both diagonals lie inside the polygon.

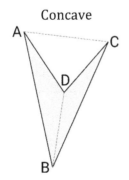
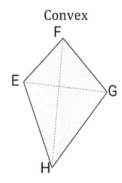

CONGRUENCE AND SIMILARITY

Congruent figures are geometric figures that have the same size and shape. All corresponding angles are equal, and all corresponding sides are equal. Congruence is indicated by the symbol ≅.

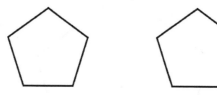

Congruent polygons

Similar figures are geometric figures that have the same shape, but do not necessarily have the same size. All corresponding angles are equal, and all corresponding sides are proportional, but they do not have to be equal. It is indicated by the symbol ~.

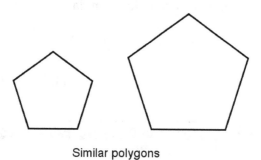

Similar polygons

Note that all congruent figures are also similar, but not all similar figures are congruent.

> **Review Video: Intro to Polygons**
> Visit mometrix.com/academy and enter code: 271869

LINE OF SYMMETRY

A line that divides a figure or object into congruent parts is called a **line of symmetry**. An object may have no lines of symmetry, one line of symmetry, or multiple (i.e., more than one) lines of symmetry.

None   One   Multiple

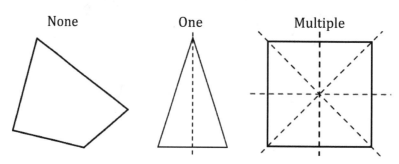

> **Review Video: Symmetry**
> Visit mometrix.com/academy and enter code: 528106

TRIANGLES

A triangle is a three-sided figure with the sum of its interior angles being $180°$ The **perimeter of any triangle** is found by summing the three side lengths; $P = a + b + c$. For an equilateral triangle, this is the same as $P = 3a$, where a is any side length, since all three sides are the same length.

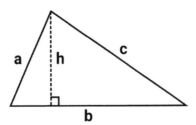

The **area of any triangle** can be found by taking half the product of one side length, referred to as the base and often given the variable b, and the perpendicular distance from that side to the opposite vertex, called the altitude or height and given the variable h. In equation form that is $A = \frac{1}{2}bh$. Another formula that works for any triangle is $A = \sqrt{s(s - a)(s - b)(s - c)}$, where s is the semiperimeter: $\frac{a+b+c}{2}$, and a, b, and c are the lengths of the three sides. Special cases include isosceles triangles: $A = \frac{1}{2}b\sqrt{a^2 - \frac{b^2}{4}}$, where b is the unique side and a is the length of one of the two congruent sides, and equilateral triangles: $A = \frac{\sqrt{3}}{4}a^2$, where a is the length of a side.

> **Review Video: Area and Perimeter of a Triangle**
> Visit mometrix.com/academy and enter code: 853779

PARTS OF A TRIANGLE

An **altitude** of a triangle is a line segment drawn from one vertex perpendicular to the opposite side. In the diagram below, $\overline{BE}$, $\overline{AD}$, and $\overline{CF}$ are altitudes. The length of an altitude is also called the height of the triangle. The three altitudes in a triangle are always concurrent. The point of concurrency of the altitudes of a triangle, O, is called the **orthocenter**. Note that in an obtuse triangle, the orthocenter will be outside the triangle, and in a right triangle, the orthocenter is the vertex of the right angle.

A **median** of a triangle is a line segment drawn from one vertex to the midpoint of the opposite side. In the diagram below, $\overline{BH}$, $\overline{AG}$, and $\overline{CI}$ are medians. This is not the same as the altitude, except the altitude to the base of an isosceles triangle and all three altitudes of an equilateral triangle. The point of concurrency of the medians of a triangle, T, is called the **centroid**. This is the same point as the orthocenter only in an equilateral triangle. Unlike the orthocenter, the centroid is always inside the triangle. The centroid can also be considered the exact center of the triangle. Any shape triangle can be perfectly balanced on a tip placed at the centroid. The centroid is also the point that is two-thirds the distance from the vertex to the opposite side.

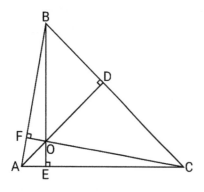 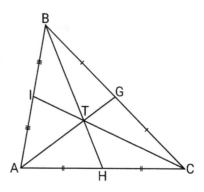

Review Video: Incenter, Circumcenter, Orthocenter, and Centroid
Visit mometrix.com/academy and enter code: 598260

QUADRILATERALS

A **quadrilateral** is a closed two-dimensional geometric figure that has four straight sides. The sum of the interior angles of any quadrilateral is 360°.

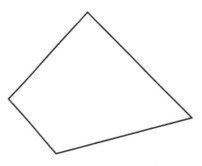

KITE

A **kite** is a quadrilateral with two pairs of adjacent sides that are congruent. A result of this is perpendicular diagonals. A kite can be concave or convex and has one line of symmetry.

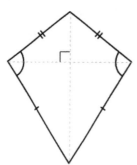 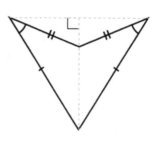

122

TRAPEZOID

Trapezoid: A trapezoid is defined as a quadrilateral that has at least one pair of parallel sides. There are no rules for the second pair of sides. So there are no rules for the diagonals and no lines of symmetry for a trapezoid.

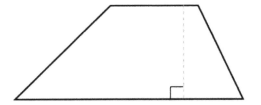 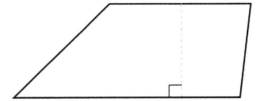

The **area of a trapezoid** is found by the formula $A = \frac{1}{2}h(b_1 + b_2)$, where h is the height (segment joining and perpendicular to the parallel bases), and b_1 and b_2 are the two parallel sides (bases). Do not use one of the other two sides as the height unless that side is also perpendicular to the parallel bases.

The **perimeter of a trapezoid** is found by the formula $P = a + b_1 + c + b_2$, where a, b_1, c, and b_2 are the four sides of the trapezoid.

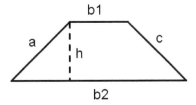

> ### Review Video: <u>Area and Perimeter of a Trapezoid</u>
> Visit mometrix.com/academy and enter code: 587523

Isosceles trapezoid: A trapezoid with equal base angles. This gives rise to other properties including: the two nonparallel sides have the same length, the two non-base angles are also equal, and there is one line of symmetry through the midpoints of the parallel sides.

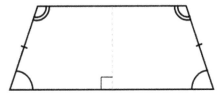

PARALLELOGRAM

Parallelogram: A quadrilateral that has two pairs of opposite parallel sides. As such it is a special type of trapezoid. The sides that are parallel are also congruent. The opposite interior angles are always congruent, and the consecutive interior angles are supplementary. The diagonals of a parallelogram divide each other. Each diagonal divides the parallelogram into two congruent triangles. A parallelogram has no line of symmetry, but does have 180-degree rotational symmetry about the midpoint.

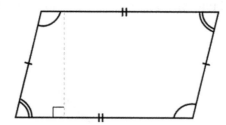

The **area of a parallelogram** is found by the formula $A = bh$, where b is the length of the base, and h is the height. Note that the base and height correspond to the length and width in a rectangle, so this formula would apply to rectangles as well. Do not confuse the height of a parallelogram with the length of the second side. The two are only the same measure in the case of a rectangle.

The **perimeter of a parallelogram** is found by the formula $P = 2a + 2b$ or $P = 2(a + b)$, where a and b are the lengths of the two sides.

> **Review Video: How to Find the Area and Perimeter of a Parallelogram**
> Visit mometrix.com/academy and enter code: 718313

RECTANGLE

Rectangle: A quadrilateral with four right angles. All rectangles are parallelograms and trapezoids, but not all parallelograms or trapezoids are rectangles. The diagonals of a rectangle are congruent. Rectangles have 2 lines of symmetry (through each pair of opposing midpoints) and 180-degree rotational symmetry about the midpoint.

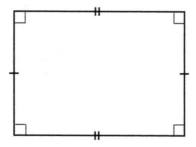

The **area of a rectangle** is found by the formula $A = lw$, where A is the area of the rectangle, l is the length (usually considered to be the longer side) and w is the width (usually considered to be the shorter side). The numbers for l and w are interchangeable.

The **perimeter of a rectangle** is found by the formula $P = 2l + 2w$ or $P = 2(l + w)$, where l is the length, and w is the width. It may be easier to add the length and width first and then double the result, as in the second formula.

RHOMBUS

Rhombus: A quadrilateral with four congruent sides. All rhombuses are parallelograms and kites; thus, they inherit all the properties of both types of quadrilaterals. The diagonals of a rhombus are perpendicular to each other. Rhombi have 2 lines of symmetry (along each of the diagonals) and

180-degree rotational symmetry. The **area of a rhombus** is half the product of the diagonals: $A = \frac{d_1 d_2}{2}$ and the perimeter of a rhombus is: $P = 2\sqrt{(d_1)^2 + (d_2)^2}$

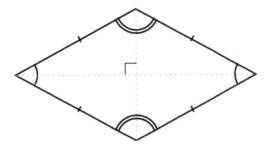

SQUARE

Square: A quadrilateral with four right angles and four congruent sides. Squares satisfy the criteria of all other types of quadrilaterals. The diagonals of a square are congruent and perpendicular to each other. Squares have 4 lines of symmetry (through each pair of opposing midpoints and along each of the diagonals) as well as 90-degree rotational symmetry about the midpoint.

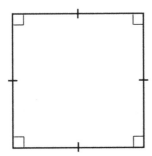

The **area of a square** is found by using the formula $A = s^2$, where s is the length of one side. The **perimeter of a square** is found by using the formula $P = 4s$, where s is the length of one side. Because all four sides are equal in a square, it is faster to multiply the length of one side by 4 than to add the same number four times. You could use the formulas for rectangles and get the same answer.

CIRCLES

The **center** of a circle is the single point from which every point on the circle is **equidistant**. The **radius** is a line segment that joins the center of the circle and any one point on the circle. All radii of a circle are equal. Circles that have the same center, but not the same length of radii are **concentric**. The **diameter** is a line segment that passes through the center of the circle and has both endpoints on the circle. The length of the diameter is exactly twice the length of the radius. Point O in the diagram below is the center of the circle, segments $\overline{OX}$, $\overline{OY}$, and $\overline{OZ}$ are radii, and segment $\overline{XZ}$ is a diameter.

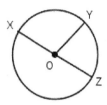

Review Video: Points of a Circle
Visit mometrix.com/academy and enter code: 420746

Review Video: The Diameter, Radius, and Circumference of Circles
Visit mometrix.com/academy and enter code: 448988

The **area of a circle** is found by the formula $A = \pi r^2$, where r is the length of the radius. If the diameter of the circle is given, remember to divide it in half to get the length of the radius before proceeding.

The **circumference** of a circle is found by the formula $C = 2\pi r$, where r is the radius. Again, remember to convert the diameter if you are given that measure rather than the radius.

Review Video: Area and Circumference of a Circle
Visit mometrix.com/academy and enter code: 243015

PRACTICE

P1. Find the area and perimeter of the following quadrilaterals:

(a) A square with side length 2.5 cm.

(b) A parallelogram with height 3 m, base 4 m, and other side 6 m.

(c) A rhombus with diagonals 15 in and 20 in.

P2. Calculate the area of a triangle with side lengths of 7 ft, 8 ft, and 9 ft.

PRACTICE SOLUTIONS

P1. (a) $A = s^2 = (2.5 \text{ cm})^2 = 6.25 \text{ cm}^2$; $P = 4s = 4 \times 2.5 \text{ cm} = 10 \text{ cm}$

(b) $A = bh = (3 \text{ m})(4 \text{ m}) = 12 \text{ m}^2$; $P = 2a + 2b = 2 \times 6 \text{ m} + 2 \times 4 \text{ m} = 20 \text{ m}$

(c) $A = \frac{d_1 d_2}{2} = \frac{(15 \text{ in})(20 \text{ in})}{2} = 150 \text{ in}^2$;
$$P = 2\sqrt{(d_1)^2 + (d_2)^2} = 2\sqrt{(15 \text{ in})^2 + (20 \text{ in})^2} = 2\sqrt{625 \text{ in}^2} = 50 \text{ in}$$

P2. Given only side lengths, we can use the semi perimeter to the find the area based on the formula, $A = \sqrt{s(s-a)(s-b)(s-c)}$, where s is the semiperimeter, $\frac{a+b+c}{2} = \frac{7+8+9}{2} = 12$ ft:

$$A = \sqrt{12(12-7)(12-8)(12-9)}$$
$$= \sqrt{(12)(5)(4)(3)}$$
$$= 12\sqrt{5} \text{ ft}^2$$

SOLIDS

The **surface area of a solid object** is the area of all sides or exterior surfaces. For objects such as prisms and pyramids, a further distinction is made between base surface area (B) and lateral surface area (LA). For a prism, the total surface area (SA) is $SA = LA + 2B$. For a pyramid or cone, the total surface area is $SA = LA + B$.

> **Review Video: How to Calculate the Volume of 3D Objects**
> Visit mometrix.com/academy and enter code: 163343

The **surface area of a sphere** can be found by the formula $A = 4\pi r^2$, where r is the radius. The volume is given by the formula $V = \frac{4}{3}\pi r^3$, where r is the radius. Both quantities are generally given in terms of π.

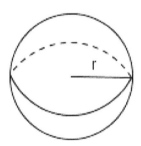

The **volume of any prism** is found by the formula $V = Bh$, where B is the area of the base, and h is the height (perpendicular distance between the bases). The surface area of any prism is the sum of the areas of both bases and all sides. It can be calculated as $SA = 2B + Ph$, where P is the perimeter of the base.

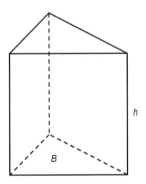

> **Review Video: Volume and Surface Area of a Prism**
> Visit mometrix.com/academy and enter code: 420158

For a **rectangular prism**, the volume can be found by the formula $V = lwh$, where V is the volume, l is the length, w is the width, and h is the height. The surface area can be calculated as $SA = 2lw + 2hl + 2wh$ or $SA = 2(lw + hl + wh)$.

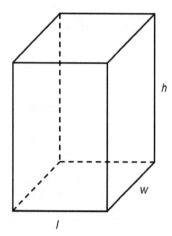

The **volume of a cube** can be found by the formula $V = s^3$, where s is the length of a side. The surface area of a cube is calculated as $SA = 6s^2$, where SA is the total surface area and s is the length of a side. These formulas are the same as the ones used for the volume and surface area of a rectangular prism, but simplified since all three quantities (length, width, and height) are the same.

The **volume of a cylinder** can be calculated by the formula $V = \pi r^2 h$, where r is the radius, and h is the height. The surface area of a cylinder can be found by the formula $SA = 2\pi r^2 + 2\pi rh$. The first

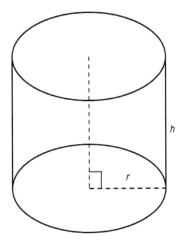

term is the base area multiplied by two, and the second term is the perimeter of the base multiplied by the height.

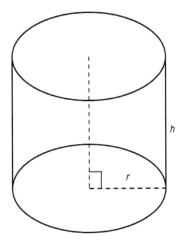

The **volume of a pyramid** is found by the formula $V = \frac{1}{3}Bh$, where B is the area of the base, and h is the height (perpendicular distance from the vertex to the base). Notice this formula is the same as $\frac{1}{3}$ times the volume of a prism. Like a prism, the base of a pyramid can be any shape.

Finding the **surface area of a pyramid** is not as simple as the other shapes we've looked at thus far. If the pyramid is a right pyramid, meaning the base is a regular polygon and the vertex is directly over the center of that polygon, the surface area can be calculated as $SA = B + \frac{1}{2}Ph_s$, where P is the perimeter of the base, and h_s is the slant height (distance from the vertex to the midpoint of one side of the base). If the pyramid is irregular, the area of each triangle side must be calculated individually and then summed, along with the base.

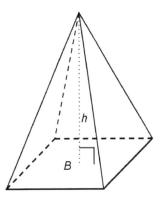

The **volume of a cone** is found by the formula $V = \frac{1}{3}\pi r^2 h$, where r is the radius, and h is the height. Notice this is the same as $\frac{1}{3}$ times the volume of a cylinder. The surface area can be calculated as $SA = \pi r^2 + \pi rs$, where s is the slant height. The slant height can be calculated using the Pythagorean theorem to be $\sqrt{r^2 + h^2}$, so the surface area formula can also be written as $SA = \pi r^2 + \pi r\sqrt{r^2 + h^2}$.

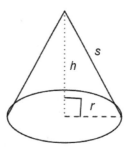

PRACTICE

P1. Find the surface area and volume of the following solids:

(a) A cylinder with radius 5 m and height 0.5 m.

(b) A trapezoidal prism with base area of 254 mm², base perimeter 74 mm, and height 10 mm.

(c) A half sphere (radius 5 yds) on the base of an inverted cone with the same radius and a height of 7 yds.

PRACTICE SOLUTIONS

P1. (a) $SA = 2\pi r^2 + 2\pi rh = 2\pi(5\text{ m})^2 + 2\pi(5\text{ m})(0.5\text{ m}) = 55\pi\text{ m}^2 \cong 172.79\text{ m}^2$;
$V = \pi r^2 h = \pi(5\text{ m})^2(0.5\text{ m}) = 12.5\pi\text{ m}^3 \cong 39.27\text{ m}^3$

(b) $SA = 2B + Ph = 2(254\text{ mm}^2) + (74\text{ mm})(10\text{ mm}) = 1248\text{ mm}^2$;
$V = Bh = (254\text{ mm}^2)(10\text{ mm}) = 2540\text{ mm}^3$

(c) We can find s, the slant height using the Pythagorean theorem, and since this solid is made of parts of simple solids, we can combine the formulas to find surface area and volume:

$$s = \sqrt{r^2 + h^2} = \sqrt{(5\text{ yd})^2 + (7\text{ yd})^2} = \sqrt{74}\text{ yd}$$

$$SA_{Total} = (SA_{sphere})/2 + SA_{cone} - SA_{base}$$
$$= \frac{4\pi r^2}{2} + (\pi rs + \pi r^2) - \pi r^2$$
$$= 2\pi(5\text{ yd})^2 + \pi(5\text{ yd})(\sqrt{74}\text{ yd})$$
$$= 5\pi(10 + \sqrt{74})\text{ yd}^2$$
$$\cong 292.20\text{ yd}^2$$

$$V_{Total} = (V_{sphere})/2 + V_{cone}$$
$$= \frac{\frac{4}{3}\pi r^3}{2} + \frac{1}{3}\pi r^2 h$$
$$= \frac{2}{3}\pi(5\text{ yd})^3 + \frac{1}{3}\pi(5\text{ yd})^2(7\text{ yd})$$
$$= \frac{5^2 \times \pi}{3}(10 + 7)\text{ yd}^3$$
$$\cong 445.06\text{ yd}^3$$

CLASSIFICATIONS OF TRIANGLES

A **scalene triangle** is a triangle with no congruent sides. A scalene triangle will also have three angles of different measures. The angle with the largest measure is opposite the longest side, and the angle with the smallest measure is opposite the shortest side. An **acute triangle** is a triangle whose three angles are all less than 90°. If two of the angles are equal, the acute triangle is also an **isosceles triangle**. An isosceles triangle will also have two congruent angles opposite the two congruent sides. If the three angles are all equal, the acute triangle is also an **equilateral triangle**. An equilateral triangle will also have three congruent angles, each 60°. All equilateral triangles are also acute triangles. An **obtuse triangle** is a triangle with exactly one angle greater than 90°. The other two angles may or may not be equal. If the two remaining angles are equal, the obtuse triangle is also an isosceles triangle. A **right triangle** is a triangle with exactly one angle equal to 90°. All right triangles follow the Pythagorean theorem. A right triangle can never be acute or obtuse.

The table below illustrates how each descriptor places a different restriction on the triangle:

Angles / Sides	Acute: All angles < 90°	Obtuse: One angle > 90°	Right: One angle = 90°
Scalene: No equal side lengths	$90° > \angle a > \angle b > \angle c$ $x > y > z$	$\angle a > 90° > \angle b > \angle c$ $x > y > z$	$90° = \angle a > \angle b > \angle c$ $x > y > z$
Isosceles: Two equal side lengths	$90° > \angle a, \angle b, or \angle c$ $\angle b = \angle c, \quad y = z$	$\angle a > 90° > \angle b = \angle c$ $x > y = z$	$\angle a = 90°, \angle b = \angle c = 45°$ $x > y = z$
Equilateral: Three equal side lengths	$60° = \angle a = \angle b = \angle c$ $x = y = z$		

Review Video: Introduction to Types of Triangles
Visit mometrix.com/academy and enter code: 511711

131

SIMILARITY AND CONGRUENCE RULES

Similar triangles are triangles whose corresponding angles are equal and whose corresponding sides are proportional. Represented by AAA. Similar triangles whose corresponding sides are congruent are also congruent triangles.

Triangles can be shown to be **congruent** in 5 ways:

- **SSS**: Three sides of one triangle are congruent to the three corresponding sides of the second triangle.
- **SAS**: Two sides and the included angle (the angle formed by those two sides) of one triangle are congruent to the corresponding two sides and included angle of the second triangle.
- **ASA**: Two angles and the included side (the side that joins the two angles) of one triangle are congruent to the corresponding two angles and included side of the second triangle.
- **AAS**: Two angles and a non-included side of one triangle are congruent to the corresponding two angles and non-included side of the second triangle.
- **HL**: The hypotenuse and leg of one right triangle are congruent to the corresponding hypotenuse and leg of the second right triangle.

> **Review Video: Similar Triangles**
> Visit mometrix.com/academy and enter code: 398538

GENERAL RULES FOR TRIANGLES

The **triangle inequality theorem** states that the sum of the measures of any two sides of a triangle is always greater than the measure of the third side. If the sum of the measures of two sides were equal to the third side, a triangle would be impossible because the two sides would lie flat across the third side and there would be no vertex. If the sum of the measures of two of the sides was less than the third side, a closed figure would be impossible because the two shortest sides would never meet. In other words, for a triangle with sides lengths A, B, and C: $A + B > C$, $B + C > A$, and $A + C > B$.

The sum of the measures of the interior angles of a triangle is always 180°. Therefore, a triangle can never have more than one angle greater than or equal to 90°.

In any triangle, the angles opposite congruent sides are congruent, and the sides opposite congruent angles are congruent. The largest angle is always opposite the longest side, and the smallest angle is always opposite the shortest side.

The line segment that joins the midpoints of any two sides of a triangle is always parallel to the third side and exactly half the length of the third side.

> **Review Video: General Rules (Triangle Inequality Theorem)**
> Visit mometrix.com/academy and enter code: 166488

PYTHAGOREAN THEOREM

The side of a triangle opposite the right angle is called the **hypotenuse**. The other two sides are called the legs. The Pythagorean theorem states a relationship among the legs and hypotenuse of a right triangle: $a^2 + b^2 = c^2$, where a and b are the lengths of the legs of a right triangle, and c is the length of the hypotenuse. Note that this formula will only work with right triangles.

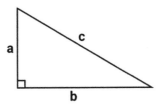

PRACTICE

P1. Given the following pairs of triangles, determine whether they are similar, congruent, or neither (note that the figures are not drawn to scale):

(a).

(b).

(c).

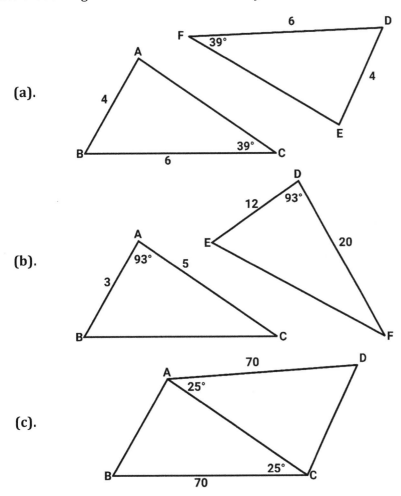

P2. Calculate the length of $\overline{MO}$ based on triangle MNO:

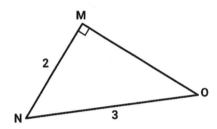

PRACTICE SOLUTIONS

P1. (a). Neither: We are given that two sides lengths and an angle are equal, however, the angle given is not between the given side lengths. That means there are two possible triangles that could satisfy the given measurements. Thus, we cannot be certain of congruence:

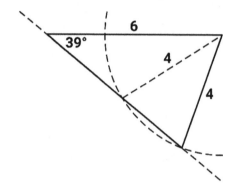

(b) Similar: Since we are given a side-angle-side of each triangle and the side lengths given are scaled evenly $\left(\frac{3}{5} \times \frac{4}{4} = \frac{12}{20}\right)$ and the angles are equal. Thus, $\triangle ABC \sim \triangle DEF$. If the side lengths were equal, then they would be congruent.

(c) Congruent: Even though we aren't given a measurement for the shared side of the figure, since it is shared it is equal. So, this is a case of SAS. Thus, $\triangle ABC \cong \triangle CDA$

P2. Since triangle MNO is a right triangle, we can use the simple form of Pythagoras theorem to find the missing side length:

$$\left(\overline{MO}\right)^2 + 2^2 = 3^2$$
$$\left(\overline{MO}\right)^2 = 9 - 4$$
$$\overline{MO} = \sqrt{5}$$

Algebra

TERMS AND COEFFICIENTS

Mathematical expressions consist of a combination of one or more values arranged in terms that are added together. As such, an expression could be just a single number, including zero. A **variable term** is the product of a real number, also called a **coefficient**, and one or more variables, each of which may be raised to an exponent. Expressions may also include numbers without a variable, called **constants** or **constant terms**. The expression $6s^2$, for example, is a single term where the coefficient is the real number 6 and the variable term is s^2. Note that if a term is written as simply a variable to some exponent, like t^2, then the coefficient is 1, because $t^2 = 1t^2$.

LINEAR EXPRESSIONS

A **single variable linear expression** is the sum of a single variable term, where the variable has no exponent, and a constant, which may be zero. For instance, the expression $2w + 7$ has $2w$ as the variable term and 7 as the constant term. It is important to realize that terms are separated by addition or subtraction. Since an expression is a sum of terms, expressions such as $5x - 3$ can be written as $5x + (-3)$ to emphasize that the constant term is negative. A real-world example of a single variable linear expression is the perimeter of a square, four times the side length, often expressed: $4s$.

In general, a **linear expression** is the sum of any number of variable terms so long as none of the variables have an exponent. For example, $3m + 8n - \frac{1}{4}p + 5.5q - 1$ is a linear expression, but $3y^3$ is not. In the same way, the expression for the perimeter of a general triangle, the sum of the side lengths: $a + b + c$, is considered to be linear, but the expression for the area of a square, the side length squared: s^2, is not.

LINEAR EQUATIONS

Equations that can be written as $ax + b = 0$, where $a \neq 0$, are referred to as **one variable linear equations**. A solution to such an equation is called a **root**. In the case where we have the equation $5x + 10 = 0$, if we solve for x we get a solution of $x = -2$. In other words, the root of the equation is -2. This is found by first subtracting 10 from both sides, which gives $5x = -10$. Next, simply divide both sides by the coefficient of the variable, in this case 5, to get $x = -2$. This can be checked by plugging -2 back into the original equation $(5)(-2) + 10 = -10 + 10 = 0$.

The **solution set** is the set of all solutions of an equation. In our example, the solution set would simply be -2. If there were more solutions (there usually are in multivariable equations) then they would also be included in the solution set. When an equation has no true solutions, this is referred to as an **empty set**. Equations with identical solution sets are **equivalent equations**. An **identity** is a term whose value or determinant is equal to 1.

> **Review Video: Linear Equations Basics**
> Visit mometrix.com/academy and enter code: 793005

Linear equations can be written many ways. Below is a list of some forms linear equations can take:

- **Standard Form**: $Ax + By = C$; the slope is $\frac{-A}{B}$ and the y-intercept is $\frac{C}{B}$
- **Slope Intercept Form**: $y = mx + b$, where m is the slope and b is the y-intercept
- **Point-Slope Form**: $y - y_1 = m(x - x_1)$, where m is the slope and (x_1, y_1) is a point on the line

- **Two-Point Form**: $\frac{y-y_1}{x-x_1} = \frac{y_2-y_1}{x_2-x_1}$, where (x_1, y_1) and (x_2, y_2) are two points on the given line
- **Intercept Form**: $\frac{x}{x_1} + \frac{y}{y_1} = 1$, where $(x_1, 0)$ is the point at which a line intersects the x-axis, and $(0, y_1)$ is the point at which the same line intersects the y-axis

> **Review Video: Slope-Intercept and Point-Slope Forms**
> Visit mometrix.com/academy and enter code: 113216

SOLVING ONE-VARIABLE LINEAR EQUATIONS

Multiply all terms by the lowest common denominator to eliminate any fractions. Look for addition or subtraction to undo so you can isolate the variable on one side of the equal sign. Divide both sides by the coefficient of the variable. When you have a value for the variable, substitute this value into the original equation to make sure you have a true equation. Consider the following example:

Kim's savings are represented by the table below. Represent her savings, using an equation.

X (Months)	Y (Total Savings)
2	$1300
5	$2050
9	$3050
11	$3550
16	$4800

The table shows a function with a constant rate of change, or slope, of 250. Given the points on the table, the slopes can be calculated as $(2050 - 1300)/(5 - 2)$, $(3050 - 2050)/(9 - 5)$, $(3550 - 3050)/(11 - 9)$, and $(4800 - 3550)/(16 - 11)$, each of which equals 250. Thus, the table shows a constant rate of change, indicating a linear function. The slope-intercept form of a linear equation is written as $y = mx + b$, where m represents the slope and b represents the y-intercept. Substituting the slope into this form gives $y = 250x + b$. Substituting corresponding x- and y-values from any point into this equation will give the y-intercept, or b. Using the point, (2, 1300), gives $1300 = 250(2) + b$, which simplifies as b = 800. Thus, her savings may be represented by the equation, $y = 250x + 800$.

RULES FOR MANIPULATING EQUATIONS
LIKE TERMS

Like terms are terms in an equation that have the same variable, regardless of whether or not they also have the same coefficient. This includes terms that *lack* a variable; all constants (i.e. numbers without variables) are considered like terms. If the equation involves terms with a variable raised to different powers, the like terms are those that have the variable raised to the same power.

For example, consider the equation $x^2 + 3x + 2 = 2x^2 + x - 7 + 2x$. In this equation, 2 and –7 are like terms; they are both constants. $3x$, x, and $2x$ are like terms: they all include the variable x raised to the first power. x^2 and $2x^2$ are like terms; they both include the variable x, raised to the second power. $2x$ and $2x^2$ are not like terms; although they both involve the variable x, the variable is not raised to the same power in both terms. The fact that they have the same coefficient, 2, is not relevant.

> **Review Video: Rules for Manipulating Equations**
> Visit mometrix.com/academy and enter code: 838871

Mometrix

CARRYING OUT THE SAME OPERATION ON BOTH SIDES OF AN EQUATION

When solving an equation, the general procedure is to carry out a series of operations on both sides of an equation, choosing operations that will tend to simplify the equation when doing so. The reason why the same operation must be carried out on both sides of the equation is because that leaves the meaning of the equation unchanged, and yields a result that is equivalent to the original equation. This would not be the case if we carried out an operation on one side of an equation and not the other. Consider what an equation means: it is a statement that two values or expressions are equal. If we carry out the same operation on both sides of the equation—add 3 to both sides, for example—then the two sides of the equation are changed in the same way, and so remain equal. If we do that to only one side of the equation—add 3 to one side but not the other—then that wouldn't be true; if we change one side of the equation but not the other then the two sides are no longer equal.

ADVANTAGE OF COMBINING LIKE TERMS

Combining like terms refers to adding or subtracting like terms—terms with the same variable— and therefore reducing sets of like terms to a single term. The main advantage of doing this is that it simplifies the equation. Often combining like terms can be done as the first step in solving an equation, though it can also be done later, such as after distributing terms in a product.

For example, consider the equation $2(x + 3) + 3(2 + x + 3) = -4$. The 2 and the 3 in the second set of parentheses are like terms, and we can combine them, yielding $2(x + 3) + 3(x + 5) = -4$. Now we can carry out the multiplications implied by the parentheses, distributing the outer 2 and 3 accordingly: $2x + 6 + 3x + 15 = -4$. The $2x$ and the $3x$ are like terms, and we can add them together: $5x + 6 + 15 = -4$. Now, the constants 6, 15, and -4 are also like terms, and we can combine them as well: subtracting 6 and 15 from both sides of the equation, we get $5x = -4 - 6 - 15$, or $5x = -25$, which simplifies further to $x = -5$.

> **Review Video: Simplifying Equations by Combining Like Terms**
> Visit mometrix.com/academy and enter code: 668506

CANCELING TERMS ON OPPOSITE SIDES OF AN EQUATION

Two terms on opposite sides of an equation can be canceled if and only if they *exactly* match each other. They must have the same variable raised to the same power and the same coefficient. For example, in the equation $3x + 2x^2 + 6 = 2x^2 - 6$, $2x^2$ appears on both sides of the equation, and can be canceled, leaving $3x + 6 = -6$. The 6 on each side of the equation can*not* be canceled, because it is added on one side of the equation and subtracted on the other. While they cannot be canceled, however, the 6 and -6 are like terms and can be combined, yielding $3x = -12$, which simplifies further to $x = -4$.

It's also important to note that the terms to be canceled must be independent terms and cannot be part of a larger term. For example, consider the equation $2(x + 6) = 3(x + 4) + 1$. We cannot cancel the xs, because even though they match each other they are part of the larger terms $2(x + 6)$ and $3(x + 4)$. We must first distribute the 2 and 3, yielding $2x + 12 = 3x + 12 + 1$. Now we see that the terms with the x's do not match, but the 12s do, and can be canceled, leaving $2x = 3x + 1$, which simplifies to $x = -1$.

PROCESS FOR MANIPULATING EQUATIONS
ISOLATING VARIABLES

To **isolate a variable** means to manipulate the equation so that the variable appears by itself on one side of the equation, and does not appear at all on the other side. Generally, an equation or

137

inequality is considered to be solved once the variable is isolated and the other side of the equation or inequality is simplified as much as possible. In the case of a two-variable equation or inequality, only one variable needs to be isolated; it will not usually be possible to simultaneously isolate both variables.

For a linear equation—an equation in which the variable only appears raised to the first power—isolating a variable can be done by first moving all the terms with the variable to one side of the equation and all other terms to the other side. (*Moving* a term really means adding the inverse of the term to both sides; when a term is *moved* to the other side of the equation its sign is flipped.) Then combine like terms on each side. Finally, divide both sides by the coefficient of the variable, if applicable. The steps need not necessarily be done in this order, but this order will always work.

> **Review Video: Solving Equations with Variables on Both Sides**
> Visit mometrix.com/academy and enter code: 402497

EQUATIONS WITH MORE THAN ONE SOLUTION

Some types of non-linear equations, such as equations involving squares of variables, may have more than one solution. For example, the equation $x^2 = 4$ has two solutions: 2 and –2. Equations with absolute values can also have multiple solutions: $|x| = 1$ has the solutions $x = 1$ and $x = -1$.

It is also possible for a linear equation to have more than one solution, but only if the equation is true regardless of the value of the variable. In this case, the equation is considered to have infinitely many solutions, because any possible value of the variable is a solution. We know a linear equation has infinitely many solutions if, when we combine like terms, the variables cancel, leaving a true statement. For example, consider the equation $2(3x + 5) = x + 5(x + 2)$. Distributing, we get $6x + 10 = x + 5x + 10$; combining like terms gives $6x + 10 = 6x + 10$, and the $6x$ terms cancel to leave $10 = 10$. This is clearly true, so the original equation is true for any value of x. We could also have canceled the 10s leaving $0 = 0$, but again this is clearly true—in general if both sides of the equation match exactly, it has infinitely many solutions.

EQUATIONS WITH NO SOLUTION

Some types of non-linear equations, such as equations involving squares of variables, may have no solution. For example, the equation $x^2 = -2$ has no solutions in the real numbers, because the square of any real number must be positive. Similarly, $|x| = -1$ has no solution, because the absolute value of a number is always positive.

It is also possible for an equation to have no solution even if does not involve any powers greater than one or absolute values or other special functions. For example, the equation $2(x + 3) + x = 3x$ has no solution. We can see that if we try to solve it. First, we distribute, leaving $2x + 6 + x = 3x$. But now if we try to combine all the terms with the variable, we find that they cancel: we have $3x$ on the left and $3x$ on the right, canceling to leave us with $6 = 0$. This is clearly false. In general, whenever the variable terms in an equation cancel leaving different constants on both sides, it means that the equation has no solution. (If we are left with the *same* constant on both sides, the equation has infinitely many solutions instead.)

FEATURES OF EQUATIONS THAT REQUIRE SPECIAL TREATMENT
LINEAR EQUATIONS

A linear equation is an equation in which variables only appear by themselves; they are not multiplied together, not with exponents other than one, and not inside absolute value signs or any other functions. For example, the equation $x + 1 - 3x = 5 - x$ is a linear equation: while x appears multiple times, it never appears with an exponent other than one, or inside any function. The two-variable equation $2x - 3y = 5 + 2x$ is also a linear equation. In contrast, the equation $x^2 - 5 = 3x$ is *not* a linear equation, because it involves the term x^2. $\sqrt{x} = 5$ is not a linear equation, because it involves a square root. $(x - 1)^2 = 4$ is not a linear equation because even though there's no exponent on the x directly, it appears as part of an expression that is squared. The two-variable equation $x + xy - y = 5$ is not a linear equation because it includes the term xy, where two variables are multiplied together.

Linear equations can always be solved (or shown to have no solution) by combining like terms and performing simple operations on both sides of the equation. Some non-linear equations can also be solved by similar methods, but others may require more advanced methods of solution, if they can be solved analytically at all.

SOLVING EQUATIONS INVOLVING ROOTS

In an equation involving roots, the first step is to isolate the term with the root, if possible, and then raise both sides of the equation to the appropriate power to eliminate it. Consider an example equation, $2\sqrt{x + 1} - 1 = 3$. In this case, begin by adding 1 to both sides, yielding $2\sqrt{x + 1} = 4$, and then dividing both sides by 2, yielding $\sqrt{x + 1} = 2$. Now square both sides, yielding $x + 1 = 4$. Finally, subtracting 1 from both sides yields $x = 3$.

Squaring both sides of an equation may, however, yield a spurious solution—a solution to the squared equation that is *not* a solution of the original equation. It's therefore necessary to plug the solution back into the original equation to make sure it works. In this case, it does: $2\sqrt{3 + 1} - 1 = 2\sqrt{4} - 1 = 2(2) - 1 = 4 - 1 = 3$.

The same procedure applies for roots other than square roots. For example, given the equation $3 + \sqrt[3]{2x} = 5$, we can first subtract 3 from both sides, yielding $\sqrt[3]{2x} = 2$ and isolating the root. Raising both sides to the third power yields $2x = 2^3$, i.e. $2x = 8$. We can now divide both sides by 2 to get $x = 4$.

> **Review Video: Solving Equations Involving Roots**
> Visit mometrix.com/academy and enter code: 297670

SOLVING EQUATIONS WITH EXPONENTS

To solve an equation involving an exponent, the first step is to isolate the variable with the exponent. We can then take the appropriate root of both sides to eliminate the exponent. For instance, for the equation $2x^3 + 17 = 5x^3 - 7$, we can subtract $5x^3$ from both sides to get $-3x^3 + 17 = -7$, and then subtract 17 from both sides to get $-3x^3 = -24$. Finally, we can divide both sides by –3 to get $x^3 = 8$. Finally, we can take the cube root of both sides to get $x = \sqrt[3]{8} = 2$.

One important but often overlooked point is that equations with an exponent greater than 1 may have more than one answer. The solution to $x^2 = 9$ isn't simply $x = 3$; it's $x = \pm 3$: that is, $x = 3$ or $x = -3$. For a slightly more complicated example, consider the equation $(x - 1)^2 - 1 = 3$. Adding one to both sides yields $(x - 1)^2 = 4$; taking the square root of both sides yields $x - 1 = 2$. We can then add 1 to both sides to get $x = 3$. However, there's a second solution: we also have the possibility that $x - 1 = -2$, in which case $x = -1$. Both $x = 3$ and $x = -1$ are valid solutions, as can be verified by substituting them both into the original equation.

> **Review Video: Solving Equations with Exponents**
> Visit mometrix.com/academy and enter code: 514557

SOLVING EQUATIONS WITH ABSOLUTE VALUES

When solving an equation with an absolute value, the first step is to isolate the absolute value term. We then consider the two possibilities: when the expression inside the absolute value is positive or when it is negative. In the former case, the expression in the absolute value equals the expression on the other side of the equation; in the latter, it equals the additive inverse of that expression—the expression times negative one. We consider each case separately, and finally check for spurious solutions.

> **Review Video: Absolute Value**
> Visit mometrix.com/academy and enter code: 314669

For instance, consider solving $|2x - 1| + x = 5$ for x. We can first isolate the absolute value by moving the x to the other side: $|2x - 1| = -x + 5$. Now, we have two possibilities. First, that $2x - 1$ is positive, and hence $2x - 1 = -x + 5$. Rearranging and combining like terms yields $3x = 6$, and hence $x = 2$. The other possibility is that $2x - 1$ is negative, and hence $2x - 1 = -(-x + 5) = x - 5$. In this case, rearranging and combining like terms yields $x = -4$. Substituting $x = 2$ and $x = -4$ back into the original equation, we see that they are both valid solutions.

Note that the absolute value of a sum or difference applies to the sum or difference as a whole, not to the individual terms: in general, $|2x - 1|$ is not equal to $|2x + 1|$ or to $|2x| - 1$.

SPURIOUS SOLUTIONS

A **spurious solution** may arise when we square both sides of an equation as a step in solving it, or under certain other operations on the equation. It is a solution to the squared or otherwise modified equation that is *not* a solution of the original equation. To identify a spurious solution, it's useful when you solve an equation involving roots or absolute values to plug the solution back into the original equation to make sure it's valid.

CHOOSING WHICH VARIABLE TO ISOLATE IN TWO-VARIABLE EQUATIONS

Similar to methods for a one-variable equation, solving a two-variable equation involves isolating a variable: manipulating the equation so that a variable appears by itself on one side of the equation, and not at all on the other side. However, in a two-variable equation, you will usually only be able to isolate one of the variables; the other variable may appear on the other side along with constant terms, or with exponents or other functions.

Often one variable will be much more easily isolated than the other, and therefore that's the variable you should choose. If one variable appears with various exponents, and the other is only raised to the first power, the latter variable is the one to isolate: given the equation $a^2 + 2b = a^3 + b + 3$, the b only appears to the first power, whereas a appears squared and cubed, so b is the variable that can be solved for: combining like terms and isolating the b on the left side of the equation, we get $b = a^3 - a^2 + 3$. If both variables are equally easy to isolate, then it's best to isolate the dependent variable, if one is defined; if the two variables are x and y, the convention is that y is the dependent variable.

> **Review Video: Solving Equations with Variables on Both Sides**
> Visit mometrix.com/academy and enter code: 402497

PRACTICE

P1. Seeing the equation $2x + 4 = 4x + 7$, a student divides the first terms on each side by 2, yielding $x + 4 = 2x + 7$, and then combines like terms to get $x = -3$. However, this is incorrect, as can be seen by substituting –3 into the original equation. Explain what is wrong with the student's reasoning.

P2. Describe the steps necessary to solve the equation $2x + 1 - x = 4 + 3x + 7$.

P3. Describe the steps necessary to solve the equation $2(x + 5) = 7(4 - x)$.

P4. Find all real solutions to the equation $1 - \sqrt{x} = 2$.

P5. Find all real solutions to the equation $|x + 1| = 2x + 5$.

P6. Solve for x: $-x + 2\sqrt{x + 5} + 1 = 3$.

P7. Ray earns $10 an hour at his job. Write an equation for his earnings as a function of time spent working. Determine how long Ray has to work in order to earn $360.

P8. Simplify the following: $3x + 2 + 2y = 5y - 7 + |2x - 1|$

PRACTICE SOLUTIONS

P1. As stated, it's easy to verify that the student's solution is incorrect: $2(-3) + 4 = -2$ and $4(-3) + 7 = -5$; clearly $-2 \neq -5$. The mistake was in the first step, which illustrates a common type of error in solving equations. The student tried to simplify the two variable terms by dividing them by 2. However, it's not valid to multiply or divide only one term on each side of an equation by a number; when multiplying or dividing, the operation must be applied to *every* term in the equation. So, dividing by 2 would yield not $x + 4 = 2x + 7$, but $x + 2 = 2x + \frac{7}{2}$. While this is now valid, that fraction is inconvenient to work with, so this may not be the best first step in solving the equation. Rather, it may have been better to first combine like terms. Subtracting $4x$ from both sides yields $-2x + 4 = 7$; subtracting 4 from both sides yields $-2x = 3$; *now* we can divide both sides by –2 to get $x = -\frac{3}{2}$.

P2. Our ultimate goal is to isolate the variable, x. To that end we first move all the terms containing x to the left side of the equation, and all the constant terms to the right side. Note that when we move a term to the other side of the equation its sign changes. We are therefore now left with $2x - x - 3x = 4 + 7 - 1$.

Next, we combine the like terms on each side of the equation, adding and subtracting the terms as appropriate. This leaves us with $-2x = 10$.

At this point, we're almost done; all that remains is to divide both sides by -2 to leave the x by itself. We now have our solution, $x = -5$. We can verify that this is a correct solution by substituting it back into the original equation.

P3. Generally, in equations that have a sum or difference of terms multiplied by another value or expression, the first step is to multiply those terms, distributing as necessary: $2(x + 5) = 2(x) + 2(5) = 2x + 10$, and $7(4 - x) = 7(4) - 7(x) = 28 - 7x$. So, the equation becomes $2x + 10 = 28 - 7x$. We can now add $7x$ to both sides to eliminate the variable from the right-hand side: $9x + 10 = 28$. Similarly, we can subtract 10 from both sides to move all the constants to the right: $9x = 18$. Finally, we can divide both sides by 9, yielding the final answer, $x = 2$.

P4. It's not hard to isolate the root: subtract one from both sides, yielding $-\sqrt{x} = 1$. Finally, multiply both sides by –1, yielding $\sqrt{x} = -1$. Squaring both sides of the equation yields $x = 1$.

However, if we plug this back into the original equation, we get $1 - \sqrt{1} = 2$, which is false. Therefore $x = 1$ is a spurious solution, and the equation has no real solutions.

P5. This equation has two possibilities: $x + 1 = 2x + 5$, which simplifies to $x = -4$; or $x + 1 = -(2x + 5) = -2x - 5$, which simplifies to $x = -2$. However, if we try substituting both values back into the original equation, we see that only $x = -2$ yields a true statement. $x = -4$ is a spurious solution; $x = -2$ is the only valid solution to the equation.

P6. Start by isolating the term with the root. We can do that by moving the $-x$ and the 1 to the other side, yielding $2\sqrt{x + 5} = 3 + x - 1$, or $2\sqrt{x + 5} = x + 2$. Dividing both sides of the equation by 2 would give us a fractional term that could be messy to deal with, so we won't do that for now. Instead, we square both sides of the equation; note that on the left-hand side the 2 is outside the square root sign, so we have to square it. As a result, we get $4(x + 5) = (x + 2)^2$. Expanding both sides gives us $4x + 20 = x^2 + 4x + 4$. In this case, we see that we have $4x$ on both sides, so we can cancel the $4x$ (which is what allows us to solve this equation despite the different powers of x). We now have $20 = x^2 + 4$, or $x^2 = 16$. Since the variable is raised to an even power, we need to take the positive and negative roots, so $x = \pm 4$: that is, $x = 4$ or $x = -4$. Substituting both values into the original equation, we see that $x = 4$ satisfies the equation but $x = -4$ does not; hence $x = -4$ is a spurious solution, and the only solution to the equation is $x = 4$.

P7. The number of dollars that Ray earns is dependent on the number of hours he works, so earnings will be represented by the dependent variable y and hours worked will be represented by the independent variable x. He earns 10 dollars per hour worked, so his earnings can be calculated as $y = 10x$. To calculate the number of hours Ray must work in order to earn \$360, plug in 360 for y and solve for x:

$$360 = 10x$$
$$x = \frac{360}{10} = 36$$

P8. To simplify this equation, we must isolate one of its variables on one side of the equation. In this case, the x appears under an absolute value sign, which makes it difficult to isolate. The y, on the other hand, only appears without an exponent—the equation is linear in y. We will therefore choose to isolate the y. The first step, then, is to move all the terms with y to the left side of the equation, which we can do by subtracting $5y$ from both sides:

$$3x + 2 - 3y = -7 + |2x - 1|$$

We can then move all the terms that do *not* include y to the right side of the equation, by subtracting $3x$ and 2 from both sides of the equation:

$$-3y = -3x - 9 + |2x - 1|$$

Finally, we can isolate the y by dividing both sides by –3.

$$y = x + 3 - \frac{1}{3}|2x - 1|$$

This is as far as we can simplify the equation; we cannot combine the terms inside and outside the absolute value sign. We can therefore consider the equation to be solved.

INEQUALITIES

Commonly in algebra and other upper-level fields of math you find yourself working with mathematical expressions that do not equal each other. The statement comparing such expressions with symbols such as < (less than) or > (greater than) is called an *inequality*. An example of an inequality is $7x > 5$. To solve for x, simply divide both sides by 7 and the solution is shown to be $x > \frac{5}{7}$. Graphs of the solution set of inequalities are represented on a number line. Open circles are used to show that an expression approaches a number but is never quite equal to that number.

> **Review Video: Solving Multi-Step Inequalities**
> Visit mometrix.com/academy and enter code: 347842

Conditional inequalities are those with certain values for the variable that will make the condition true and other values for the variable where the condition will be false. **Absolute inequalities** can have any real number as the value for the variable to make the condition true, while there is no real number value for the variable that will make the condition false. Solving inequalities is done by following the same rules for solving equations with the exception that when multiplying or dividing by a negative number the direction of the inequality sign must be flipped or reversed. **Double inequalities** are situations where two inequality statements apply to the same variable expression. An example of this is $-c < ax + b < c$.

> **Review Video: Conditional and Absolute Inequalities**
> Visit mometrix.com/academy and enter code: 980164

DETERMINING SOLUTIONS TO INEQUALITIES

To determine whether a coordinate is a solution of an inequality, you can substitute the values of the coordinate into the inequality, simplify, and check whether the resulting statement holds true. For instance, to determine whether $(-2, 4)$ is a solution of the inequality $y \geq -2x + 3$, substitute the values into the inequality, $4 \geq -2(-2) + 3$. Simplify the right side of the inequality and the result is $4 \geq 7$, which is a false statement. Therefore, the coordinate is not a solution of the inequality. You can also use this method to determine which part of the graph of an inequality is shaded. The graph of $y \geq -2x + 3$ includes the solid line $y = -2x + 3$ and, since it excludes the point $(-2, 4)$ to the left of the line, it is shaded to the right of the line.

FLIPPING INEQUALITY SIGNS

When given an inequality, we can always turn the entire inequality around, swapping the two sides of the inequality and changing the inequality sign. For instance, $x + 2 > 2x - 3$ is equivalent to $2x - 3 < x + 2$. Aside from that, normally the inequality does not change if we carry out the same operation on both sides of the inequality. There is, however, one principal exception: if we *multiply* or *divide* both sides of the inequality by a *negative number*, the inequality is flipped. For example, if we take the inequality $-2x < 6$ and divide both sides by -2, the inequality flips and we are left with $x > -3$. This *only* applies to multiplication and division, and only with negative numbers. Multiplying or dividing both sides by a positive number, or adding or subtracting any number regardless of sign, does not flip the inequality. Another special case that flips the inequality sign is when reciprocals are used. For instance, $3 > 2$ but the relation of the reciprocals is $\frac{1}{2} < \frac{1}{3}$.

COMPOUND INEQUALITIES

A **compound inequality** is an equality that consists of two inequalities combined with *and* or *or*. The two components of a proper compound inequality must be of opposite type: that is, one must be greater than (or greater than or equal to), the other less than (or less than or equal to). For instance, "$x + 1 < 2$ or $x + 1 > 3$" is a compound inequality, as is "$2x \geq 4$ and $2x \leq 6$." An *and* inequality can be written more compactly by having one inequality on each side of the common part: "$2x \geq 1$ and $2x \leq 6$," can also be written as $1 \leq 2x \leq 6$.

In order for the compound inequality to be meaningful, the two parts of an *and* inequality must overlap; otherwise no numbers satisfy the inequality. On the other hand, if the two parts of an *or* inequality overlap, then *all* numbers satisfy the inequality and as such is usually not meaningful.

Solving a compound inequality requires solving each part separately. For example, given the compound inequality "$x + 1 < 2$ or $x + 1 > 3$," the first inequality, $x + 1 < 2$, reduces to $x < 1$, and the second part, $x + 1 > 3$, reduces to $x > 2$, so the whole compound inequality can be written as "$x < 1$ or $x > 2$." Similarly, $1 \leq 2x \leq 6$ can be solved by dividing each term by 2, yielding $\frac{1}{2} \leq x \leq 3$.

Review Video: Compound Inequalities
Visit mometrix.com/academy and enter code: 786318

SOLVING INEQUALITIES INVOLVING ABSOLUTE VALUES

To solve an inequality involving an absolute value, first isolate the term with the absolute value. Then proceed to treat the two cases separately as with an absolute value equation, but flipping the inequality in the case where the expression in the absolute value is negative (since that essentially involves multiplying both sides by -1.) The two cases are then combined into a compound inequality; if the absolute value is on the greater side of the inequality, then it is an *or* compound inequality, if on the lesser side, then it's an *and*.

Consider the inequality $2 + |x - 1| \geq 3$. We can isolate the absolute value term by subtracting 2 from both sides: $|x - 1| \geq 1$. Now, we're left with the two cases $x - 1 \geq 1$ or $x - 1 \leq -1$: note that in the latter, negative case, the inequality is flipped. $x - 1 \geq 1$ reduces to $x \geq 2$, and $x - 1 \leq -1$ reduces to $x \leq 0$. Since in the inequality $|x - 1| \geq 1$ the absolute value is on the greater side, the two cases combine into an *or* compound inequality, so the final, solved inequality is "$x \leq 0$ or $x \geq 2$."

Review Video: Solving Absolute Value Inequalities
Visit mometrix.com/academy and enter code: 997008

SOLVING INEQUALITIES INVOLVING SQUARE ROOTS

Solving an inequality with a square root involves two parts. First, we solve the inequality as if it were an equation, isolating the square root and then squaring both sides of the equation. Second, we restrict the solution to the set of values of x for which the value inside the square root sign is non-negative.

For example, in the inequality, $\sqrt{x - 2} + 1 < 5$, we can isolate the square root by subtracting 1 from both sides, yielding $\sqrt{x - 2} < 4$. Squaring both sides of the inequality yields $x - 2 < 16$, so $x < 18$. Since we can't take the square root of a negative number, we also require the part inside the square root to be non-negative. In this case, that means $x - 2 \geq 0$. Adding 2 to both sides of the inequality yields $x \geq 2$. Our final answer is a compound inequality combining the two simple inequalities: $x \geq 2$ and $x < 18$, or $2 \leq x < 18$.

Note that we only get a compound inequality if the two simple inequalities are in opposite directions; otherwise we take the one that is more restrictive.

The same technique can be used for other even roots, such as fourth roots. It is *not*, however, used for cube roots or other odd roots—negative numbers *do* have cube roots, so the condition that the quantity inside the root sign cannot be negative does not apply.

> **Review Video: Solving Inequalities Involving Square Roots**
> Visit mometrix.com/academy and enter code: 800288

SPECIAL CIRCUMSTANCES

Sometimes an inequality involving an absolute value or an even exponent is true for all values of x, and we don't need to do any further work to solve it. This is true if the inequality, once the absolute value or exponent term is isolated, says that term is greater than a negative number (or greater than or equal to zero). Since an absolute value or a number raised to an even exponent is *always* non-negative, this inequality is always true.

GRAPHICAL SOLUTIONS TO EQUATIONS AND INEQUALITIES

When equations are shown graphically, they are usually shown on a **Cartesian coordinate plane**. The Cartesian coordinate plane consists of two number lines placed perpendicular to each other and intersecting at the zero point, also known as the origin. The horizontal number line is known as the x-axis, with positive values to the right of the origin, and negative values to the left of the origin. The vertical number line is known as the y-axis, with positive values above the origin, and negative values below the origin. Any point on the plane can be identified by an ordered pair in the form (x, y), called coordinates. The x-value of the coordinate is called the abscissa, and the y-value of the coordinate is called the ordinate. The two number lines divide the plane into **four quadrants**: I, II, III, and IV.

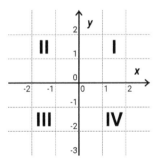

Note that in quadrant I $x > 0$ and $y > 0$, in quadrant II $x < 0$ and $y > 0$, in quadrant III $x < 0$ and $y < 0$, and in quadrant IV $x > 0$ and $y < 0$.

Recall that if the value of the slope of a line is positive, the line slopes upward from left to right. If the value of the slope is negative, the line slopes downward from left to right. If the y-coordinates are the same for two points on a line, the slope is 0 and the line is a **horizontal line**. If the x-coordinates are the same for two points on a line, there is no slope and the line is a **vertical line**. Two or more lines that have equivalent slopes are **parallel lines**. **Perpendicular lines** have slopes that are negative reciprocals of each other, such as $\frac{a}{b}$ and $\frac{-b}{a}$.

GRAPHING SIMPLE INEQUALITIES

To graph a simple inequality, we first mark on the number line the value that signifies the end point of the inequality. If the inequality is strict (involves a less than or greater than), we use a hollow circle; if it is not strict (less than or equal to or greater than or equal to), we use a solid circle. We

145

then fill in the part of the number line that satisfies the inequality: to the left of the marked point for less than (or less than or equal to), to the right for greater than (or greater than or equal to).

For example, we would graph the inequality $x < 5$ by putting a hollow circle at 5 and filling in the part of the line to the left:

GRAPHING COMPOUND INEQUALITIES

To graph a compound inequality, we fill in both parts of the inequality for an *or* inequality, or the overlap between them for an *and* inequality. More specifically, we start by plotting the endpoints of each inequality on the number line. For an *or* inequality, we then fill in the appropriate side of the line for each inequality. Typically, the two component inequalities do not overlap, which means the shaded part is *outside* the two points. For an *and* inequality, we instead fill in the part of the line that meets both inequalities.

For the inequality "$x \leq -3$ or $x > 4$," we first put a solid circle at –3 and a hollow circle at 4. We then fill the parts of the line *outside* these circles:

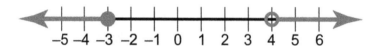

GRAPHING INEQUALITIES INCLUDING ABSOLUTE VALUES

An inequality with an absolute value can be converted to a compound inequality. To graph the inequality, first convert it to a compound inequality, and then graph that normally. If the absolute value is on the greater side of the inequality, we end up with an *or* inequality; we plot the endpoints of the inequality on the number line and fill in the part of the line *outside* those points. If the absolute value is on the smaller side of the inequality, we end up with an *and* inequality; we plot the endpoints of the inequality on the number line and fill in the part of the line *between* those points.

For example, the inequality $|x + 1| \geq 4$ can be rewritten as $x \geq 3$ or $x \leq -5$. We place solid circles at the points 3 and -5 and fill in the part of the line *outside* them:

GRAPHING EQUATIONS IN TWO VARIABLES

One way of graphing an equation in two variables is to plot enough points to get an idea for its shape, and then draw the appropriate curve through those points. A point can be plotted by substituting in a value for one variable and solving for the other. If the equation is linear, we only need two points, and can then draw a straight line between them.

> **Review Video: Graphing Linear Functions**
> Visit mometrix.com/academy and enter code: 699478

For example, consider the equation $y = 2x - 1$. This is a linear equation—both variables only appear raised to the first power—so we only need two points. When $x = 0$, $y = 2(0) - 1 = -1$.

When $x = 2$, $y = 2(2) - 1 = 3$. We can therefore choose the points $(0, -1)$ and $(2, 3)$, and draw a line between them:

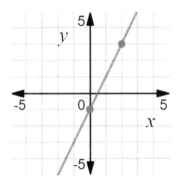

PRACTICE

P1. Analyze the following inequalities:

(a) $2 - |x + 1| < 3$
(b) $2(x - 1)^2 + 7 \leq 1$

P2. Graph the following on a number line:

(a) $x \geq 3$
(b) $-2 \leq x \leq 6$
(c) $|x| < 2$

PRACTICE SOLUTIONS

P1. (a) Subtracting 2 from both sides yields $-|x + 1| < 1$; multiplying by -1—and flipping the inequality, since we're multiplying by a negative number—yields $|x + 1| > -1$. But since the absolute value cannot be negative, it's *always* greater than -1, so this inequality is true for all values of x.

(b) Subtracting 7 from both sides yields $2(x - 1)^2 \leq -6$; dividing by 2 yields $(x - 1)^2 \leq -3$. But $(x - 1)^2$ must be nonnegative, and hence cannot be less than or equal to -3; this inequality has no solution.

P2. (a) We would graph the inequality $x \geq 3$ by putting a solid circle at 3 and filling in the part of the line to the right:

(b) The inequality $-2 \leq x \leq 6$ is equivalent to "$x \geq -2$ and $x \leq 6$." To plot this compound inequality, we first put solid circles at -2 and 6, and then fill in the part of the line *between* these circles:

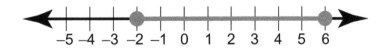

(c) The inequality $|x| < 2$ can be rewritten as "$x > -2$ and $x < 2$." We place hollow circles at the points –2 and 2 and fill in the part of the line between them:

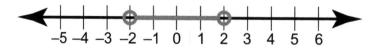

BASIC FUNCTIONS

When expressing functional relationships, the **variables** x and y are typically used. These values are often written as the **coordinates** (x, y). The x-value is the independent variable and the y-value is the dependent variable. A **relation** is a set of data in which there is not a unique y-value for each x-value in the dataset. This means that there can be two of the same x-values assigned to different y-values. A relation is simply a relationship between the x and y-values in each coordinate but does not apply to the relationship between the values of x and y in the data set. A **function** is a relation where one quantity depends on the other. For example, the amount of money that you make depends on the number of hours that you work. In a function, each x-value in the data set has one unique y-value because the y-value depends on the x-value.

> **Review Video: <u>Definition of a Function</u>**
> Visit mometrix.com/academy and enter code: 784611

A function has exactly one value of **output variable** (dependent variable) for each value of the **input variable** (independent variable). The set of all values for the input variable (here assumed to be x) is the domain of the function, and the set of all corresponding values of output variable (here assumed to be y) is the range of the function. When looking at a graph of an equation, the easiest way to determine if the equation is a function or not is to conduct the vertical line test. If a vertical line drawn through any value of x crosses the graph in more than one place, the equation is not a function.

FINDING THE DOMAIN AND RANGE OF A FUNCTION

The **domain** of a function $f(x)$ is the set of all input values for which the function is defined. The **range** of a function $f(x)$ is the set of all possible output values of the function—that is, of every possible value of $f(x)$, for any value of x in the function's domain. For a function expressed in a table, every input-output pair is given explicitly. To find the domain, we just list all the x values and to find the range, we just list all the values of $f(x)$. Consider the following example:

x	-1	4	2	1	0	3	8	6
$f(x)$	3	0	3	–1	–1	2	4	6

In this case, the domain would be {-1, 4, 2, 1, 0, 3, 8, 6}, or, putting them in ascending order, {-1, 0, 1, 2, 3, 4, 6, 8}. (Putting the values in ascending order isn't strictly necessary, but generally makes the set easier to read.) The range would be {3, 0, 3, –1, –1, 2, 4, 6}. Note that some of these values appear more than once. This is entirely permissible for a function; while each value of x must be matched to a unique value of $f(x)$, the converse is not true. We don't need to list each value more than once, so eliminating duplicates, the range is {3, 0, –1, 2, 4, 6}, or, putting them in ascending order, {–1, 0, 2, 3, 4, 6}.

Note that by definition of a function, no input value can be matched to more than one output value. It is good to double check to make sure that the data given follows this and is therefore actually a function.

DETERMINING A FUNCTION

You can determine whether an equation is a **function** by substituting different values into the equation for x. You can display and organize these numbers in a data table. A **data table** contains the values for x and y, which you can also list as coordinates. In order for a function to exist, the table cannot contain any repeating x-values that correspond with different y-values. If each x-coordinate has a unique y-coordinate, the table contains a function. However, there can be repeating y-values that correspond with different x-values. An example of this is when the function contains an exponent. For example, if $x^2 = y$, $2^2 = 4$, and $(-2)^2 = 4$.

WRITING A FUNCTION RULE USING A TABLE

If given a set of data, place the corresponding x and y-values into a table and analyze the relationship between them. Consider what you can do to each x-value to obtain the corresponding y-value. Try adding or subtracting different numbers to and from x and then try multiplying or dividing different numbers to and from x. If none of these **operations** give you the y-value, try combining the operations. Once you find a rule that works for one pair, make sure to try it with each additional set of ordered pairs in the table. If the same operation or combination of operations satisfies each set of coordinates, then the table contains a function. The rule is then used to write the equation of the function in "$y = f(x)$" form.

DIRECT AND INVERSE VARIATIONS OF VARIABLES

Variables that vary directly are those that either both increase at the same rate or both decrease at the same rate. For example, in the functions $y = kx$ or $y = kx^n$, where k and n are positive, the value of y increases as the value of x increases and decreases as the value of x decreases.

Variables that vary inversely are those where one increases while the other decreases. For example, in the functions $y = \frac{k}{x}$ or $y = \frac{k}{x^n}$ where k and n are positive, the value of y increases as the value of x decreases and decreases as the value of x increases.

In both cases, k is the constant of variation.

PROPERTIES OF FUNCTIONS

There are many different ways to classify functions based on their structure or behavior. Important features of functions include:

- **End behavior**: the behavior of the function at extreme values ($f(x)$ as $x \to \pm\infty$)
- **y-intercept**: the value of the function at $f(0)$
- **Roots**: the values of x where the function equals zero ($f(x) = 0$)
- **Extrema**: minimum or maximum values of the function or where the function changes direction ($f(x) \geq k$ or $f(x) \leq k$)

CLASSIFICATION OF FUNCTIONS

An **invertible function** is defined as a function, $f(x)$, for which there is another function, $f^{-1}(x)$, such that $f^{-1}(f(x)) = x$. For example, if $f(x) = 3x - 2$ the inverse function, $f^{-1}(x)$, can be found:

$$x = 3(f^{-1}(x)) - 2$$
$$\frac{x+2}{3} = f^{-1}(x)$$

$$f^{-1}(f(x)) = \frac{3x - 2 + 2}{3}$$
$$= \frac{3x}{3}$$
$$= x$$

Note that $f^{-1}(x)$ is a valid function over all values of x.

In a **one-to-one function**, each value of x has exactly one value for y on the coordinate plane (this is the definition of a function) and each value of y has exactly one value for x. While the vertical line test will determine if a graph is that of a function, the horizontal line test will determine if a function is a one-to-one function. If a horizontal line drawn at any value of y intersects the graph in more than one place, the graph is not that of a one-to-one function. Do not make the mistake of using the horizontal line test exclusively in determining if a graph is that of a one-to-one function. A one-to-one function must pass both the vertical line test and the horizontal line test. As such, one-to-one functions are invertible functions.

A **many-to-one function** is a function whereby the relation is a function, but the inverse of the function is not a function. In other words, each element in the domain is mapped to one and only one element in the range. However, one or more elements in the range may be mapped to the same element in the domain. A graph of a many-to-one function would pass the vertical line test, but not the horizontal line test. This is why many-to-one functions are not invertible.

A **monotone function** is a function whose graph either constantly increases or constantly decreases. Examples include the functions $f(x) = x$, $f(x) = -x$, or $f(x) = x^3$.

An **even function** has a graph that is symmetric with respect to the y-axis and satisfies the equation $f(x) = f(-x)$. Examples include the functions $f(x) = x^2$ and $f(x) = ax^n$, where a is any real number and n is a positive even integer.

An **odd function** has a graph that is symmetric with respect to the origin and satisfies the equation $f(x) = -f(-x)$. Examples include the functions $f(x) = x^3$ and $f(x) = ax^n$, where a is any real number and n is a positive odd integer.

> **Review Video: Even and Odd Functions**
> Visit mometrix.com/academy and enter code: 278985

Constant functions are given by the equation $f(x) = b$, where b is a real number. There is no independent variable present in the equation, so the function has a constant value for all x. The graph of a constant function is a horizontal line of slope 0 that is positioned b units from the x-axis. If b is positive, the line is above the x-axis; if b is negative, the line is below the x-axis.

Identity functions are identified by the equation $f(x) = x$, where every value of the function is equal to its corresponding value of x. The only zero is the point $(0, 0)$. The graph is a line with slope of 1.

In **linear functions**, the value of the function changes in direct proportion to x. The rate of change, represented by the slope on its graph, is constant throughout. The standard form of a linear equation is $ax + cy = d$, where a, c, and d are real numbers. As a function, this equation is commonly in the form $y = mx + b$ or $f(x) = mx + b$ where $m = -\frac{a}{c}$ and $b = \frac{d}{c}$. This is known as the slope-intercept form, because the coefficients give the slope of the graphed function (m) and its y-intercept (b). Solve the equation $mx + b = 0$ for x to get $x = -\frac{b}{m}$, which is the only zero of the function. The domain and range are both the set of all real numbers.

> **Review Video: Linear Functions**
> Visit mometrix.com/academy and enter code: 200735

Algebraic functions are those that exclusively use polynomials and roots. These would include polynomial functions, rational functions, square root functions, and all combinations of these functions, such as polynomials as the radicand. These combinations may be joined by addition, subtraction, multiplication, or division, but may not include variables as exponents.

> **Review Video: Common Functions**
> Visit mometrix.com/academy and enter code: 629798

ABSOLUTE VALUE FUNCTIONS

An **absolute value function** is in the format $f(x) = |ax + b|$. Like other functions, the domain is the set of all real numbers. However, because absolute value indicates positive numbers, the range is limited to positive real numbers. To find the zero of an absolute value function, set the portion inside the absolute value sign equal to zero and solve for x. An absolute value function is also known as a piecewise function because it must be solved in pieces—one for if the value inside the absolute value sign is positive, and one for if the value is negative. The function can be expressed as:

$$f(x) = \begin{cases} ax + b \text{ if } ax + b \geq 0 \\ -(ax + b) \text{ if } ax + b < 0 \end{cases}$$

This will allow for an accurate statement of the range. The graph of an example absolute value function, $f(x) = |2x - 1|$, is below:

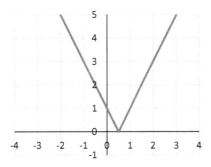

PIECEWISE FUNCTIONS

A **piecewise function** is a function that has different definitions on two or more different intervals. The following, for instance, is one example of a piecewise-defined function:

$$f(x) = \begin{cases} x^2, & x < 0 \\ x, & 0 \leq x \leq 2 \\ (x-2)^2, & x > 2 \end{cases}$$

To graph this function, we'd simply graph each part separately in the appropriate domain. The final graph would look like this:

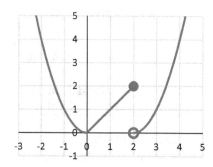

Note the filled and hollow dots at the discontinuity at $x = 2$. This is important to show which side of the graph that point corresponds to. Because $f(x) = x$ on the closed interval $0 \leq x \leq 2$, $f(2) = 2$. The point $(2, 2)$ is therefore marked with a filled circle, and the point $(2, 0)$, which is the endpoint of the rightmost $(x - 2)^2$ part of the graph but *not actually part of the function*, is marked with a hollow dot to indicate this.

Review Video: <u>Piecewise Functions</u>
Visit mometrix.com/academy and enter code: 707921

RATIONAL FUNCTIONS

A **rational function** is a function that can be constructed as a ratio of two polynomial expressions: $f(x) = \frac{p(x)}{q(x)}$, where $p(x)$ and $q(x)$ are both polynomial expressions and $q(x) \neq 0$. The domain is the set of all real numbers, except any values for which $q(x) = 0$. The range is the set of real numbers that satisfies the function when the domain is applied. When you graph a rational function, you will have vertical asymptotes wherever $q(x) = 0$. If the polynomial in the numerator is of lesser degree than the polynomial in the denominator, the x-axis will also be a horizontal asymptote. If the numerator and denominator have equal degrees, there will be a horizontal asymptote not on the x-axis. If the degree of the numerator is exactly one greater than the degree of the denominator, the graph will have an oblique, or diagonal, asymptote. The asymptote will be along the line $y = \frac{p_n}{q_{n-1}} x + \frac{p_{n-1}}{q_{n-1}}$, where p_n and q_{n-1} are the coefficients of the highest degree terms in their respective polynomials.

SQUARE ROOT FUNCTIONS

A **square root function** is a function that contains a radical and is in the format $f(x) = \sqrt{ax + b}$. The domain is the set of all real numbers that yields a positive radicand or a radicand equal to zero. Because square root values are assumed to be positive unless otherwise identified, the range is all real numbers from zero to infinity. To find the zero of a square root function, set the radicand equal to zero and solve for x. The graph of a square root function is always to the right of the zero and always above the x-axis.

Example graph of a square root function, $f(x) = \sqrt{2x + 1}$:

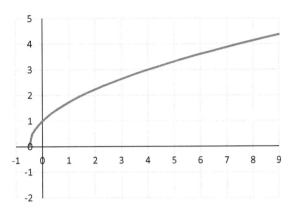

PRACTICE

P1. Martin needs a 20% medicine solution. The pharmacy has a 5% solution and a 30% solution. He needs 50 mL of the solution. If the pharmacist must mix the two solutions, how many milliliters of 5% solution and 30% solution should be used?

P2. Describe two different strategies for solving the following problem:

Kevin can mow the yard in 4 hours. Mandy can mow the same yard in 5 hours. If they work together, how long will it take them to mow the yard?

P3. A car, traveling at 65 miles per hour, leaves Flagstaff and heads east on I-40. Another car, traveling at 75 miles per hour, leaves Flagstaff 2 hours later, from the same starting point and also heads east on I-40. Determine how many hours it will take the second car to catch the first car by:

(a) Using a table.

(b) Using algebra.

PRACTICE SOLUTIONS

P1. To solve this problem, a table may be created to represent the variables, percentages, and total amount of solution. Such a table is shown below:

	mL solution	% medicine	Total mL medicine
5% solution	x	0.05	$0.05x$
30% solution	y	0.30	$0.30y$
Mixture	$x + y = 50$	0.20	$(0.20)(50) = 10$

The variable x may be rewritten as $50 - y$, so the equation $0.05(50 - y) + 0.30y = 10$ may be written and solved for y. Doing so gives $y = 30$. So, 30 mL of 30% solution are needed. Evaluating the expression, $50 - y$ for an x-value of 20, shows that 20 mL of 5% solution are needed.

P2. Two possible strategies both involve the use of rational equations to solve. The first strategy involves representing the fractional part of the yard mowed by each person in one hour and setting this sum equal to the ratio of 1 to the total time needed. The appropriate equation is $1/4 + 1/5 = 1/t$, which simplifies as $9/20 = 1/t$, and finally as $t = 20/9$. So the time it will take them to mow the yard, when working together, is a little more than 2.2 hours.

A second strategy involves representing the time needed for each person as two fractions and setting the sum equal to 1 (representing 1 yard). The appropriate equation is $t/4 + t/5 = 1$, which simplifies as $9t/20 = 1$, and finally as $t = 20/9$. This strategy also shows the total time to be a little more than 2.2 hours.

P3. (a) One strategy might involve creating a table of values for the number of hours and distances for each car. The table may be examined to find the same distance traveled and the corresponding number of hours taken. Such a table is shown below:

Car A		Car B	
x (hours)	y (distance)	x (hours)	y (distance)
0	0	0	
1	65	1	
2	130	2	0
3	195	3	75
4	260	4	150
5	325	5	225
6	390	6	300
7	455	7	375
8	520	8	450
9	585	9	525
10	650	10	600
11	715	11	675
12	780	12	750
13	845	13	825
14	910	14	900
15	975	15	975

The table shows that after 15 hours, the distance traveled is the same. Thus, the second car catches up with the first car after a distance of 975 miles and 15 hours.

(b) A second strategy might involve setting up and solving an algebraic equation. This situation may be modeled as $65x = 75(x - 2)$. This equation sets the distances traveled by each car equal to one another. Solving for x gives $x = 15$. Thus, once again, the second car will catch up with the first car after 15 hours.

Statistics and Probability

MEASURES OF CENTRAL TENDENCY

A **measure of central tendency** is a statistical value that gives a reasonable estimate for the center of a group of data. There are several different ways of describing the measure of central tendency. Each one has a unique way it is calculated, and each one gives a slightly different perspective on the data set. Whenever you give a measure of central tendency, always make sure the units are the same. If the data has different units, such as hours, minutes, and seconds, convert all the data to the same unit, and use the same unit in the measure of central tendency. If no units are given in the data, do not give units for the measure of central tendency.

MEAN

The **statistical mean** of a group of data is the same as the arithmetic average of that group. To find the mean of a set of data, first convert each value to the same units, if necessary. Then find the sum of all the values, and count the total number of data values, making sure you take into consideration each individual value. If a value appears more than once, count it more than once. Divide the sum of the values by the total number of values and apply the units, if any. Note that the mean does not have to be one of the data values in the set, and may not divide evenly.

$$\text{mean} = \frac{\text{sum of the data values}}{\text{quantity of data values}}$$

For instance, the mean of the data set {88, 72, 61, 90, 97, 68, 88, 79, 86, 93, 97, 71, 80, 84, 89} would be the sum of the fifteen numbers divided by 15:

$$\frac{88 + 72 + 61 + 90 + 97 + 68 + 88 + 79 + 86 + 93 + 97 + 71 + 80 + 84 + 89}{15} = \frac{1242}{15}$$
$$= 82.8$$

While the mean is relatively easy to calculate and averages are understood by most people, the mean can be very misleading if it is used as the sole measure of central tendency. If the data set has outliers (data values that are unusually high or unusually low compared to the rest of the data values), the mean can be very distorted, especially if the data set has a small number of values. If unusually high values are countered with unusually low values, the mean is not affected as much. For example, if five of twenty students in a class get a 100 on a test, but the other 15 students have an average of 60 on the same test, the class average would appear as 70. Whenever the mean is skewed by outliers, it is always a good idea to include the median as an alternate measure of central tendency.

A **weighted mean**, or weighted average, is a mean that uses "weighted" values. The formula is weighted mean $= \frac{w_1 x_1 + w_2 x_2 + w_3 x_3 \dots + w_n x_n}{w_1 + w_2 + w_3 + \dots + w_n}$. Weighted values, such as $w_1, w_2, w_3, \dots w_n$ are assigned to each member of the set $x_1, x_2, x_3, \dots x_n$. When calculating the weighted mean, make sure a weight value for each member of the set is used.

MEDIAN

The **statistical median** is the value in the middle of the set of data. To find the median, list all data values in order from smallest to largest or from largest to smallest. Any value that is repeated in the set must be listed the number of times it appears. If there are an odd number of data values, the median is the value in the middle of the list. If there is an even number of data values, the median is the arithmetic mean of the two middle values.

For example, the median of the data set {88, 72, 61, 90, 97, 68, 88, 79, 86, 93, 97, 71, 80, 84, 88} is 86 since the ordered set is {61, 68, 71, 72, 79, 80, 84, **86**, 88, 88, 88, 90, 93, 97, 97}.

The big disadvantage of using the median as a measure of central tendency is that is relies solely on a value's relative size as compared to the other values in the set. When the individual values in a set of data are evenly dispersed, the median can be an accurate tool. However, if there is a group of rather large values or a group of rather small values that are not offset by a different group of values, the information that can be inferred from the median may not be accurate because the distribution of values is skewed.

MODE

The **statistical mode** is the data value that occurs the greatest number of times in the data set. It is possible to have exactly one mode, more than one mode, or no mode. To find the mode of a set of data, arrange the data like you do to find the median (all values in order, listing all multiples of data values). Count the number of times each value appears in the data set. If all values appear an equal number of times, there is no mode. If one value appears more than any other value, that value is the mode. If two or more values appear the same number of times, but there are other values that appear fewer times and no values that appear more times, all of those values are the modes.

For example, the mode of the data set {**88**, 72, 61, 90, 97, 68, **88**, 79, 86, 93, 97, 71, 80, 84, **88**} is 88.

The main disadvantage of the mode is that the values of the other data in the set have no bearing on the mode. The mode may be the largest value, the smallest value, or a value anywhere in between in the set. The mode only tells which value or values, if any, occurred the greatest number of times. It does not give any suggestions about the remaining values in the set.

> **Review Video: Mean, Median, and Mode**
> Visit mometrix.com/academy and enter code: 286207

DISPERSION

A **measure of dispersion** is a single value that helps to "interpret" the measure of central tendency by providing more information about how the data values in the set are distributed about the measure of central tendency. The measure of dispersion helps to eliminate or reduce the disadvantages of using the mean, median, or mode as a single measure of central tendency, and give a more accurate picture of the dataset as a whole. To have a measure of dispersion, you must know or calculate the range, standard deviation, or variance of the data set.

RANGE

The **range** of a set of data is the difference between the greatest and lowest values of the data in the set. To calculate the range, you must first make sure the units for all data values are the same, and then identify the greatest and lowest values. If there are multiple data values that are equal for the highest or lowest, just use one of the values in the formula. Write the answer with the same units as the data values you used to do the calculations.

> **Review Video: Statistical Range**
> Visit mometrix.com/academy and enter code: 778541

PRACTICE

P1. Given the following graph, determine the range of patient ages:

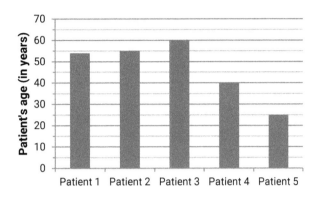

P2. Calculate the mean for the dataset $\{10, 13, 11, 5, 8, 18\}$

PRACTICE SOLUTIONS

P1. Patient 1 is 54 years old; Patient 2 is 55 years old; Patient 3 is 60 years old; Patient 4 is 40 years old; and Patient 5 is 25 years old. The range of patient ages is the age of the oldest patient minus the age of the youngest patient. In other words, $60 - 25 = 35$. The range of ages is 35 years.

P2. The mean is calculated using the equation: $\text{mean} = \frac{\text{sum of the data values}}{\text{quantity of data values}}$

$$\frac{10 + 13 + 12 + 5 + 8 + 18}{6} = \frac{66}{6} = 11$$

PROBABILITY

Probability is the likelihood of a certain outcome occurring for a given event. An **event** is any situation that produces a result. It could be something as simple as flipping a coin or as complex as launching a rocket. Determining the probability of an outcome for an event can be equally simple or complex. As such, there are specific terms used in the study of probability that need to be understood:

- **Compound event**—an event that involves two or more independent events (rolling a pair of dice and taking the sum)
- **Desired outcome** (or success)—an outcome that meets a particular set of criteria (a roll of 1 or 2 if we are looking for numbers less than 3)
- **Independent events**—two or more events whose outcomes do not affect one another (two coins tossed at the same time)
- **Dependent events**—two or more events whose outcomes affect one another (two cards drawn consecutively from the same deck)
- **Certain outcome**—probability of outcome is 100% or 1
- **Impossible outcome**—probability of outcome is 0% or 0

- **Mutually exclusive outcomes**—two or more outcomes whose criteria cannot all be satisfied in a single event (a coin coming up heads and tails on the same toss)
- **Random variable**—refers to all possible outcomes of a single event which may be discrete or continuous.

> **Review Video: Intro to Probability**
> Visit mometrix.com/academy and enter code: 212374

THEORETICAL PROBABILITY

Theoretical probability can usually be determined without actually performing the event. The likelihood of an outcome occurring, or the probability of an outcome occurring, is given by the formula:

$$P(A) = \frac{\text{Number of acceptable outcomes}}{\text{Number of possible outcomes}}$$

Note that $P(A)$ is the probability of an outcome A occurring, and each outcome is just as likely to occur as any other outcome. If each outcome has the same probability of occurring as every other possible outcome, the outcomes are said to be equally likely to occur. The total number of acceptable outcomes must be less than or equal to the total number of possible outcomes. If the two are equal, then the outcome is certain to occur and the probability is 1. If the number of acceptable outcomes is zero, then the outcome is impossible and the probability is 0. For example, if there are 20 marbles in a bag and 5 are red, then the theoretical probability of randomly selecting a red marble is 5 out of 20, ($\frac{5}{20} = \frac{1}{4}$, 0.25, or 25%).

COMPLEMENT OF AN EVENT

Sometimes it may be easier to calculate the possibility of something not happening, or the **complement of an event**. Represented by the symbol $\bar{A}$, the complement of A is the probability that event A does not happen. When you know the probability of event A occurring, you can use the formula $P(\bar{A}) = 1 - P(A)$, where $P(\bar{A})$ is the probability of event A not occurring, and $P(A)$ is the probability of event A occurring.

ADDITION RULE

The **addition rule** for probability is used for finding the probability of a compound event. Use the formula $P(A \text{ or } B) = P(A) + P(B) - P(A \text{ and } B)$, where $P(A \text{ and } B)$ is the probability of both events occurring to find the probability of a compound event. The probability of both events occurring at the same time must be subtracted to eliminate any overlap in the first two probabilities.

MULTIPLICATION RULE

The **multiplication rule** can be used to find the probability of two independent events occurring using the formula $P(A \text{ and } B) = P(A) \times P(B)$, where $P(A \text{ and } B)$ is the probability of two independent events occurring, $P(A)$ is the probability of the first event occurring, and $P(B)$ is the probability of the second event occurring.

The multiplication rule can also be used to find the probability of two dependent events occurring using the formula $P(A \text{ and } B) = P(A) \times P(B|A)$, where $P(A \text{ and } B)$ is the probability of two dependent events occurring and $P(B|A)$ is the probability of the second event occurring after the first event has already occurred. Before using the multiplication rule, you MUST first determine whether the two events are *dependent* or *independent*.

Use a **combination of the multiplication** rule and the rule of complements to find the probability that at least one outcome of the element will occur. This is given by the general formula $P(\text{at least one event occurring}) = 1 - P(\text{no outcomes occurring})$. For example, to find the probability that at least one even number will show when a pair of dice is rolled, find the probability that two odd numbers will be rolled (no even numbers) and subtract from one. You can always use a tree diagram or make a chart to list the possible outcomes when the sample space is small, such as in the dice-rolling example, but in most cases it will be much faster to use the multiplication and complement formulas.

Review Video: Multiplication Rule
Visit mometrix.com/academy and enter code: 782598

PRACTICE

P1. Determine the theoretical probability of the following events:

(a) Rolling an even number on a regular 6-sided die.

(b) Not getting a red ball when selecting one from a bag of 3 red balls, 4 black balls, and 2 green balls.

PRACTICE SOLUTIONS

P1. (a). The values on the faces of a regular die are 1, 2, 3, 4, 5, and 6. Since three of these are even numbers (2, 4, 6), The probability of rolling an even number is $\frac{3}{6} = \frac{1}{2} = 0.5 = 50\%$.

(b) The bag contains a total of 9 balls, 6 of which are not red, so the probability of selecting one non-red ball would be $\frac{6}{9} = \frac{2}{3} \cong 0.667 \cong 66.7\%$.

DISPLAYING INFORMATION

FREQUENCY TABLES

Frequency tables show how frequently each unique value appears in the set. A **relative frequency table** is one that shows the proportions of each unique value compared to the entire set. Relative frequencies are given as percentages; however, the total percent for a relative frequency table will not necessarily equal 100 percent due to rounding. An example of a frequency table with relative frequencies is below.

Favorite Color	Frequency	Relative Frequency
Blue	4	13%
Red	7	22%
Green	3	9%
Purple	6	19%
Cyan	12	38%

Review Video: Data Interpretation of Graphs
Visit mometrix.com/academy and enter code: 200439

CIRCLE GRAPHS

Circle graphs, also known as *pie charts*, provide a visual depiction of the relationship of each type of data compared to the whole set of data. The circle graph is divided into sections by drawing radii to create central angles whose percentage of the circle is equal to the individual data's percentage of the whole set. Each 1% of data is equal to 3.6° in the circle graph. Therefore, data represented by a 90° section of the circle graph makes up 25% of the whole. When complete, a circle graph often looks like a pie cut into uneven wedges. The pie chart below shows the data from the frequency table referenced earlier where people were asked their favorite color.

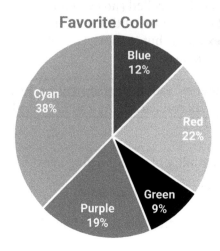

Favorite Color

PICTOGRAPHS

A **pictograph** is a graph, generally in the horizontal orientation, that uses pictures or symbols to represent the data. Each pictograph must have a key that defines the picture or symbol and gives the quantity each picture or symbol represents. Pictures or symbols on a pictograph are not always shown as whole elements. In this case, the fraction of the picture or symbol shown represents the same fraction of the quantity a whole picture or symbol stands for. For example, a row with $3\frac{1}{2}$ ears of corn, where each ear of corn represents 100 stalks of corn in a field, would equal $3\frac{1}{2} \times 100 = 350$ stalks of corn in the field.

> **Review Video: Pictographs**
> Visit mometrix.com/academy and enter code: 147860

LINE GRAPHS

Line graphs have one or more lines of varying styles (solid or broken) to show the different values for a set of data. The individual data are represented as ordered pairs, much like on a Cartesian plane. In this case, the *x*- and *y*-axes are defined in terms of their units, such as dollars or time. The individual plotted points are joined by line segments to show whether the value of the data is increasing (line sloping upward), decreasing (line sloping downward) or staying the same (horizontal line). Multiple sets of data can be graphed on the same line graph to give an easy visual comparison. An example of this would be graphing achievement test scores for different groups of students over the same time period to see which group had the greatest increase or decrease in performance from year-to-year (as shown below).

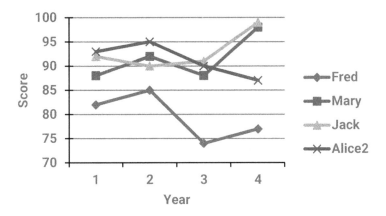

LINE PLOTS

A **line plot**, also known as a *dot plot*, has plotted points that are not connected by line segments. In this graph, the horizontal axis lists the different possible values for the data, and the vertical axis lists the number of times the individual value occurs. A single dot is graphed for each value to show the number of times it occurs. This graph is more closely related to a bar graph than a line graph. Do not connect the dots in a line plot or it will misrepresent the data.

STEM AND LEAF PLOTS

A **stem and leaf plot** is useful for depicting groups of data that fall into a range of values. Each piece of data is separated into two parts: the first, or left, part is called the stem; the second, or right, part is called the leaf. Each stem is listed in a column from smallest to largest. Each leaf that has the common stem is listed in that stem's row from smallest to largest. For example, in a set of two-digit numbers, the digit in the tens place is the stem, and the digit in the ones place is the leaf. With a stem and leaf plot, you can easily see which subset of numbers (10s, 20s, 30s, etc.) is the largest. This information is also readily available by looking at a histogram, but a stem and leaf plot also allows you to look closer and see exactly which values fall in that range. Using a sample set of test scores (82, 88, 92, 93, 85, 90, 92, 95, 74, 88, 90, 91, 78, 87, 98, 99), we can assemble a stem and leaf plot like the one below.

Test Scores

7	4	8							
8	2	5	7	8	8				
9	0	0	1	2	2	3	5	8	9

BAR GRAPHS

A **bar graph** is one of the few graphs that can be drawn correctly in two different configurations – both horizontally and vertically. A bar graph is similar to a line plot in the way the data is organized on the graph. Both axes must have their categories defined for the graph to be useful. Rather than placing a single dot to mark the point of the data's value, a bar, or thick line, is drawn from zero to the exact value of the data, whether it is a number, percentage, or other numerical value. Longer bar lengths correspond to greater data values. To read a bar graph, read the labels for the axes to find the units being reported. Then look where the bars end in relation to the scale given on the corresponding axis and determine the associated value.

The bar chart below represents the responses from our favorite color survey.

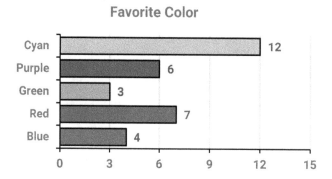

HISTOGRAMS

At first glance, a **histogram** looks like a vertical bar graph. The difference is that a bar graph has a separate bar for each piece of data and a histogram has one continuous bar for each *range* of data. For example, a histogram may have one bar for the range 0–9, one bar for 10–19, etc. While a bar graph has numerical values on one axis, a histogram has numerical values on both axes. Each range is of equal size, and they are ordered left to right from lowest to highest. The height of each column on a histogram represents the number of data values within that range. Like a stem and leaf plot, a histogram makes it easy to glance at the graph and quickly determine which range has the greatest quantity of values. A simple example of a histogram is below.

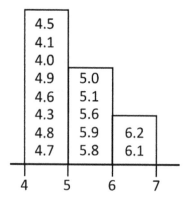

BIVARIATE DATA

Bivariate data is simply data from two different variables. (The prefix *bi-* means *two.*) In a *scatter plot*, each value in the set of data is plotted on a grid similar to a Cartesian plane, where each axis represents one of the two variables. By looking at the pattern formed by the points on the grid, you can often determine whether or not there is a relationship between the two variables, and what that relationship is, if it exists. The variables may be directly proportionate, inversely proportionate, or show no proportion at all. It may also be possible to determine if the data is linear, and if so, to find an equation to relate the two variables. The following scatter plot shows the relationship between preference for brand "A" and the age of the consumers surveyed.

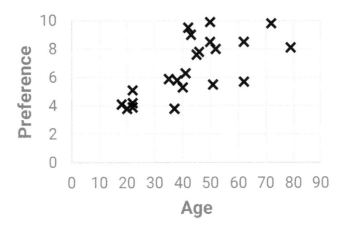

Scatter Plots

Scatter plots are also useful in determining the type of function represented by the data and finding the simple regression. Linear scatter plots may be positive or negative. Nonlinear scatter plots are generally exponential or quadratic. Below are some common types of scatter plots:

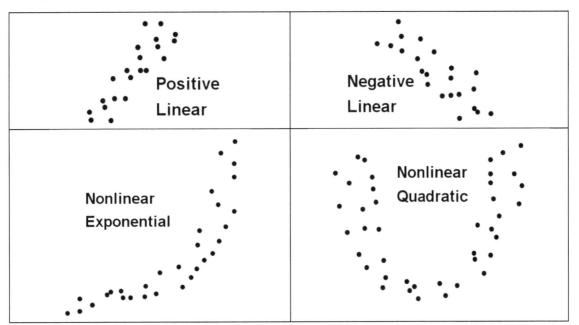

> **Review Video: What is a Scatter Plot?**
> Visit mometrix.com/academy and enter code: 596526

Quantitative Skills Test

The questions on this section of the test are largely applied math—that is, they require you to use concepts and principles of arithmetic, algebra, and geometry you already know in order to solve new types of problems. In light of this, there is no additional instructional content for this section, but practice problems are provided to help you become familiar with the types of questions you are likely to see on the test.

Practice

NUMBER SERIES

P1. Find the next number in the series: 64, 57, 60, 53, 56, ___

P2. What is the missing number in the sequence: 11, 22, 33, ___, 55, 66

P3. Find the next number in the series: 1, 4, 9, 16, ___

QUANTITATIVE REASONING

P1. What is the sum of 13^2 and 9^2?

P2. What is the product of $\frac{4}{5}$ and the average of 10 and 20?

GEOMETRIC COMPARISON

P1. Which of the following values are equivalent?

1. The diameter of a circle with circumference 12π
2. The area of a rectangle with a length of 3 and a width of 4
3. The radius of a circle with area 144π

P2. Which of the following values are equivalent?

1. The volume of a cube with side length 3
2. The volume of a sphere with radius 3
3. The area of a circle with radius 6

NON-GEOMETRIC COMPARISON

P1. Which of the following statements are equivalent?

1. $4\sqrt{36} - 7$
2. $2 \cdot 20 - 23$
3. $6^2 - 14$

P2. Which of the following statements are equivalent?

1. $\sqrt{4x^2} + 9x \cdot 0$
2. $2(x^2 + 4) - \sqrt{36x^4}$
3. $6(x + 2) - 2(2x + 6)$

Practice Solutions

NUMBER SERIES

P1. The pattern is: subtract 7 from the previous number and then add 3. 53 + 3 = 56, so the next number is 56 – 7 = 49.

P2. The pattern is adding 11 to the previous number, so the missing number is 44.

P3. The pattern is the list of perfect squares starting with 1. $4^2 = 16$, so the next number must be $5^2 = 25$.

QUANTITATIVE REASONING

P1. This is the same as $13^2 + 9^2$. $13^2 = 169$ and $9^2 = 81$ so $169 + 81 = 250$.

P2. First find the average of 10 and 20; $\frac{10+20}{2} = \frac{30}{2} = 15$. The word 'product' indicates multiplication, so $\frac{4}{5} \times 15 = 12$.

GEOMETRIC COMPARISON

P1. To solve this problem, first calculate the value of each statement, then compare them to one another:

1. The formula for circumference is $C = \pi d$. With a circumference of 12π, the diameter (d) is equal to 12.
2. The area of a rectangle is found by multiplying its length by its width, $3 \times 4 = 12$.
3. The area of a circle is found using the formula $A = \pi r^2$. With an area of 144π, the radius (r) is $\sqrt{144} = 12$.

The value of each statement is 12, so they are all equivalent.

P2. To solve this problem, first calculate the value of each statement, then compare them to one another:

1. The volume of a cube with side length 3 is found by cubing 3, $3^3 = 27$.
2. The volume of a sphere is found using the formula $V = \frac{4}{3}\pi r^3$. Plugging in 3 for the radius results in $V = \frac{4}{3}\pi(3)^3 = \frac{4}{3}\pi(27) = 36\pi$.
3. The area of a circle is found using the formula $A = \pi r^2$. Plugging in a radius of 6 results in: $A = \pi(6)^2 = 36\pi$.

Therefore, the values of statements II and III are equivalent.

NON-GEOMETRIC COMPARISON

P1.

$$4\sqrt{36} - 7 = 4 \cdot 6 - 7 = 24 - 7 = 17$$

$$2 \cdot 20 - 23 = 40 - 23 = 17$$

$$6^2 - 14 = 36 - 14 = 22$$

Therefore, statements I and II are equivalent.

P2.

$$\sqrt{4x^2} + 9x \cdot 0 = 2x + 9x \cdot 0 = 2x + 0 = 2x$$

$$2(x^2 + 4) - \sqrt{36x^4} = 2x^2 + 8 - \sqrt{36x^4} = 2x^2 + 8 - 6x^2 = 8 - 4x^2$$

$$6(x - 2) - 2(2x + 6) = 6x + 12 - 4x - 12 = 2x$$

Therefore, statements I and III are equivalent.

HSPT Optional Assessments

The HSPT also offers three optional assessments, one or more of which may be part of your exam. Be sure to check with your school about which, if any, of the optional assessments they expect you to take:

1. Science
2. Catholic Religion
3. Mechanical Aptitude

Note that while these optional assessments will not be part of your composite score, your school may still use the results for placement decisions.

Practice Test

Want to take this practice test in an online interactive format?
Check out the bonus page, which includes interactive practice questions and much more: **mometrix.com/bonus948/hspt**

SCAN HERE

Verbal Skills

1. Enliven means the opposite of

   a. Depress
   b. Imagine
   c. Accost
   d. Refrain

2. Which word does not belong with the others?

   a. Artificial
   b. Synthetic
   c. Natural
   d. Man-made

3. Frog is to amphibian as hydrogen is to:

   a. Aerospace
   b. Element
   c. Galaxy
   d. Instrumental

4. Bernie arrived late for the performance. Tom arrived before Darius. Tom arrived after Bernie. If the first two statements are true, then the third is:

   a. True
   b. False
   c. Unknown
   d. Unimportant

5. Aural most nearly means

   a. Hearing
   b. Language
   c. Circular
   d. Drill

6. Which word does not belong with the others?

   a. Painter
   b. Artist
   c. Musician
   d. Dancer

7. Shun means the *opposite* of

    a. Return

    b. Embrace

    c. Manipulate

    d. Retract

8. Apple is to seed as person is to

    a. Parent

    b. Embryo

    c. Nourishment

    d. Cell

9. Ellie was born one minute after Dean. Dean was born before Rob. Rob was born after Ellie. If the first two statements are true, then the third is:

    a. True

    b. False

    c. Unknown

    d. A contradiction

10. Punishment is to reprimand as impetuous is to

    a. Cautious

    b. Considerate

    c. Hasty

    d. Meticulous

11. Mediocre means the *opposite* of

    a. Stunted

    b. Forgiven

    c. Median

    d. Excellent

12. Which word does not belong with the others?

    a. Toaster

    b. Oven

    c. Appliance

    d. Coffee maker

13. Intricate most nearly means

    a. Woven

    b. Complex

    c. Unified

    d. Simple

14. Temperature is to heat as pound is to

    a. Weight

    b. Height

    c. Measurement

    d. Heavy

15. **Furrow means the *opposite* of**

    a. Sculpt
    b. Extension
    c. Replace
    d. Mound

16. **Counsel most nearly means**

    a. Doctor
    b. Committee
    c. Judge
    d. Advise

17. **Mackenzie left the daycare right after Austin. Nora left right before Austin. Mackenzie left before Austin. If the first two statements are true, then the third is:**

    a. True
    b. False
    c. Unknown
    d. An opinion

18. **Light is to hologram as film is to**

    a. Aesthetic
    b. Panoramic
    c. Photographer
    d. Video camera

19. **Passive means the *opposite* of**

    a. Active
    b. Attend
    c. Lassitude
    d. Forlorn

20. **Index is to book as elegy is to**

    a. Artifact
    b. Audition
    c. Equinox
    d. Funeral

21. **Underdog is to audacious as conspirator is to**

    a. Altruistic
    b. Elusive
    c. Illegible
    d. Passive

22. **Secede means the *opposite* of**

    a. Accessible
    b. Recall
    c. Merge
    d. Bail

23. Which word does not belong with the others?

   a. Gasoline
   b. Inflammable
   c. Ignitable
   d. Combustible

24. Samuel invented more patents than his brother James. Horace had twice as many patents as James. Samuel and Horace had the same number of patents. If the first two statements are true, then the third is:

   a. True
   b. False
   c. Unknown
   d. Unimportant

25. Coarse most nearly means

   a. Soft
   b. Polite
   c. Harsh
   d. Direction

26. Impartial most nearly means

   a. Interested
   b. Objective
   c. Passionate
   d. Unfair

27. Intermission is to drama as plant is to

   a. Compliment
   b. Constellation
   c. Habitat
   d. Memorabilia

28. Which word does not belong with the others?

   a. Brick
   b. Bottleneck
   c. Burden
   d. Benchmark

29. Jog is to marathon as hypothesis is to

   a. Discovery
   b. Forgery
   c. Irate
   d. Surreal

30. Deter most nearly means

   a. Stop
   b. Assist
   c. Grind
   d. Sway

31. Esther drove the same distance as Marcus. Lee drove twice as far as Marcus. Esther drove farther than Lee. If the first two statements are true, then the third is:

a. True
b. False
c. Unknown
d. An opinion

32. Which word does not belong with the others?

a. Aptitude
b. Inability
c. Readiness
d. Prowess

33. Alleviate means the *opposite* of

a. Hover
b. Worsen
c. Intend
d. Large

34. Antipathy is to sympathy as convivial is to

a. Avarice
b. Gloomy
c. Harmonious
d. Sociable

35. Refined most nearly means

a. Aromatic
b. Blatant
c. Cultured
d. Frightened

36. University Press received more submissions than Institutes Press. Institutes Press received fewer submissions than Academy Press. Academy Press received more submissions than University Press. If the first two statements are true, then the third is:

a. True
b. False
c. Unknown
d. Redundant

37. Espionage is to discreet as kindling is to

a. Grotesque
b. Majestic
c. Novelty
d. Ominous

38. Pallid most nearly means

   a. Healthy
   b. Sickly
   c. Rosy
   d. Deep

39. Jovial means the *opposite* of

   a. Revive
   b. Depressed
   c. Obscure
   d. Pretend

40. Otis caught more beads than Steve at Mardi Gras. Steve got as many beads as Carrie. Carrie got fewer beads than Otis. If the first two statements are true, then the third is:

   a. True
   b. False
   c. Unknown
   d. Redundant

41. Insufficient means the *opposite* of

   a. Deaden
   b. Distract
   c. Suction
   d. Adequate

42. Novice most nearly means

   a. Beginner
   b. Expert
   c. Naught
   d. Veteran

43. Foster most nearly means

   a. Nurture
   b. Woods
   c. Home
   d. Retain

44. Metal Leather sold far fewer records than The Animal Instincts. The Gang Mentality sold ten times the records The Animal Instincts sold. The Gang Mentality sold fewer records than Metal Leather. If the first two statements are true, then the third is:

   a. True
   b. False
   c. Unknown
   d. Incomplete

45. Initiate means the *opposite* of

    a. Stop
    b. Headlong
    c. Internal
    d. Sequence

46. Marry most nearly means

    a. Jolly
    b. Resolve
    c. Divorce
    d. Join

47. Which word does not belong with the others?

    a. Independence
    b. Irresponsibility
    c. Duty
    d. Maturity

48. General means the *opposite* of

    a. Military
    b. Decisive
    c. Abstract
    d. Particular

49. Paltry most nearly means

    a. Cheap
    b. Valuable
    c. Peaceful
    d. Plenty

50. Optimum most nearly means

    a. Ideal
    b. Visual
    c. Silent
    d. Temporal

51. Pledge means the *opposite* of

    a. Breach
    b. Compromise
    c. Vivid
    d. Sanction

52. Which word does not belong with the others?

    a. Counselor
    b. Nurse
    c. Lawyer
    d. Novelist

53. Reece was married the month before Lee. Darren got married after Lee. Reece got married after Darren. If the first two statements are true, then the third is:

    a. True
    b. False
    c. Unknown
    d. Incomplete

54. Attest most nearly means

    a. Disprove
    b. Abstain
    c. Extract
    d. Vouch

55. Outspoken most nearly means

    a. Demure
    b. Introverted
    c. Candid
    d. Precise

56. Kevin watched fewer television shows than Allen. John watched more television shows than Allen. John watched the greatest amount of television shows of the three. If the first two statements are true, then the third is:

    a. True
    b. False
    c. Unknown
    d. A contradiction

57. Pantomime most nearly means

    a. Mimic
    b. Clothes
    c. Jester
    d. Book

58. Serendipity means the *opposite* of

    a. Ambivalence
    b. Misfortune
    c. Providence
    d. Fluke

59. Pandemonium most nearly means

    a. Chaos
    b. Animal
    c. Monetary
    d. Masculine

60. Which word does not belong with the others?

    a. Restaurant
    b. Airport
    c. Cape Cod
    d. Hotel

Quantitative Skills

1. Which of the following numbers is greatest?

    a. $\frac{1}{3}$

    b. 0.25

    c. 0.099

    d. $\frac{2}{7}$

2. Determine the number of diagonals of a dodecagon.

    a. 12
    b. 24
    c. 54
    d. 108

3. Which number should come next in the series: 4, 13, 22, 31, …?

    a. 40
    b. 39
    c. 34
    d. 42

4. Jonas jogs three times faster than he walks. Which graph BEST represents the situation?

a.
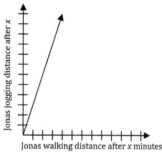

c.
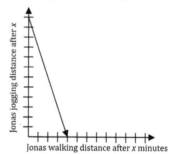

b.
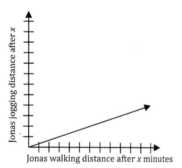

d.
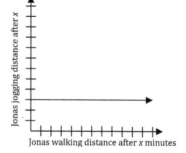

5. Jerry needs to load four pieces of equipment onto a factory elevator that has weight limit of 800 pounds. Jerry weighs 200 pounds. What would the average weight of each item have to be so that the elevator's weight limit is not exceeded?

    a.   128 pounds
    b.   150 pounds
    c.   175 pounds
    d.   180 pounds

6. Examine the figure below, which shows two lines passing through the center O of a circle, and select the best answer.

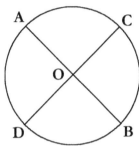

    a. $\overline{AO}$ is greater than $\overline{OC}$ but less than $\overline{CD}$
    b. $\overline{AB}$ is greater than $\overline{CD}$ and greater than $\overline{DO}$
    c. $\overline{AB}$ is greater than $\overline{OC}$ but less than $\overline{CD}$
    d. $\overline{AO}$ is the same length as $\overline{OC}$ but less than $\overline{CD}$

7. A rectangle is twice as long as it is wide. If the width is 3 meters, what is the area in m²?

    a. $12\ m^2$
    b. $6\ m^2$
    c. $9\ m^2$
    d. $18\ m^2$

8. Chan receives a bonus from his job. He pays 30% in taxes, gives 20% to charity, uses another 20% to pay off an old debt, and sets aside 10% in a savings account. He has $600 remaining from his bonus. What was the total amount of Chan's bonus?

    a. $2400
    b. $2800
    c. $3000
    d. $3600

9. An airplane travels at 300 mph relative to the air. It moves against a headwind of 15 mph. What is its speed relative to the ground?

    a.   300 mph
    b.   315 mph
    c.   270 mph
    d.   285 mph

10. A jar contains pennies and nickels. The ratio of nickels to pennies is 6:2. What percent of the coins are pennies?

    a. 25%

    b. 33.3%

    c. 40%

    d. 50%

11. Given the equation, $ax + b = c$, what is the value of x?

    a. $\frac{c+b}{a}$

    b. $\frac{ca}{b}$

    c. $c - ba$

    d. $\frac{c-b}{a}$

12. For the number set {7, 12, 5, 16, 23, 44, 18, 9, Z}, which of the following values could be equal to Z if Z is the median of the set?

    a. 10

    b. 11

    c. 14

    d. 17

13. The sides of a triangle are equal to an integer number of units. Two sides are 4 and 6 units long, respectively; what is the minimum value for the triangle's perimeter?

    a. 10 units

    b. 11 units

    c. 12 units

    d. 13 units

14. Which of the following choices is the missing number from this series: 1, 2, 4, __, 16?

    a. 6

    b. 8

    c. 10

    d. 12

15. If $x = 2y - 3$ and $2x + \frac{1}{2}y = 3$, then $y = ?$

    a. $-\frac{2}{3}$

    b. 1

    c. 2

    d. $\frac{18}{7}$

16. Which of the following numbers is the smallest?

    a. 2^8

    b. 3^3

    c. 16^1

    d. 24

Mometrix

17. There are 64 squares on a checkerboard. Bobby puts one penny on the first square, two on the second square, four on the third, eight on the fourth. He continues to double the number of coins at each square until he has covered all 64 squares. How many coins must he place on the last square?

    a. 2^{63}
    b. $2^{63} + 1$
    c. $2^{64} - 1$
    d. 2^{64}

18. Which number comes next in the series: 12, 7, 8, 13, 4, 19, 0, ...?

    a. 25
    b. 0
    c. 19
    d. -2

19. Examine (I), (II), and (III), and find the best answer.

    (I) 20% of 80
    (II) 50% of 70
    (III) 40% of 90

    a. (II) > (III)
    b. (II) > (I)
    c. (I) < (II) and (II) = (III)
    d. (I) = (II) = (III)

20. A commuter survey counts the people riding in cars on a highway in the morning. Each car contains only one man, only one woman, or both one man and one woman. Out of 25 cars, 13 contain a woman and 20 contain a man. How many contain both a man and a woman?

    a. 4
    b. 7
    c. 8
    d. 13

21. The length of Square A is 3 feet longer than the length of Square B. If the difference between their areas is 75 ft^2, what is the length of Square B?

    a. 11 feet
    b. 12 feet
    c. 13 feet
    d. 14 feet

22. Given points A and B on a number line, where $A = -3$ and $B = 7$, find point C, located between A and B, such that C is four times farther from A than it is from B.

    a. -1
    b. 1
    c. 3
    d. 5

23. Which number comes next in the series: 1, 4, 9, 16, ... ?

    a. 20
    b. 24
    c. 25
    d. 32

24. Which of the following sums is the greatest?

    a. $3 + 4 + 16$
    b. $6 + 4 + 5 + 7$
    c. $4 + 5 + 9$
    d. $10 + 4 + 8$

25. Examine (I), (II), and (III), and find the best answer.

    (I) $\frac{1}{3}$ of 24
    (II) $\frac{1}{5}$ of 30
    (III) $\frac{3}{4}$ of 20

    a. (II) < (III)
    b. (I) < (II) < (III)
    c. (I) = (II) and (II) < (III)
    d. (I) = (II) and (II) > (III)

26. The cost, in dollars, of shipping x computers to California for sale is $3000 + 100x$. The amount received when selling these computers is $400x$ dollars. What is the least number of computers that must be shipped and sold so that the amount received is at least equal to the shipping cost?

    a. 10
    b. 15
    c. 20
    d. 25

27. If p and n are positive, consecutive integers such that $p > n$, and $p + n = 15$, what is the value of n?

    a. 5
    b. 6
    c. 7
    d. 8

28. What number should come next in the series 3, 6, 8, 16, 18, 36, ... ?

    a. 38
    b. 72
    c. 57
    d. 44

29. Examine (I), (II), and (III), and find the best answer. Consider only the magnitude of each measurement.

    (I) The perimeter of a rectangle with length of 6 cm and width of 4 cm
    (II) The perimeter of a square with sides 4 cm long
    (III) The area of a square with sides 4 cm long

    a. (II) > (III)
    b. (I) = (II) = (III)
    c. (II) = (III)
    d. (II) < (III)

30. On a floor plan drawn at a scale of 1:100, the area of a rectangular room is 30 cm². What is the actual area of the room?

    a. 30 m^2
    b. 300 cm^2
    c. $3{,}000 \text{ m}^2$
    d. $30{,}000 \text{ cm}^2$

31. The repeating pattern shown below uses the same four figures over and over again.

    Fig. 1   Fig. 2   Fig. 3   Fig. 4   Fig. 5   Fig. 6 ...

Which of the four figures will the figure in the 31ˢᵗ position look like?

    a. Figure 1
    b. Figure 2
    c. Figure 3
    d. Figure 4

32. Examine (I), (II), and (III), and find the best answer.

    (I) $\frac{2}{3}$
    (II) $\frac{20}{30}$
    (III) $\frac{30}{45}$

    a. (II) > (III)
    b. (I) = (II) = (III)
    c. (II) = (III)
    d. (II) < (III)

33. Which of the following sums is the least?

    a. $4 + 3 + 4 + 5$
    b. $3 + 6 + 8$
    c. $9 + 5 + 3$
    d. $1 + 8 + 7 + 2$

34. Examine the diagram of a square and find the best answer.

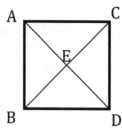

a. $\overline{AD}$ is equal to $\overline{CD}$
b. $\overline{CE}$ is equal to $\overline{AE}$
c. $\overline{BD}$ is equal to $\overline{ED}$
d. $\overline{CB}$ is equal to $\overline{BD}$

35. Hannah draws two supplementary angles. One angle measures 34°. What is the measure of the other angle?

a. 56°
b. 66°
c. 146°
d. 326°

36. Examine (I), (II), and (III), and find the best answer.

(I) 0.04
(II) 4%
(III) $\frac{2}{50}$

a. (II) > (III)
b. (I) = (II) = (III)
c. (II) = (III)
d. (II) < (III)

37. What number should fill the blank in the series 8, 12, 16, __, 24?

a. 18
b. 20
c. 22
d. 26

38. A long-distance runner does a first lap around a track in exactly 50 seconds. As she tires, each subsequent lap takes 20% longer than the previous one. How long does she take to run 3 laps?

a. 72 seconds
b. 150 seconds
c. 180 seconds
d. 182 seconds

39. In the figure below, the distance from *A* to *D* is 48. The distance from *A* to *B* is equal to the distance from *B* to *C*. If the distance from *C* to *D* is twice the distance of *A* to *B*, how far apart are *B* and *D*?

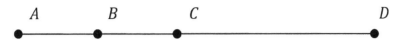

a. 12
b. 16
c. 24
d. 36

40. Examine (I), (II), and (III), and find the best answer.

   (I) $(3 \times 4) + 5$
   (II) $(4 + 5) \times 6$
   (III) $(3 \times 5) + 6$

a. (II) > (III)
b. (I) = (II) = (III)
c. (II) = (III)
d. (I) < (II) and (II) > (III)

41. Janice makes *x* phone calls. Elaina makes 23 more phone calls than Janice. June makes 14 more phone calls than Janice. In terms of *x*, what is the sum of their phone calls minus 25 calls?

a. $3x + 37$
b. $3x + 12$
c. $x + 12$
d. $3x - 25$

42. What number should come next in the series 41, 44, 48, 53, 59, ... ?

a. 64
b. 65
c. 66
d. 67

43. Given the sequence represented in the table below, where *n* represents the position of the term and a_n represents the value of the term, which of the following describes the relationship between the position number and the value of the term?

n	1	2	3	4	5	6
a_n	5	2	−1	−4	−7	−10

a. Multiply *n* by 2 and subtract 4
b. Multiply *n* by 2 and subtract 3
c. Multiply *n* by −3 and add 8
d. Multiply *n* by −4 and add 1

44. Jeremy put a heavy chalk mark on the tire of his bicycle. His bike tire is 27 inches in diameter. When he rolled the bike, the chalk left marks on the sidewalk. Which expression can be used to best determine the distance, in inches, the bike rolled from the first mark to the fourth mark?

   a. $3(27\pi)$
   b. $4\pi(27)$
   c. $(27 \div 3)\pi$
   d. $(27 \div 4)\pi$

45. A data set has five values: 5, 10, 12, 13, and one unknown value. The average of the data set is 9.6. What is the unknown value?

   a. 4
   b. 6
   c. 7.2
   d. 8

46. If $a - 16 = 8b + 6$, what does $a + 3$ equal?

   a. $b + 3$
   b. $8b + 9$
   c. $8b + 22$
   d. $8b + 25$

47. What two numbers should come next in the series 1, 1, 2, 3, 5, 8, 13, ... ?

   a. $18, 24$
   b. $20, 28$
   c. $21, 29$
   d. $21, 34$

48. Examine the diagram of a circle and find the best answer. The chord shown is a diameter of the circle. The shorter line segment is a radius of the circle. The labels (I), (II), and (III) correspond to segments of the circle

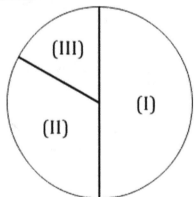

   a. $(I) = (II) = (III)$
   b. $(I) > (II) < (III)$
   c. $(II) = (I) - (III)$
   d. $(I) + (III) = (II)$

49. **Examine (I), (II), and (III), and find the best answer.**

    (I) 5^2
    (II) 2^5
    (III) 25

a. (III) > (II)
b. (I) = (II) = (III)
c. (II) = (III)
d. (I) = (III) and (III) < (II)

50. **Examine (I), (II), and (III), and find the best answer.**

    (I) A number that is 3 less than 2 times 15
    (II) A number that is equal to 3 cubed
    (III) A number that is 3 more than 80% of 30

a. (II) > (III)
b. (I) = (II) = (III)
c. (II) = (III)
d. (I) < (II) and (II) > (III)

51. **Student scores on Mrs. Thompson's last math test are shown below. Which of the following is the best representation of class performance?**

    76, 39, 87, 85, 91, 93, 86, 90, 77, 89, 74, 82, 68, 86, 79

a. mean
b. median
c. mode
d. range

52. **What number should be next in the series 108, 104, 98, 90, 80, ... ?**

a. 68
b. 72
c. 76
d. 64

Reading

COMPREHENSION

Questions 1 – 6 refer to the following selection from Pride and Prejudice by Jane Austen:

It is a truth universally acknowledged, that a single man in possession of a good fortune, must be in want of a wife.

However little known the feelings or views of such a man may be on his first entering a neighbourhood, this truth is so well fixed in the minds of the surrounding families, that he is considered the rightful property of someone or other of their daughters.

"My dear Mr. Bennet," said his lady to him one day, "have you heard that Netherfield Park is let at last?"

Mr. Bennet replied that he had not.

"But it is," returned she; "for Mrs. Long has just been here, and she told me all about it."

Mr. Bennet made no answer.

"Do you not want to know who has taken it?" cried his wife impatiently.

"You want to tell me, and I have no objection to hearing it."

This was invitation enough.

"Why, my dear, you must know, Mrs. Long says that Netherfield is taken by a young man of large fortune from the north of England; that he came down on Monday in a chaise and four to see the place, and was so much delighted with it, that he agreed with Mr. Morris immediately; that he is to take possession before Michaelmas, and some of his servants are to be in the house by the end of next week."

"What is his name?"

"Bingley."

"Is he married or single?"

"Oh! Single, my dear, to be sure! A single man of large fortune; four or five thousand a year. What a fine thing for our girls!"

"How so? How can it affect them?"

"My dear Mr. Bennet," replied his wife, "how can you be so tiresome!" You must know that I am thinking of his marrying one of them."

"Is that his design in settling here?"

"Design! Nonsense, how can you talk so! But it is very likely that he may fall in love with one of them, and therefore you must visit him as soon as he comes."

188

"I see no occasion for that. You and the girls may go, or you may send them by themselves, which perhaps will be still better, for as you are as handsome as any of them, Mr. Bingley may like you the best of the party."

1. What is the central idea of this selection?

a. A new neighbor is due to arrive who may become good friends with Mr. and Mrs. Bennet.
b. A new neighbor is due to arrive who may be a prospective husband for one of the Bennet daughters.
c. A new neighbor is due to arrive who may be a good business connection for Mr. Bennet.
d. A new neighbor is due to arrive who has already expressed an interest in marrying one of the Bennet daughters.

2. How does Mrs. Bennet feel about the arrival of Mr. Bingley?

a. Mrs. Bennet is excited about the arrival of Mr. Bingley.
b. Mrs. Bennet is nervous about the arrival of Mr. Bingley.
c. Mrs. Bennet is afraid the arrival of Mr. Bingley will upset Mr. Bennet.
d. Mrs. Bennet is indifferent to the arrival of Mr. Bingley.

3. Which of the following statements best describes Mrs. Bennet's feelings about her husband as indicated by this selection?

a. Mrs. Bennet is tired of her husband.
b. Mrs. Bennet is exasperated by her husband.
c. Mrs. Bennet is afraid of her husband.
d. Mrs. Bennet is indifferent toward her husband.

4. This selection is set in England at the beginning of the 19th century. Drawing on information from this selection, what could you conclude was a primary goal for young women in England during this time period?

a. To marry
b. To marry a man with money
c. To entertain the neighbors
d. To be courted by as many men as possible

5. "It is a truth universally acknowledged, that a single man in possession of a good fortune, must be in want of a wife."
Which of the following most nearly matches the meaning of the underlined phrase?

a. Everyone knows
b. The universe has decided
c. It is a documented fact
d. It is best to tell the truth

6. "Is that his design in settling here?"
What does the word design mean in the context of this selection?

a. Intention
b. Drawing
c. Creation
d. Improvisation

Questions 7 – 10 refer to the following paragraph:

> Margaritte stood nervously in the wings of the stage, waiting for her cue. The music from the orchestra swelled around her. She could almost see the colors and shapes it made in the air. With one foot, Margaritte kept time with the beat. Any minute now, it would be her turn. The note sounded, and Margaritte flew from the wings.

7. Which of the following would be the best introductory sentence for this paragraph?

a. Margaritte wore her favorite pink tutu.
b. Margaritte looked at the other dancers waiting with her backstage.
c. Margaritte had been taking dance lessons since she was nine years old.
d. Margaritte was about to begin the most important performance of her dancing career.

8. Which of the following would be the best sentence to add sensory detail to this paragraph?

a. The people in the audience looked like a garden in their colorful attire.
b. The stage was draped in black so that the dancers' costumes stood out.
c. The sound of the music reverberated in Margaritte's chest, becoming a part of her.
d. Margaritte's tights felt itchy against her legs.

9. Which of the following would be the best sentence to add descriptive detail to this paragraph?

a. The music formed the shapes of birds that soared above the stage and disappeared over the audience.
b. This was Margaritte's favorite music to dance to.
c. Tapping her toe to the beat of the music, Margaritte found herself growing increasingly nervous.
d. Margaritte felt the audience would see her nervousness as soon as she stepped onto the stage.

10. Which of the following would be the best concluding sentence for this paragraph?

a. Margaritte danced onto the stage as the music swirled around her.
b. Margaritte danced onto the stage; her moment had finally come.
c. When the dance recital was over, Margaritte was tired.
d. The other dancers moved onto the stage with Margaritte.

Questions 11 – 13 refer to the following paragraph:

> Many fears about snakes arise from misconceptions. People are often afraid that all snakes are venomous creatures looking for people to bite. However, of the approximately 2400 species of snakes, only 270 are venomous. Venomous snakes have fangs, hollow teeth with tiny holes at the bottom through which venom is released. Although venomous snakes should be treated carefully, there is no need to fear that a snake will bite you without provocation. Like many other animals, snakes will only attack when they feel threatened.

11. Which of the following would be the best introductory sentence for this paragraph?
   a. Many people think snakes have slimy skin, but they do not.
   b. Gaining knowledge about snakes is the best way to learn to live harmoniously with these misunderstood reptiles.
   c. A rattlesnake will sound its rattle to warn people not to come near.
   d. Snakes shed their skin when it gets too small.

12. Which of the following sentences is not essential to explain the primary premise of the paragraph?
   a. People are often afraid that all snakes are venomous creatures looking for people to bite.
   b. However, of the approximately 2400 species of snakes, only 270 are venomous.
   c. Venomous snakes have fangs, hollow teeth with tiny holes at the bottom through which venom is released.
   d. Although venomous snakes should be treated carefully, there is no need to fear that a snake will bite you without provocation.

13. Which of the following would be the best concluding sentence for this paragraph?
   a. There is no need to be fearful of snakes as long as you are careful.
   b. People in the desert are the only ones who should be afraid of snakes.
   c. You should learn the names of each species of snake.
   d. Snakes are more afraid of people than people are of them.

Questions 14 – 18 pertain to the following short story:

Puck

(1) It was the second week of an unseasonably cool July. The sun had finally made a rare weekend appearance, and the suburban neighborhood sizzled with possibility. As the day slipped lazily into evening, sun-baked residents trickled back to their homes from the lakeshore and the park and the community pool. The air smelled of sunscreen, charcoal smoke, sweat, overcooked meat.

(2) Will Jensen tossed a football across the yard to his best friend, Troy Coons. Dusk was settling around them, but the thought of retreating to the confines of the house seemed sacrilegious.

(3) "Can you believe we're going to college in a few weeks?" Troy asked, lobbing the ball back to Will.

(4) "What I can't believe is that you and I will be six hundred miles apart," Will said, catching the ball easily. "I don't think we've gone more than three days without seeing each other since kindergarten."

(5) "Except for when you had chicken pox," Troy said. "And the time I went to Hawaii with my grandparents. Remember how we begged them to let you come in my luggage?"

(6) Will laughed and tossed the ball back. "Those things don't count," he argued.

(7) The ball went sideways and Troy lunged for it, tripping over a ragged little terrier lounging lazily on the lawn. Troy collapsed in a tangled heap and the ball bounced down, just beyond his outstretched hand.

(8) "Puck!" Troy groaned. "No dogs on the field!"

(9) Will sauntered over and scooped up the little dog. He plopped down onto the crisp brown grass and laughed at Troy. Will reached over and rolled the ball toward Troy.

(10) "Don't blame Puck for your clumsiness," Will said, idly scratching the dog's fuzzy scalp. "How was he supposed to know you'd come stumbling through his daydreams?"

(11) Troy chuckled. Then they sat in silence as darkness swirled around them. Light glowed from windows thrown hopefully open to the faint breeze. Above them, the stars winked on in the charcoal sky. In the distance, leftover fireworks crackled and fizzed. The night was ripe with memories to be made.

(12) "Are you taking Puck with you?" Troy finally asked, breaking the silence.

(13) "Nah. No dogs in the dorm. Besides, Puck would hate being locked up in a room. He's spent the last sixteen years being king of the castle. He'll be happier here. That way he can greet me whenever I make it back home."

(14) Will lifted Puck and held him in mid-air. Puck wriggled playfully and licked Will's nose with his doughy pink tongue. Will laughed and set him down.

(15) "I sure will miss him, though," Will said, wiping Puck's saliva from his nose. "Puck's been a part of every memory I've had since I was really little."

(16) Troy faked a sniffle. "Stop, man. Just stop. I'm tearing up over here."

(17) Will punched Troy's arm good-naturedly. "Shut up!"

(18) A low, loud car careened around the corner, shattering the stupor of the summer night. Puck ran barking toward the car as it wove across the street like a wayward pinball.

(19) Seized with sudden panic, Will scrambled to his feet. "Puck, no! Come back!"

(20) As Will reached the sidewalk, Puck darted into the street. In a terrible, slow-motion montage, Will heard the tires squeal and Puck's bark turn to a startled yelp. Then the car sped away, and silence smothered the chaos.

(21) Will ran into the street. People peeked from doorways and windows, searching for the source of the commotion. Will fell beside Puck's limp body. Puck whimpered quietly and struggled to lick Will's hand. Then he was still.

(22) "No, Puck! No!" Will screamed. Shock rang in his ears and he was dizzy with emotion. Troy put a hand on Will's shoulder, but Will shook it off. He didn't want to be comforted. He wanted to wallow and writhe in the pool of pain that was slowly spreading through his soul.

(23) Every memory he had with Puck flooded his mind. This was not how it was supposed to be. Puck was supposed to be waiting for him when he came home from

college. He was supposed to watch at the window as Will drove away and be there wagging with excitement whenever Will came home. He was supposed to be the constant in Will's changing life. This was not part of the plan.

(24) Will stayed in the road for a long time, crouched over Puck's familiar, lifeless body. He felt numb, empty, and emotionless. Finally, Will's mother led him gently from the street. Troy and Will's father gathered Puck's body carefully into a sheet. Neighbors watched in sympathy as the sorrowful party crossed the lawn.

(25) They walked in silence as darkness swirled around them. Lights still glowed from windows thrown hopefully open to the faint breeze. Above them, stars still winked on in the charcoal sky. In the distance, leftover fireworks still crackled and fizzed. Everything was the same, and nothing was the same. Puck was gone. And Will knew things would never really be the same again.

14. In paragraph 2, what does "sacrilegious" mean?
   a. Absurdly inappropriate
   b. Nasty and evil
   c. A waste of time
   d. Holy and good

15. Which of the following best describes Will's attitude in paragraph 15?
   a. Angry
   b. Cheerful
   c. Sentimental
   d. Annoyed

16. What type of figurative language is used to describe the stars in paragraph 11?
   a. Simile
   b. Personification
   c. Metaphor
   d. Paradox

17. How is Puck's death an example of irony?
   a. Will was worried about missing Puck while Will was away at college, and now he will miss him forever
   b. Will wanted Puck to die so Will didn't have to think about him while he was away at college
   c. Puck was always quiet and docile, but he was strangely driven to run after that one car
   d. Troy hated Puck, and he wanted Puck to be hit by the passing car

18. Which of the following is a main idea in this story?
   a. The passing car is playing loud music
   b. Troy misses the ball when he trips over Puck
   c. Will and Troy like to play football
   d. Will has had Puck for a very long time

Questions 19 – 23 pertain to the following passage:

Comets

Comets are bodies that orbit the sun. They are distinguishable from asteroids by the presence of comas or tails. In the outer solar system, comets remain frozen and are so small that they are difficult to detect from Earth. As a comet approaches the inner solar system, solar radiation causes the materials within the comet to vaporize and trail off the nuclei. The released dust and gas forms a fuzzy atmosphere called the coma, and the force exerted on the coma causes a tail to form, pointing away from the sun.

Comet nuclei are made of ice, dust, rock and frozen gases and vary widely in size: from 100 meters or so to tens of kilometers across. The comas may be even larger than the Sun. Because of their low mass, they do not become spherical and have irregular shapes.

There are over 3,500 known comets, and the number is steadily increasing. This represents only a small portion of the total comets existing, however. Most comets are too faint to be visible without the aid of a telescope; the number of comets visible to the naked eye is around one a year.

Comets leave a trail of solid debris behind them. If a comet's path crosses the Earth's path, there will likely be meteor showers as Earth passes through the trail of debris.

Many comets and asteroids have collided into Earth. Some scientists believe that comets hitting Earth about 4 billion years ago brought a significant proportion of the water in Earth's oceans. There are still many near-Earth comets.

Most comets have oval shaped orbits that take them close to the Sun for part of their orbit and then out further into the Solar System for the remainder of the orbit. Comets are often classified according to the length of their orbital period: short period comets have orbital periods of less than 200 years, long period comets have orbital periods of more than 200 years, single apparition comets have trajectories which cause them to permanently leave the solar system after passing the Sun once.

19. What does the passage claim distinguishes comets from asteroids?
   a. The make-up of their nuclei
   b. The presence of comas or tails
   c. Their orbital periods
   d. Their irregular shapes

20. According to the passage, which of the following is true?
   a. There are 350 known comets, and the number is steadily increasing.
   b. There are 3,500 known comets, and the number is staying the same.
   c. There are 3,500 known comets, and many more comets that aren't known.
   d. Most comets are visible to the naked eye.

21. According to the passage, why do comets have irregular shapes?
    a. Because they are not spherical
    b. Because they have orbital periods
    c. Because of their low mass
    d. Because of their tails

22. What does the passage claim about the size of comets?
    a. Some are tens of kilometers across and can be seen without the use of a telescope
    b. Some are tens of kilometers across, and the coma is never larger than the Sun.
    c. Some are 100 meters across, and the coma is never larger than the Sun.
    d. The smallest comet is at least a kilometer, and the coma can be larger than the Sun.
    e. Some are tens of kilometers across, and the coma can be larger than the sun.

23. According to the last paragraph, what does the name <u>"single apparition comets"</u> mean?
    a. They only appear during the part of their orbit that is nearer to the Sun.
    b. They stay in the solar system even though they are only apparent once.
    c. Their orbital periods are so long they only appear once across millennia.
    d. They only remain in the solar system long enough to pass the Sun once.

Questions 24 – 29 pertain to the following passage:

"The Gettysburg Address" by Abraham Lincoln

Four score and seven years ago our fathers brought forth, upon this continent, a new nation, conceived in Liberty, and dedicated to the proposition that all men are created equal.

Now we are engaged in a great civil war, testing whether that nation, or any nation so conceived, and so dedicated, can long endure. We are met here on a great battlefield of that war. We have come to dedicate a portion of it as a final resting place for those who here gave their lives that that nation might live. It is altogether fitting and proper that we should do this.

But in a larger sense we cannot dedicate - we cannot consecrate - we cannot hallow this ground. The brave men, living and dead, who struggled here, have consecrated it far above our poor power to add or detract. The world will little note, nor long remember, what we say here, but can never forget what they did here.

It is for us, the living, rather to be dedicated here to the unfinished work which they have, thus far, so nobly carried on. It is rather for us to be here dedicated to the great task remaining before us - that from these honored dead we take increased devotion to that cause for which they here gave the last full measure of devotion - that we here highly resolve that these dead shall not have died in vain; that this nation shall have a new birth of freedom; and that this government of the people, by the people, for the people, shall not perish from the earth.

24. What is the main message of this speech?

  a. Those who died in this battle honor this land we are dedicating today better than anyone else.
  b. As we honor those who died in this battle, we should move forward with renewed dedication to ensuring the nation our founding fathers created continues to function the way they intended.
  c. We need to put the regrets of the past aside, without remembering the sacrifices of those who gave their lives for our country.
  d. The war we are fighting is far from over, as evidenced by the number of lives lost in this battle.

25. The phrase "the world will little note" means what?

  a. The world will not soon forget.
  b. The world will record what we say here.
  c. The world will not spread this information to distant places.
  d. The world will not pay much attention.

26. There were nearly 100 years between the American Revolution and the Civil War. The speech connects ideas about these two conflicts by saying that the ideas of the Civil War

  a. Threaten those of the Revolution.
  b. Are similar to those of the Revolution.
  c. Are newer than those of the Revolution.
  d. Are better than those of the Revolution.

27. Why does Lincoln most likely talk about the past before he talks about the present?

  a. To incite listeners of his message to protest
  b. To remember what has been lost in the past
  c. To establish context for his main message
  d. To try to get listeners to side with his position

28. What is the following sentence addressing?

  Now we are engaged in a great civil war, testing whether that nation, or any nation so conceived, and so dedicated, can long endure.

  a. Whether or not a nation based on ideas of freedom and equality can survive for any significant length of time
  b. Whether or not the Union will be able to preserve the existing structure of the United States by preventing the Confederacy from seceding
  c. Whether or not the Confederacy will be successful in seceding from the United States and surviving on its own
  d. Whether or not Lincoln should continue dedicating troops to the war

29. In paragraph 4, the word "vain" most nearly means:

  a. Decisive
  b. Frivolous
  c. Momentous
  d. Practical

Questions 30 – 34 pertain to the following passage:

Black History Month

Black History Month is still a meaningful observance. Despite the election of our first African American president being a huge achievement, education about African American history is still unmet to a substantial degree. Black History Month is a powerful tool in working towards meeting that need. There is no reason to give up that tool now, and it can easily coexist with an effort to develop a more comprehensive and inclusive yearly curriculum.

Having a month set aside for the study of African American history doesn't limit its study and celebration to that month; it merely focuses complete attention on it for that month. There is absolutely no contradiction between having a set-aside month and having it be present in the curriculum the rest of the year.

Equally important is that the debate itself about the usefulness of Black History Month can, and should, remind parents that they can't necessarily count on schools to teach African American history as thoroughly as many parents would want.

Although Black History Month has, to an extent, become a shallow ritual, it doesn't have to be. Good teachers and good materials could make the February curriculum deeply informative, thought-provoking, and inspiring. The range of material that can be covered is rich, varied, and full of limitless possibilities.

Finally, it is worthwhile to remind ourselves and our children of the key events that happened during the month of February. In 1926, Woodson organized the first Black History Week to honor the birthdays of essential civil rights activists Abraham Lincoln and Frederick Douglass. W. E. B. DuBois was born on February 23, 1868. The 15th Amendment, which granted African Americans the right to vote, was passed on February 3, 1870. The first black U.S. senator, Hiram R. Revels, took his oath of office on February 25, 1870. The National Association for the Advancement of Colored People (NAACP) was founded on February 12, 1909. Malcolm X was shot on February 21, 1965.

30. Based on this passage, what would be the author's argument against the study and celebration of Black History Month being limited to one month of the year?
   a. Black History Month is still a meaningful observance.
   b. Black History Month is a powerful tool in meeting the need for education about African American history.
   c. Having a month set aside for the study of African American history does not limit its study and celebration to that month.
   d. Black History Month does not have to be a shallow ritual.

31. Why does the author believe that the debate itself about Black History Month can be useful?

    a. The people on opposing sides can come to an intelligent resolution about whether to keep it.

    b. African American history is discussed in the media when the debate is ongoing.

    c. The debate is a reminder to parents that they can't count on schools to teach their children about African American history.

    d. Black History Month doesn't have to be a shallow ritual.

32. What does the author say about the range of material that can be taught during Black History Month?

    a. It is rich and varied.

    b. It is important.

    c. It is an unmet need.

    d. It is comprehensive.

33. The author's tone in this passage can be described as:

    a. Doubtful

    b. Emboldening

    c. Jovial

    d. Menacing

34. Which of the following can be inferred from the last paragraph?

    a. The most important events in black history happened in the 19th century.

    b. Black history has been influenced by more men than women.

    c. There are several avenues from which to draw on larger lessons of black history.

    d. The most influential black figures served in politics.

Questions 35 – 42 pertain to the following passage:

Plastics

Plastics have long been considered one of the great conveniences of the modern era, but evidence is mounting to indicate that these conveniences have come at an incredible cost. The chief benefit of plastics is their durability, but this benefit turns out to be the same reason plastic has become a significant problem: It takes between two and four hundred years to decompose. All of this plastic has accumulated into a catastrophic mess and has also caused disease in humans.

Between Hawaii and Japan, a giant mass of plastic twice the size of Texas slowly swirls with the currents of the Pacific Ocean. This area has come to be known as the Great Pacific Garbage Patch, and its effects on the ecology of the ocean are unimaginable. According to United Nations researchers, a hundred thousand sea mammals and a million seabirds die each year. They are found with cigarette lighters, syringes, and other plastics that they mistake for food in their stomachs.

Evidence also indicates that the plastic we store our food in poses health risks. For instance, phthalates (pronounced "THEY-lates") have been shown to have detrimental effects on the reproductive system, yet they are found in many plastic products—including baby bottles and water bottles. They have also been linked to various forms of cancer. Additionally, a chemical called bisphenol A that is found in many plastics can mimic the effects of the hormone estrogen, which can also affect the reproductive system.

In short, plastics may turn out to be a lot less convenient than they seem!

35. Which of the following best describes the author's purpose in writing this passage?
a. To persuade readers to accept the author's point of view.
b. To explain the benefits of plastic.
c. To explain the risks of plastic bottles.
d. To inform the reader of the effects of phthalates in plastics.

36. In the first paragraph, the word "chief" most nearly means:
a. Main
b. Least likely
c. Benefit
d. Leader of a Native American tribe

37. Which of the following statements can be inferred from paragraph two?
a. The Great Pacific Garbage Patch is not a significant threat to humans.
b. No one has determined why sea mammals and seabirds are dying at an alarming rate.
c. The Great Pacific Garbage Patch is too large to be cleaned up by one country.
d. Ocean currents carry the plastic to the middle of the ocean.

38. Which of the following statements best summarizes the main idea of this passage?
a. The benefits of plastics outweigh their risks.
b. Plastics pose a significant threat to humans and other living creatures.
c. Phthalates should not be used in baby bottles.
d. Plastics decompose very slowly.

39. In the third paragraph, the word "mimic" most nearly means:
a. Reduce
b. Cancerous
c. Intensify
d. Resemble

40. What particular risk does the author say the Great Pacific Garbage Patch poses to marine animals?
a. It affects yearly temperature averages.
b. Animals accidentally ingest the plastics and die.
c. The animals' habitat is poisoned by phthalates.
d. Seabirds cannot get to the fish below the garbage.

41. Why does this passage not discuss more of plastics' benefits?
a. Plastics have no benefits.
b. The passage emphasizes the dangers over the benefits in order to prove that plastics are harmful.
c. The passage devotes a significant amount of attention to the benefits of plastics.
d. Discussing the benefits would contradict the author's point that plastics are a necessary evil.

42. In the first paragraph, the word "durability" most nearly means:

a. Decomposition
b. Permanence
c. Coloration
d. Poisonous

VOCABULARY

Choose the appropriate synonym for each underlined word in the following phrases:

43. The peevish instructor

a. Ill-tempered
b. Foreign
c. Unpredictable
d. Tired

44. The mortified clerk

a. Cold
b. Embarrassed
c. Drowsy
d. Excited

45. His keen remorse

a. Relative
b. Sharp
c. Long
d. Large

46. The secluded village

a. Loud
b. Remote
c. Populous
d. Religious

47. The fortified perimeter

a. Boundary
b. Distance
c. Intimacy
d. Jewel

48. The painful slight

a. Daydream
b. Passive
c. Formality
d. Insult

49. Our <u>monetary</u> goals

   a. Financial
   b. Impossible
   c. Particular
   d. Academic

50. The <u>volatile</u> chemical

   a. Harmless
   b. Inert
   c. Small
   d. Explosive

51. <u>Ruddy</u> cheeks

   a. Red
   b. Weary
   c. Swollen
   d. Watery

52. The <u>stellar</u> student

   a. Predictable
   b. Unimpressed
   c. Outstanding
   d. Indifferent

53. The <u>spare</u> tire

   a. Small
   b. Extra
   c. Old
   d. Flat

54. A <u>shrill</u> tone

   a. High-pitched
   b. Low
   c. Punitive
   d. Soft

55. The <u>enthralled</u> audience

   a. Bored
   b. Released
   c. Noisy
   d. Captivated

56. Time for <u>recuperation</u>

   a. Healing
   b. Replacement
   c. Drinking
   d. Discipline

57. <u>Meager</u> wages

a. Desired
b. Owed
c. Insufficient
d. Exact

58. A <u>severe</u> storm

a. Relentless
b. Slight
c. Cold
d. Immediate

59. To <u>replicate</u> exactly

a. Amphibian
b. Approximate
c. Apply
d. Reproduce

60. To <u>repudiate</u> under oath

a. Lie
b. Commit
c. Desist
d. Renounce

61. To <u>absolve</u> someone's misdeeds

a. Forgive
b. Accept
c. Repeat
d. Reject

62. The <u>impregnable</u> fortress

a. Defeated
b. Indecipherable
c. Visible
d. Impenetrable

Mathematics

1. Which number is the least common multiple of 2 and 4?

    a. 2
    b. 4
    c. 8
    d. 12

2. Equation A is $5y - 100x = 25$. What are the slope and y-intercept of the line?

    a. The slope is 100, and the y-intercept is 5.
    b. The slope is 5, and the y-intercept is 100.
    c. The slope is 20, and the y-intercept is 5.
    d. The slope is 25, and the y-intercept is 5.

3. If an odd number is added to an even number, the result must be

    a. odd
    b. even
    c. positive
    d. zero

4. Which of the following is equal to 6.19×10^3?

    a. .00619
    b. .0619
    c. 619
    d. 6,190

5. What is the area of a square with a perimeter of 16 ft?

    a. 4 ft^2
    b. 16 ft^2
    c. 32 ft^2
    d. 256 ft^2

6. The sum of two negative numbers

    a. is always negative.
    b. is always positive.
    c. sometimes is positive and sometimes is negative.
    d. is always zero.

7. Which of the following is equal to $4\sqrt{2^4}$?

    a. 4
    b. 8
    c. 16
    d. 32

8. The Charleston Recycling Company collects 50,000 tons of recyclable material every month. The chart shows the kinds of materials that are collected by the company's five trucks.

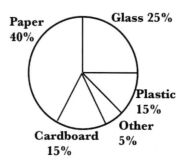

About how much paper is recycled every month?
   a.   15,000 tons
   b.   20,000 tons
   c.   25,000 tons
   d.   40,000 tons

9. Which of the following is equal to 12.5%?
   a. $\frac{1}{4}$

   b. $\frac{1}{8}$

   c. $\frac{1}{12}$

   d. $\frac{1}{16}$

10. A circle has an area equal to 36π. What is its diameter?
   a.   4
   b.   6
   c.   12
   d.   4π

11. Which of the following numbers is NOT prime?
   a.   3
   b.   6
   c.   17
   d.   41

12. The number 5 is multiplied by its reciprocal. What is the result?
   a.   0

   b.   1

   c. $\frac{1}{5}$

   d.   5

13. A dartboard is divided into 8 black and 8 white wedge-shaped sectors, so that when a dart is thrown it has a 50% chance of landing on white and a 50% chance of landing on black. If a dart is thrown 3 times in a row and lands on black each time, what is the chance that it will land again on black if it is thrown a fourth time?

    a. 12.5%
    b. 25%
    c. 50%
    d. 100%

14. How many integers exist between the numbers -4.2 and $+6.1$?

    a. 2
    b. 6
    c. 10
    d. 11

15. Joseph purchased 12 pounds of peaches at 80 cents per pound. He calculated the total amount as $12 \times \$0.80 = \$9.60$. Another method Joseph could have used to calculate the total cost of the peaches is:

    a. $(10 \times \$0.80) + (2 \times \$0.80)$
    b. $(12 \times \$0.40) + (2 \times \$0.80)$
    c. $(12 \times \$0.20) + (12 \times \$0.20)$
    d. $(2 \times \$0.80) + (10 \times \$0.40)$

16. What is the volume of the cube?

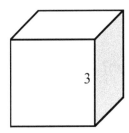

    a. 9 cubic units
    b. 15 cubic units
    c. 27 cubic units
    d. 33 cubic units

17. Which of the following expressions represents "five times a number m squared"?

    a. $\frac{5}{m^2}$
    b. $5m^2$
    c. $(5m)^2$
    d. $5 + m^2$

18. The square root of 6 is between

    a. 0 and 1
    b. 1 and 2
    c. 2 and 3
    d. 3 and 4

19. The radius of a circle with an area of 31 square units is doubled. What is the area of the new circle?

    a. 62 square units
    b. 93 square units
    c. 124 square units
    d. 132 square units

20. Juan got grades of 68 and 73 on his first two math tests. What grade must he get on the third test if all are weighted equally and he wants to raise his grade to a 75 average?

    a. 84
    b. 82
    c. 80
    d. 78

21. The ratio of left-handed to right-handed ballplayers on the girls' softball team is 2:3. If there are 12 left-handed players on the team, how many girls are on the roster in all?

    a. 18
    b. 24
    c. 30
    d. 32

22. Round 17.188 to the nearest hundredth.

    a. 17.1
    b. 17.2
    c. 17.18
    d. 17.19

23. Which function represents the graph?

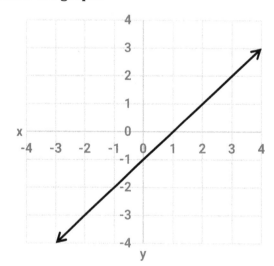

    a. $y = x + 1$
    b. $y = x - 1$
    c. $y = -x + 1$
    d. $y = -x - 1$

24. Refer to the following chart. Which month shows the greatest increase in rainfall compared to the preceding month?

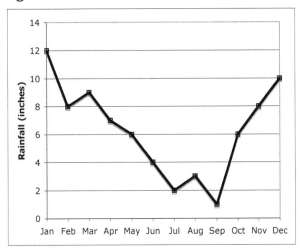

a. January
b. March
c. August
d. October

25. If $3x + 5 = 11$, then $x = ?$

a. 6
b. 3
c. 2
d. 1

26. Jamet had $6.50 in his wallet when he left home. He spent $4.25 on drinks and $2.00 on a magazine. Later, his friend repaid him $2.50 that he had borrowed the previous day. How much does Jamet have in his wallet now?

a. $12.25
b. $14.25
c. $3.25
d. $2.75

27. A sailboat is 19 meters long. What is its approximate length in inches?

a. 254
b. 1,094
c. 4,826
d. 748

28. Mrs. Patterson's classroom has sixteen empty chairs in it. All the chairs are occupied when every student is present. If 2/5 of the students are absent, how many students make up her entire class?

a. 16
b. 32
c. 24
d. 40

29. Rachel spent $24.15 on vegetables. She bought 2 pounds of onions, 3 pounds of carrots, and $1\frac{1}{2}$ pounds of mushrooms. If the onions cost $3.69 per pound, and the carrots cost $4.29 per pound, what is the price per pound of mushrooms?

    a. $2.60
    b. $2.25
    c. $2.80
    d. $3.10

30. Elijah drove 45 miles to his job in an hour and ten minutes in the morning. On the way home, however, traffic was much heavier, and the same trip took an hour and a half. What was his average speed in miles per hour for the round trip?

    a. 30 mph
    b. 32.5 mph
    c. 33.75 mph
    d. 35 mph

31. Lauren had $80 in her savings account. When she got her paycheck, she made a deposit that brought the total to $120. By what percentage did the total amount in her account increase as a result of this deposit?

    a. 50%
    b. 40%
    c. 35%
    d. 80%

32. Which of these is a solution to the inequality $4x - 12 < 4$?

    a. $x < 2$
    b. $x > 2$
    c. $x > 4$
    d. $x < 4$

33. If $a = -6$ and $b = 7$, then $4a(3b + 5) + 2b = ?$

    a. -638
    b. -485
    c. -850
    d. -610

34. Mark is driving to Phoenix, a distance of 210 miles. He drives the first ten miles in 12 minutes. If he continues at the same rate, how long will it take him, in total, to reach his destination?

    a. 3 hours 15 minutes
    b. 4 hours 12 minutes
    c. 3 hours 45 minutes
    d. 4 hours 20 minutes

35. An airplane leaves Atlanta at 2 PM and flies north at 250 miles per hour. A second airplane leaves Atlanta 30 minutes later and flies north at 280 miles per hour. At what time will the second airplane overtake the first?

    a. 6:00 PM
    b. 6:20 PM

   c. 6:40 PM

   d. 6:50 PM

36. The table shows the cost of renting a bicycle for 1, 2, or 3 hours. Which of the following equations best represents the data, if *C* represents the cost and *h* represents the time of the rental?

Hours	1	2	3
Cost	$3.60	$7.20	$10.80

   a. $C = 3.60h$

   b. $C = h + 3.60$

   c. $C = 3.60h + 10$

   d. $C = \dfrac{10.80}{h}$

37. Joshua has to earn more than 92 points on the state test in order to qualify for an academic scholarship. Each question is worth 4 points, and the test has a total of 30 questions. Let *x* represent the number of test questions.

Which of the following inequalities can be solved to determine the number of questions Joshua must answer correctly?

   a. $4x < 30$

   b. $4x < 92$

   c. $4x > 30$

   d. $4x > 92$

38. What is the area of the shaded region? (Each square represents one unit.)

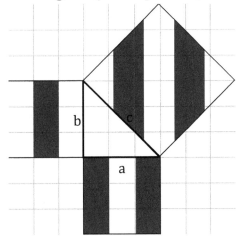

   a. 16 units

   b. 18 units

   c. 24 units

   d. 36 units

39. A tire on a car rotates at 500 RPM (revolutions per minute) when the car is traveling at 50 km/hr (kilometers per hour). What is the circumference of the tire, in meters?

    a. $\dfrac{10}{12\pi}$

    b. $\dfrac{125}{3}$

    c. $\dfrac{100}{2\pi}$

    d. $\dfrac{10}{6}$

40. If $\dfrac{4}{x-3} - \dfrac{2}{x} = 1$, then $x = ?$

    a. −6

    b. −1

    c. −6 or −1

    d. −1 or 6

41. Richard buys two cups of coffee every day except Saturday and Sunday. On Saturday he buys only one cup, and on Sunday he buys none. If a cup of coffee costs $2.25, how much does Richard spend on coffee every week?

    a. $25.00

    b. $23.50

    c. $24.75

    d. $25.25

42. Candice is reading a map. She measures a distance along a road as 6.5 inches. If the scale of the map is such that one mile is represented as 2 inches, what is the real distance along the road that Candice has measured?

    a. 4 miles

    b. 3.25 miles

    c. 6.5 miles

    d. 13 miles

43. Bob spends $17.90 on sodas and snacks for his study group. The expenses are to be split evenly between five people. How much is each person's share?

    a. $3.45

    b. $3.58

    c. $3.65

    d. $3.73

44. What percentage of 72 is 9?

    a. 16%

    b. 12.5%

    c. 11%

    d. 8%

45. The histogram below represents the overall GRE scores for a sample of college students. Which of the following is a true statement?

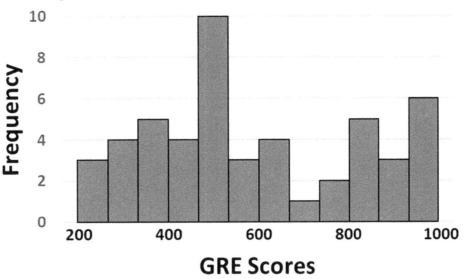

a. The range of GRE scores is approximately 600.
b. The average GRE score is 750.
c. The median GRE score is approximately 500.
d. The fewest number of college students had an approximate score of 800.

46. A train takes 40 minutes to go 55 miles. Moving at the same constant speed, how long will the train require to go 220 miles?

a. 4 hours 20 minutes
b. 3 hours 40 minutes
c. 2 hours 40 minutes
d. 2 hours 20 minutes

47. A clothing store offers a red tag sale during which items are offered at 5% off the marked price. Margaret selects a dress with a marked price of $120. How much will she have to pay for it?

a. $115
b. $110
c. $96
d. $114

48. On his last math test, Sam got 2 questions correct for every 3 questions he missed. If the test had a total of 60 questions, how many questions did Sam answer correctly?

a. 12
b. 24
c. 36
d. 40

49. Based on the figure below, if $\overline{BG} = 6x - 4$ and $\overline{GD} = 2x + 8$, what is the length of $\overline{GD}$?

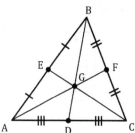

    a. 10
    b. 14
    c. 28
    d. 56

50. An automobile gets 34 miles per gallon of gasoline on typical roads. If it gets this fuel efficiency on a drive of 629 miles, how many gallons of gasoline will it burn?

    a. 17
    b. 18.5
    c. 19.25
    d. 20.5

51. In the figure below, lines a and b are parallel. Find the value of x.

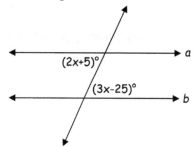

    a. $x = 22$
    b. $x = 30$
    c. $x = 40$
    d. $x = 55$

52. A company is building a track for a local high school. There are two straight sections and two semi-circular turns. Given the dimensions, which of the following most closely measures the perimeter of the entire track?

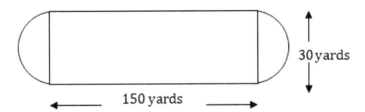

a. 120 yards
b. 180 yards
c. 300 yards
d. 395 yards

53. Rafael has a business selling computers. He buys computers from the manufacturer for $450 each and sells them for $800. Each month, he must also pay fixed costs of $3000 for rent and utilities for his store. If he sells n computers in a month, which of the following equations can be used to find his profit?

a. $P = n(800 - 450)$
b. $P = n(800 - 450 - 3000)$
c. $P = 3000 \, n(800 - 450)$
d. $P = n(800 - 450) - 3000$

54. Which of the following statements is true?

a. Perpendicular lines have slopes of opposite signs.
b. Perpendicular lines have the same slopes.
c. Perpendicular lines have reciprocal slopes.
d. Perpendicular lines have reciprocal slopes of opposite signs.

55. A bag contains six marbles: two green, two blue, and two red. If two marbles are drawn at random, what is the probability that they are of the same color?

a. 3%
b. 20%
c. 25%
d. 33%

56. Which of the following is the factored form of the expression, $x^2 + 3x - 28$?

a. $(x - 14)(x + 2)$
b. $(x + 6)(x - 3)$
c. $(x + 4)(x - 1)$
d. $(x - 4)(x + 7)$

57. Nancy had $17.25 from her part-time job. She spent $3.15 on a magazine and $6.75 on snacks and drinks. How much does she have left?

a. $7.35
b. $9.15
c. $7.20
d. $7.40

58. A dress is marked down by 20% and placed on a clearance rack, on which is posted a sign reading, "Take an extra 25% off already reduced merchandise." What fraction of the original price is the final sale price of the dress?

    a. $\frac{1}{4}$

    b. $\frac{2}{5}$

    c. $\frac{3}{5}$

    d. $\frac{9}{20}$

59. It takes two men 8 hours to paint a wall that is 10 feet high and 18 feet long. How long does it take three men working at the same pace to paint a wall that is 10 feet high and 27 feet long?

    a. 6 hours
    b. 8 hours
    c. 9 hours
    d. 10 hours

60. Vivian has $50. She goes to the store and buys a calculator. then she buys a book that costs half what the calculator cost. Then she buys a pen that costs half what the book cost. She has $15 left. How much did she spend on the calculator?

    a. $14
    b. $15
    c. $18
    d. $20

61. A rectangular box is twice as long as it is wide. If it were 3 inches shorter and 3 inches wider, it would be square. What is the width in inches of the box?

    a. 4
    b. 6
    c. 8
    d. 12

62. In a game of chance, 3 dice are thrown at the same time. What is the probability that all three will land with a 6?

    a. 1 in 6
    b. 1 in 18
    c. 1 in 216
    d. 1 in 30

63. Richard sells cell phones. He is paid a commission of 10% for every phone he sells. The phones cost $140 each. How many phones must Richard sell in order to be paid $840?

    a. 40
    b. 50
    c. 60
    d. 70

214

64. What is the value of $(2 \times 10^{-2}) \times (5 \times 10^3)$?

    a.   1

    b.   10

    c.   100

    d.   1000

Language

USAGE, PUNCTUATION, AND GRAMMAR

Identify the sentence that contains an error in usage, punctuation or grammar. If there are no errors, choose answer choice "d."

1.

   a. Fear of the number thirteen is called "triskaidekaphobia."

   b. The earwig's name originates in the myth that the insect burrows into the human ear to lay its eggs.

   c. The longest word recorded in an English dictionary are "Pneumonoultramicroscopic-silicovolcanokoniosis."

   d. No mistake.

2.

   a. "Stewardesses," "desegregated," and "reverberated" are the longest words a person can type using only his or her left hand.

   b. The largest catfish ever catch is 646 pounds, the size of an adult brown bear.

   c. A flyswatter has holes in it to reduce air resistance.

   d. No mistake.

3.

   a. The canoe cut a clear swath through the algae.

   b. Though widely ridiculed when first proposed, Alfred Wegener's theory of plate tectonics is now an accepted explanation of how continents are formed.

   c. Though a highly influentially anthropologist, Claude Levi-Strauss often took criticism for spending little time in the field studying real cultures.

   d. No mistake.

4.

   a. Fiction writer David Foster Wallace, author of the influential novel *Infinite Jest*, also authored a book surveying all of the significant theories of infinity in the history of mathematics.

   b. The photograph made the Eiffel Tower look like it was balanced on Oswald's palm.

   c. It is easy to get confused when calculating time differences between time zones a useful way to remember them is that the Atlantic Ocean starts with A, as in A.M., and the Pacific Ocean starts with P, as in P.M.

   d. No mistake.

5.

   a. Arnold was disappointed to discover the model airplane he purchased online was half the size he expected.

   b. Computer storage has come a long way since the days of punched paper tape.

   c. The surrealists were a group of artists who believed that art should reflect the subconscious mind, their images are often very dreamlike, showing businessmen falling like rain over a city and melting clocks.

   d. No mistake.

6.

   a. A "moor" is a plot of uncultivated land, similar to prairies in the U.S.

   b. "Orange is my favorite color, but not my favorite fruit." said Lisa.

   c. Some historians believe that the United States would have been too large for one government to control if the telegraph had not been invented in 1837.

   d. No mistake.

7.

   a. The largest volcano in our solar system is found on Mars.

   b. The deepest canyon, too.

   c. The volcano, called the Olympus Mons, is 342 miles in width and 17 miles tall; the canyon, called the Valles Marinaris, is 2,500 miles long.

   d. No mistake.

8.

   a. Pocahontas spent the last year's of her young life in England under the name Rebecca.

   b. Dorine beat me in tennis for three straight matches.

   c. Much of the light given off by stars is blocked by cosmic dust before it reaches the Earth's atmosphere.

   d. No mistake.

9.

   a. The Pima Indians of Arizona have remarkably high rates of diabetes and obesity some scientists believe the gene that causes this present-day health crisis was actually of great value to the Pima's ancestors who had to be able to retain glucose during periods of famine.

   b. Recent research has discovered that some types of incense can create effects in the human brain similar to antidepressants.

   c. Though debate on the topic has been ongoing, some believe that many amphibian species may be on the brink of extinction.

   d. No mistake.

10.

   a. The driver's side fender of my car is caved in because the high-speed winds pulled the door open too quickly.

   b. While there is some truth to the belief that Inuits have many words for snow, it is often overlooked that there are quite a few words for snow in English too: snow, slush, flurry, snowflake, and even more if you count the slang of snowboarders.

   c. Director Alfred Hitchcock make over 60 films in his career.

   d. No mistake.

11.

   a. A good pediatrician should try not to laugh at the fears of new parents.

   b. Some of the most difficult words to spell include "bureaucracy," "sacrilegious," and "millennium."

   c. Sales of digitally downloaded albums have risen from 5.5 million in 2004 to 65.8 million in 2008.

   d. No mistake.

12.

   a. The earliest recording of a human voice was made by Thomas Edison in 1877, when they recorded himself reciting "Mary Had a Little Lamb."

   b. In 2009, *The Simpsons* became the longest running series in television history.

   c. Many say that Reunion Tower in downtown Dallas, Texas, resembles a microphone or a golf ball on a tee.

   d. No mistake.

13.

   a. The *trireme* was a Greek battleship that got its name from the three banks of oars that helped propel the ship into battle.

   b. Our basement floods once a yearly.

   c. The *novitiate* is the period of time before a monk or priest takes his vows to make sure he is suited for the religious life.

   d. No mistake.

14.

   a. The trumpet player said, "I played the song right, just not the notes."

   b. Woody Allen said, "I don't want to achieve immortality through my work. I want to achieve it through not dying."

   c. Samuel Goldwyn is said to have replied to a secretary who asked whether she should destroy files over ten years old, "Yes, but keep copies."

   d. No mistake.

15.

   a. When asked to take a reduction in pay from $20,000 to $7,500 a year, baseball legend Vernon Gomez replied, "You keep the salary and pay me the cut."

   b. The spread of Islam began around 600 A.D. and reached from the Middle East to North Africa, Spain, Central Asia, and India?

   c. Hadrian, Emperor of Rome, is credited with halting the expansion of the Roman Empire to concentrate instead on defending its boundaries.

   d. No mistake.

16.

   a. The Sahara Desert was rarely crossed until the introduction of the camel in 100 A.D.

   b. International time standards were not put in place until 1883.

   c. The names of the days of the week originate in either Latin or Saxon names for deities, Sunday, for instance, is Saxon for "Sun's Day," while Thursday derives from "Thor's Day."

   d. No mistake.

17.

a. The origin of the clock is usually traced back to Galileo, who in 1583 reportedly watched a chandelier swinging during a church service and imagined a way to use a pendulum as a time-keeping device.

b. Irvin Hertzel ran a statistical analysis of Monopoly squares and found that players land on some spots more often than others, specifically Illinois Ave., Go, B & O Railroad, and Free Parking.

c. Held in Georgia, the Masters is an annual golf tournament that professional golfers consider the most valuable title in golf.

d. No mistake.

18.

a. Ironically, the namesake of the Nobel Peace Prize, Alfred Nobel, are most noted for his invention of dynamite in the 1860s.

b. The terms of our lease agreement were long and hard to understand.

c. Many terms in our legal system are Latin in origin, such as "nolo contendere" (no contest) and "actus rea" (a wrongful act).

d. No mistake.

19.

a. Loud sounds can causing damage to the hair cells that turn sound waves into electrical signals that the brain perceives as sound.

b. Debate has raged for over 200 years about whether the U.S. should adopt the metric system.

c. The metric system recognizes only seven base units of measurement, including the meter for length, the kilogram for mass, and lesser known units used by specialists like the mole for substance and the candela for light intensity.

d. No mistake.

20.

a. The metric system uses a "base-ten" system of measurement, which means its prefixes indicate multiples of ten.

b. If you ever need to measure something but do not have access to a ruler, these facts can help: The average credit card is $3\frac{3}{8}$ inches by $2\frac{1}{8}$ inches, the diameter of a quarter is around one inch, and the diameter of a penny is about $\frac{3}{4}$ inch.

c. Carbon monoxide Poisoning can cause disorientation and delirium, and it can induce a coma.

d. No mistake.

21.

a. Capgras Syndrome causes the strange delusion that people such as family members and friends are not who they appear to be but are instead imposters.

b. Yvette belonged to three organizations whose schedules constantly conflicted.

c. Owen's shirt was stained pink from his popsicle, purple from jelly, and blue from Kool-Aid.

d. No mistake.

22.

    a. They closed the parking deck at midnight, so we could not get no cars out until morning.

    b. "Associationism" is the name given to the theory that memories are linked together so that when one is triggered, associated memories are activated as well.

    c. Some psychologists believe that many emotional disorders, including depression and anxiety, can be traced back to unrealistic expectations and assumptions.

    d. No mistake.

23.

    a. Joni designed the grocery stores sign, but Evan painted it.

    b. The "figure-ground phenomenon" is a term used to describe the way we perceive some objects to be in the foreground and others to be in the background.

    c. The Latin professor called his students "quidnuncs" when they asked too many questions about the course; the term is Latin for "what now?"

    d. No mistake.

24.

    a. Outside the apartment, the bus stop is a source of constant noise.

    b. Few people remembered Sydney's birthday except Jon, whose birthday was the same day.

    c. Erin brought cookies and juice on the last day of class.

    d. No mistake.

25.

    a. In math, the "Goldbach conjecture" states that every even number greater than two is the sum of two primes.

    b. Enjil was a complex Sumerian sky god who was at times characterized as wrathful and at others as kind and generous.

    c. Twenty-four leaders of the Nazi party was brought to trial at the end of World War II in what became known as the Nuremberg Trials.

    d. No mistake.

26.

    a. In radio broadcasting, a short jingle called a "bumper" announces the name of the station after commercials.

    b. "There weren't any jobs listed in the newspaper this morning," Ed told his father.

    c. Water is called "hard water" if it do not quickly create lather upon contact with soap because of mineral compounds dissolved in the water.

    d. No mistake.

27.

    a. Halley's Comet, which completes its orbit around the sun once every 76 years, was last seen in 1986 and will not be visible again until 2062.

    b. Ice crystals in the atmosphere, which can create a halo around the sun or moon.

    c. "Abiogenesis" is a term that refers to the discredited belief that living things can be created from nonliving things.

    d. No mistake.

28.

   a. The term "Algebra" comes from the title of a book written in the ninth century that explains how to balance equations.

   b. Atomic clocks keep time by measuring the vibrations of Atoms and molecules.

   c. The chemical formula for the caffeine molecule contains calcium, hydrogen, oxygen, and nitrogen.

   d. No mistake.

29.

   a. Heat was once believes to be a type of fluid called "caloric," which flowed into objects and raised their temperature.

   b. Streams of protons and neutrons that escape the sun during solar flares are called "solar wind."

   c. The "heat death of the universe" is a theory that predicts the universe will eventually run out of usable energy.

   d. No mistake.

30.

   a. The epicenter of an earthquake is the point on the Earth's surface that is above the hypocenter, or the point inside the Earth where the earthquake occurs.

   b. Apart from a sine wave created by an electronic device, most sounds are not "pure" because they contain many different vibrations at different frequencies pure tones vibrate at only one frequency.

   c. Though Chicago is known as the "Windy City" with winds that average 10.4 miles per hour, its winds are far slower than those of Mt. Washington, New Hampshire, where winds average 35.3 miles per hour.

   d. No mistake.

31.

   a. Arthur, realizing that bugs were turning the roots of his zucchini plants to mush.

   b. The Earth moves at different speeds depending on where one stands in relation to the poles; the North Pole spins at about zero miles per hour, while the equator spins at over 1,000 miles per hour.

   c. Because maps must distort the size of certain continents to represent a sphere stretched over a two-dimensional plane, Greenland is often depicted as similar in size to South America, even though it is about eight times smaller.

   d. No mistake.

32.

   a. The Earth is believed to be about 4.6 billion years old.

   b. Sequoyah, who created a written script for the Cherokee language, compared the task to "catching a wild animal and taming it."

   c. The discovery of gold on Cherokee land in 1828 is considered a significant motivation for the passage of the Indian Removal Act of 1830, which forced Native Americans from their homes.

   d. No mistake.

33.

    a. In 1803, Robert Livingston and James Monroe, two of Thomas Jefferson's aides, purchased all of the French territories in America.

    b. They paid the remarkably low price of $15 million to Napoleon, who wanted to sell the land to finance his military campaigns.

    c. This figure amounts to about four cents per acre, or eight dollars per square mile.

    d. No mistake.

34.

    a. The narwhal is a member of the dolphin family, easily recognized by its long, spiraling tusk, it is often compared to the mythical unicorn.

    b. The ocean is saltier in regions where the temperature is higher due to a higher rate of evaporation.

    c. The garter snake is often called a "gardener snake" or a "guarder snake" because of the similar sounds of the words.

    d. No mistake.

35.

    a. Long distance calls were placed by an operator until 1951.

    b. The first drive-in movie theater opened in 1933.

    c. The first Ferris' Wheel was built in Chicago, Illinois.

    d. No mistake.

36.

    a. Trees in the Olympic rain forest in northwest Washington State is covered with a thick green moss that is nourished by the 150 annual inches of rainfall.

    b. The sand dunes were prettiest at sunset, when the shadows ran across the landscape like dark ribbons.

    c. Some of the students were sleeping during reading time.

    d. No mistake.

37.

    a. Most published writing goes through many drafts and many readers before it is printed.

    b. Blogs, however, are rarely edited as carefully.

    c. As a result, readers have different expectations of online publications.

    d. No mistake.

38.

    a. When asked what his songs were about, Bob Dylan replied, "Well, some of them are about five minutes, and some of them are about eleven minutes."

    b. I found several fossils of large trilobites on a field trip with my geology class.

    c. I was, hoping to avoid the customs official who was yelling at all of the other travelers.

    d. No mistake.

39.

    a. Reykjavik is the Capitol of Iceland.

    b. It is pronounced "Rake-ya-veek."

    c. The letter "j" is pronounced like a "y" in English.

    d. No mistake.

Mometrix

40.

   a. Jen asked the professor for an extension on her first essay.
   b. She was asking for more time.
   c. The professor added three pages to the required length.
   d. No mistake.

SPELLING

Choose the sentence that contains a spelling error. If there are no errors, choose answer choice "d."

41.

   a. My favorite Beatles' record is <u>Revolver</u>.
   b. My favorite Beatles' song is "Strawberry Fields."
   c. My favorite Beatle is John Lennon.
   d. No mistake.

42.

   a. I had to have a tooth pulled after a bike accident.
   b. When I received the dentist's bill, I was disgruntled.
   c. I was graitful that I couldn't feel a thing.
   d. No mistake.

43.

   a. Mrs. Albom, the music teacher, financed her summer vacation by bagging groceries at Wal-Mart after school.
   b. We put down a tarp and shook the branches to get the mulberries.
   c. The citric acid used in Vitamin C tablets makes them taste sower.
   d. No mistake.

44.

   a. Despite being born a slave, Benjamin Banneker went on to play a pivotal role in the planning of Washington D. C.
   b. Andrew Johnson is the only president to serve as a sinator after his time as president, which is ironic because the senate had attempted to impeach him when he was president.
   c. The St. Burchardi Church in Halberstadt, Germany, is currently performing a composition by John Cage entitled "As Slow as Possible," a piece that takes 639 years to complete.
   d. No mistake.

45.

   a. Jan tried to remember her groshery list by turning it into a song that went, "carrots and cashews and rolled toilet tissues."
   b. I thought for sure I had killed the basil plant, but it revived with a little water.
   c. The washing machine died with a load of wet clothes in it.
   d. No mistake.

46.

  a. The rock polisher ran all nite and day for months.
  b. When the bouquet of flowers started to die, it left a little mound of yellow dust under each flower.
  c. Nora wants to become a veterinarian when she grows up.
  d. No mistake.

47.

  a. Eleanor wove baskets from reeds that she pulled from the bank of the nearby lake.
  b. The dog howled whenever the ambulances passed.
  c. Gas station coffee alway tastes watered down to me.
  d. No mistake.

48.

  a. Peter Elbow is famous for his book titled *Writing without Teachers*, in which he promotes "freewriting," or writing for short periods of time without any concern for spelling, grammar, or logic.
  b. John Wilkes Booth's intention in assassinating President Lincoln was to avenge the Confederacy, but in effect, his actions hurt the South because Lincoln did not live to oversee his plan for reconstruction.
  c. Perspective painting uses techniques to give the two-dimentional surface of a painting the appearance of three-dimentional spays.
  d. No mistake.

49.

  a. We entered the church from the south, but the family we were supposed to meet was waiting on the north side of the building.
  b. The stained glass cast colorful shadows across the carpet.
  c. I filled out the tax forms incorrectly, and that mistake cost me a quadruple-digit figure.
  d. No mistake.

50.

  a. Enrique loved to sketch copies of the images he found in *National Geographic*.
  b. Over 60% of the Netherlands lies below sea level.
  c. Jon submitted three poems to the contest and won one thousand dollars.
  d. No mistake.

COMPOSITION

51. Where should the following sentence be placed in the paragraph below?

Many people have proposed explanations for this drop.

1] Surveys of criminal activity in the United States have shown that the 1990s marked a significant drop in crimes such as vehicle theft, rape, and murder. 2] Economist Rick Nevin argues that one contributing factor is the ban on lead gasoline in the 70s because lead poisoning in children has been linked with criminal behavior later in life. 3] Other theories include the controversial claim that legalizing abortion has led to fewer unwanted children and, as a result, fewer potential criminals. 4] Some politicians, including Rudy Giuliani, even take personal responsibility, identifying their policies as effective deterrents to crime.

   a. After sentence 1
   b. After sentence 2
   c. After sentence 3
   d. After sentence 4

52. Where should the following sentence be placed in the paragraph below?

Insects that carry the disease can develop resistance to the chemicals, or insecticides, that are used to kill the mosquitoes.

1] Malaria, a disease spread by insects and parasites, has long proven to be difficult to treat. 2] Part of the explanation has to do with adaptation, or the ability of one generation to pass its strengths on to another. 3] Some insects are simply not affected by these insecticides. 4] Unfortunately, these are the insects that survive and go on to reproduce, creating another generation of insects that are immune to the current insecticides. 5] Many researchers have abandoned hope for insecticides as a cure for malaria, turning their attention instead to other forms of defense, such as protein-blockers that protect humans from the effects of the disease instead of from the carriers.

   a. After sentence 1
   b. After sentence 2
   c. After sentence 3
   d. After sentence 4

53. Choose the word or words that best fill the blank.

Disney films often use the same voice actors; _____, Sterling Holloway was the voice for Winnie the Pooh, the stork in *Dumbo*, the snake Kaa in *Jungle Book*, and the Cheshire Cat in *Alice in Wonderland.*

   a. but
   b. for instance
   c. thus
   d. so

54. Choose the word or words that best fill the blank.

Many similarities exist between the film *Star Wars IV: A New Hope* and a Japanese film called *The Hidden Fortress*; _____ , *Star Wars* director George Lucas openly acknowledges the film as a significant influence.

a. however
b. or
c. in fact
d. yet

55. Choose the word or words that best fill the blank.

Marty did not realize until he arrived to perform in Philadelphia that he had left his guitar in Pittsburgh; _____, he was fortunate to find a music store that agreed to rent him one for the evening.

a. however
b. because
c. after
d. while

56. Choose the sentence that is correct and most clearly written.

a. The novelist David Markson is known for his experimental works, such as "This Is Not a Novel."
b. Experimental works such as "This Is Not a Novel" have been wrote by David Markson.
c. Novelist David Markson is knew for his experimental works, such as "This Is Not a Novel."
d. David Markson is a novelist who is known for experimentation his works include "This Is Not a Novel."

57. Choose the sentence that is correct and most clearly written.

a. I intended to mow the yard, but I wanted to wait until evening when it are cooler.
b. I intended to mow the yard, but I wanted to wait until evening when it would be cooler.
c. I intended to mow the yard, but not until it getting cooler in the evening.
d. I intended to mow the yard, but I waits until evening when it was cooler.

58. Choose the sentence that is correct and most clearly written.

a. We used to dump our lawn clippings, but now we compost them for the garden.
b. Dumping our lawn clippings used to be something done by us, but now composting is done by us for the garden.
c. We used to dumps our lawn clippings, but now we composts them for the garden.
d. We used to dump our lawn clippings, but now I compost them for the garden.

59. Which sentence does not belong in the following paragraph?

1] Though Thomas Jefferson's taste for expensive home furnishings and wine contributed to the substantial debts he faced toward the end of his life, many other factors also contributed. 2] For instance, when Jefferson's father-in-law died, all of his debts were transferred to Jefferson. 3] Additionally, though his holdings in land and slaves were considerable, they were never especially profitable. 4] Jefferson is believed to have fathered children with one of his slaves. 5] Finally, less than a decade before his death, Jefferson unwisely agreed to endorse a $20,000 loan for a friend, and when the friend unexpectedly died a year later, Jefferson inherited yet another large debt. 6] Jefferson's personal experience with debt may have been part of his motivation in criticizing policies that would increase the national debt.

a. Sentence 2
b. Sentence 3
c. Sentence 4
d. Sentence 5

60. Which sentence does not belong in the following paragraph?

1] Renowned scientist Richard Feynman once said that the atomic theory is one of the most profound discoveries scientists have made. 2] Feynman was also an accomplished percussionist who could play nine beats with one hand while playing ten with the other! 3] "All things are made of atoms," explained Feynman, "little particles that...move around in perpetual motion, attracting each other when they are a little distance apart, but repelling upon being squeezed into one another." 4] He then made the claim that this idea is one of the most illuminating ideas in the history of science: "In that one sentence, you will see, there is an enormous amount of information about the world, if just a little imagination and thinking are applied."

a. Sentence 1
b. Sentence 2
c. Sentence 3
d. Sentence 4

Answers and Explanations

Verbal Skills

1. A: To depress is the opposite of enliven, which means to excite or invigorate.

2. C: Natural is the opposite of the other words in the series. Artificial, synthetic, and man-made are all words for non-natural processes.

3. B: The category of amphibians contains frogs. The order of this analogy begins with something that is specific and moves to the general category. Since you are given the specific item of *hydrogen*, then you are looking for the general category which would be choice B: *element*.

4. C: We can diagram this sentence as follows: Tom > Darius, which tells us that Tom arrived before Darius. We do not have enough information to determine when Bernie arrived in relation to the other two people.

5. A: Aural refers to the auditory sense, or hearing.

6. B: "Artist" is the general category that all the other items in the series belong to; painters, musicians, and dancers are all kinds of artists.

7. B: Shun means reject or ignore, the opposite of embrace.

8. B: An apple develops from a seed; a person develops from an embryo.

9. C: We can diagram this sentence as follows: Dean > Ellie; Dean > Rob. In other words, Dean was born before Ellie and before Rob. We do not have enough information to determine whether Ellie > Rob is true.

10. C: This analogy focuses on synonyms. *Reprimand* and *punishment* are close synonyms. *Impetuous* is a sudden or impulsive action with little or no thoughtful planning. So, the best choice is *hasty* which means rapid or very quick.

11. D: Mediocre means unexceptional, which is the opposite of excellent.

12. C: "Appliance" is a general category that the other words in the list belong to. Toasters, ovens, and coffee makers are all appliances.

13. B: Intricate most nearly means complex.

14. A: Temperature is used to measure heat; pounds are used to measure weight.

15. D: Furrow, a word that refers to a line cut into the ground, means the opposite of mound.

16. D: The verb counsel most nearly means to advise.

17. B: We can diagram the first two sentences as follows: Mackenzie > Austin; Nora > Austin. The third sentence, which we could diagram as Mackenzie < Austin, contradicts the first sentence.

228

18. D: A *hologram* is an image that is made up of beams of *light* from a laser. So, we could say that the order of this analogy is a piece of a whole. The start of the next comparison is *film* which would be a piece of a *video camera*.

19. A: Passive means inactive, or the opposite of active.

20. D: As a reference at the end of a *book*, an *index* may be provided that contains key terms or phrases with page numbers where those terms or phrases can be found. So, we can say that an *index* is a part to the whole of a *book*. The comparison involves an *elegy* which can be a song or a poem that expresses terrible sadness for the death of a person. This *elegy* would then be a part to the whole of a *funeral* service.

21. B: When a strong opponent competes against an unlikely challenger, we sometimes call the unlikely challenger an *underdog* who will face the incredible odds of defeating the strong opponent. An attribute or characteristic of an underdog can be their *audacious* (i.e., confident or bold) attitude. Now, a *conspirator* is a person who is participating in a plan that has some illegal intent. So, a conspirator has the characteristic of being *elusive* (i.e., easily escaping capture).

22. C: To secede is to split apart, the opposite of merge.

23. A: The words inflammable, ignitable, and combustible all describe choice A, gasoline.

24. C: We can diagram the first two sentences as follows: Samuel > James; Horace > James. These sentences do not give us enough information to prove sentence three, Samuel=Horace.

25. C: Coarse, or rough, most nearly means harsh.

26. B: To be impartial is to be objective, detached or unbiased.

27. C: An *intermission* is a pause between acts of a play. Two common types of plays are *dramas* and comedies. So, we can determine that an *intermission* is a piece to the whole of a *drama*. Now, the comparison begins with *plant* as in vegetation. So, the best answer choice is *habitat* (i.e., the place where animal and plant life are naturally living) which fills the role of being the whole to the piece of *plant*.

28. C: The other words start with the letter "B" and end with the letter "K." So, the correct answer starts with the letter "B," but it ends with the letter "N."

29. A: This analogy is a matter of degree as starting with something basic and escalating to something more significant. The question begins with *jog* which is basic and general, and this is matched with *marathon* which is a 26.2 mile race that takes several hours to complete. So, the best choice is choice A which starts with a basic *hypothesis* (i.e., educated guess) and escalates to a *discovery*.

30. A: Deter most nearly means stop.

31. B: The first two sentences can be diagrammed as follows: Esther=Marcus; Lee > Marcus. If Lee drove farther than Marcus, he also drove farther than Esther. The third sentence, which we can diagram as Esther > Lee, contradicts sentences one and two, so it is false.

32. B: Inability is an antonym to the other answer choices.

33. B: Alleviate means to ease or lessen, which is the opposite of worsen.

34. B: This analogy focuses on antonyms. *Antipathy* and *sympathy* are opposites as *antipathy* means a strong feeling of opposition, and *sympathy* is the act of understanding another person's feeling or situation. You are given *convivial* which means sociable or cheerful, and you know that you are looking for the antonym of sociable and cheerful. So, *gloomy* means depressed or miserable, and this is the clear opposite to *convivial*.

35. C: To be refined is to be cultured and well-bred.

36. C: We can diagram the first two sentences as follows: University Press > Institutes Press and Institutes Press < Academy Press, which tells us that University Press and Academy Press received more submissions than Institutes Press. Yet, we cannot be sure which publishing house received the most submissions.

37. D: *Espionage* is the service of spying on opposition in order to gain intelligence. So, the nature (or characteristic) of this task is easily understood to be *discreet* (i.e., tactful and cautious). The analogy continues with *kindling* which are the pieces of material used to start a fire. In many situations, a fire is characteristic of something tragic that is about to happen to someone or something. A name for this foreboding sense of tragedy can be *ominous*. In short, a characteristic of *kindling* is *ominous*.

38. B: A person who is said to be pallid is feeble or sickly.

39. B: Jovial means happy, which is the opposite of depressed.

40. A: We can diagram the first two sentences as follows: Otis > Steve=Carrie. The third sentence claims that Otis > Carrie, which is consistent with the first two sentences.

41. D: Insufficient means inadequate, which is the opposite of adequate.

42. A: A novice is someone who is new to the circumstances, or the person is a beginner.

43. A: Foster most nearly means to care for, or nurture.

44. B: We can diagram the first two sentences as follows: The Gang Mentality > Metal Leather > The Animal Instincts. The third sentence, Gang Mentality < Metal Leather, is inconsistent with the first two.

45. A: Initiate means to start, the opposite of to stop.

46. D: Marry most nearly means join.

47. B: Independence, responsibility, and maturity are positive qualities typically associated with adulthood. Irresponsibility is a negative quality that is often associated with youth.

48. D: General means the opposite of particular.

49. A: Something paltry is cheap, base, or common.

50. A: Optimum most nearly means ideal.

51. A: A pledge is a promise, the opposite of breach, which is the violation or breaking of a promise.

52. D: The work of counselors, nurses, and lawyers call for working with people directly. The work of a novelist may include interviews or research with people, but their work is more solitary than the others.

53. B: The first two sentences can be diagrammed as follows: Reece > Lee > Darren. Sentence three, Darren > Reece, is inconsistent with the first two sentences. It is false.

54. D: To attest is to vouch for or to certify.

55. C: Outspoken most nearly means candid.

56. A: We can diagram the first two sentences as follows: Kevin < Allen and John > Allen. Then, the third sentence claims that, John > Allen > Kevin which is consistent with the first two sentences.

57. A: Pantomime most nearly means mimic.

58. B: Serendipity is the accidental finding of something that is deemed valuable. So, misfortune is an antonym to serendipity.

59. A: Pandemonium most nearly means chaos.

60. C: The other answer choices are general nouns. Choice C is specific noun. Cape Cod is a cape off the coast of Massachusetts.

Quantitative Skills

1. A: Convert all the numbers to fractions and compare. The number 0.099 can be rounded to 0.1. Then, the first 3 choices are: a) $\frac{1}{3}$; b) $\frac{1}{4}$; c) $\frac{1}{100}$. Since the numerators are equal, the number with the smallest denominator is greatest. To compare that with choice D, note that $\frac{1}{3} = \frac{2}{6}$ and $\frac{2}{6} > \frac{2}{7}$.

2. C: One strategy is to draw polygons with fewer sides and look for a pattern in the number of the polygons' diagonals.

Polygon	Sides	Diagonals	Δ Diagonals
	3	0	-
	4	2	2
	5	5	3
	6	9	4

A quadrilateral has two more diagonals than a triangle, a pentagon has three more diagonals than a quadrilateral, and a hexagon has four more diagonals than a pentagon. Continue this pattern to find that a dodecagon has 54 diagonals.

3. A: Each element of the series adds 9 to the preceding one. In algebraic terms, $P_n = P_{n-1} + 9$, where P_n is the nth element of the series. Since $31 + 9 = 40$, 40 is the correct answer.

4. A: $(0, 0)$ is a point because if Jonas doesn't walk, then his running speed is also 0. Another point is $(1, 3)$ because if Jonas moves a distance of 1 unit after walking x minutes, then he moves a distance of 3 units after x minutes from jogging.

5. B: To solve, first subtract Jerry's weight from the total permitted: $800 - 200 = 600$. Divide 600 by 4 (the four pieces of equipment) to get 150, the average weight.

6. D: Since the line segments pass through the center of the circle, both $\overline{AB}$ and $\overline{CD}$ are diameters of equal length, and the four line segments radiating outwards from O are all equal-length radii.

7. D: The area of a rectangle is calculated as the product of the width and length. If the length is twice the width of 3 m, it must be 6 m long. Then, $3 \times 6 = 18$ m^2.

8. C: The correct answer is $3000. Besides the $600 he has remaining; Chan has paid out a total of 80% (30% + 20% + 20% + 10%) of his bonus for the expenses described in the question. Therefore, the $600 represents the remaining 20%. Thus, his total bonus is $\frac{100}{20} \times \$600 = \$3000$.

9. D: Since the airplane is moving against a headwind, it will be slowed relative to the ground. Therefore, its final speed will be 300 mph − 15 mph = 285 mph.

10. A: If the ratio of pennies to nickels is 2:6, the ratio of the pennies to the combined coins is 2: $(2 + 6)$, or 2:8. This is $\frac{1}{4}$ or, expressed as a percentage, 25%.

11. D: The literal equation may be solved for x by first subtracting b from both sides of the equation. Doing so gives $ax = c - b$. Dividing both sides of the equation by a gives $x = \frac{c-b}{a}$.

12. C: The median of a set of numbers is one for which the set contains an equal number of greater and lesser values. Besides Z, there are 8 numbers in the set, so that 4 must be greater and 4 lesser than Z. The 4 smallest values are 5, 7, 9, and 12. The 4 largest are 16, 18, 23, and 44. So Z must fall between 12 and 16.

13. D: The sides of a triangle must all be greater than zero. The sum of the lengths of the two shorter sides must be greater than the length of the third side. Since we are looking for the minimum value of the perimeter, assume the longer of the two given sides, which is 6, is the longest side of the triangle. Then the third side must be greater than $6 - 4 = 2$. Since the sides are integers, the last side must be 3 units long. Thus, the minimum length for the perimeter is $4 + 6 + 3 = 13$ units.

14. B: The series consists of numbers each of which is double the number preceding. The number prior to the blank is 4: $2 \times 4 = 8$. The number following the blank is 16: $2 \times 8 = 16$.

15. C: The given equations form a system of linear equations. Since the first equation is already given in terms of x, it will be easier to solve the system using the substitution method. Start by substituting $2y - 3$ for x in the second equation:

$$2x + \frac{1}{2}y = 3$$
$$2(2y - 3) + \frac{1}{2}y = 3$$

Next, solve the resulting equation for y. Distribute the 2 and then combine like y-terms in the result:

$$4y - 6 + \frac{1}{2}y = 3$$
$$\frac{9}{2}y - 6 = 3$$

Finally, isolate the variable y by adding 6 to both sides and then dividing both sides by the coefficient of y, which is $\frac{9}{2}$ (or, equivalently, multiply by 2 and divide by 9):

$$\frac{9}{2}y = 9$$
$$y = 2$$

16. C: A number raised to the first power is multiplied by itself only once, so $16^1 = 16$. 2^8 is 2 multiplied by itself eight times, so $2^8 = 256$. Similarly, $3^3 = 27$.

17. A: This table shows the numbers of coins added to the first few squares and the equivalent powers of 2:

Square	1	2	3	4
Coins	1	2	4	8
Power of 2	2^0	2^1	2^2	2^3

In this series, the number of coins on each is the consecutive powers of 2. The reason is that the number doubles with each consecutive square. However, the series of powers begins with 0 for the first square. For the 64th square, the number of coins will be 2^{63}.

18. A: The series alternates between subtracting 4 from the number occurring two positions earlier (12, 8, 4, 0) and adding 6 to the number occurring two positions earlier (7, 13, 19, 25). Therefore, 25 is the next number.

19. B: 20% of 80 = 16; 50% of 70 = 35; and 40% of 90 = 36. Since 36 > 35 > 16, B is correct.

20. C: The correct answer is 8. The total 20 + 13 = 33, but only 25 cars have been scored. Therefore, 33 − 25, or 8 cars must have had both a man and a woman inside.

21. A: First establish a variable, s, for the length of the smaller square. Since the larger square is 3 feet longer than the smaller one, its length is $s + 3$. Given that the difference between the areas of the two squares is 75, and the area of any square is equal to its side lengths squared, the following equation can be established and solved:

$$(s + 3)^2 - s^2 = 75$$
$$(s + 3)(s + 3) - s^2 = 75$$
$$s^2 + 6s + 9 - s^2 = 75$$
$$6s + 9 = 75$$

Isolate the variable and divide both sides by its coefficient to solve for s:

$$6s = 66$$
$$s = 11$$

22. D: If point C is four times farther from A than from B, it means that the ratio of distances from C to A and B is 4:1, respectively. Therefore, the line segment can be broken up into $4 + 1 = 5$ equal segments. The total distance between points A and B is $7 - (-3) = 10$ units. If we divide 10 by 5, each equal segment is 2 units in length. We can then multiply the ratio by 2 to get the actual distances of C from A and B, $(4 \times 2) : (1 \times 2) = 8 : 2$. So, C is located 8 units from A and 2 units from B. Since A is located at -3, it means that $-3 + 8 = 5$. Answer A is the location if C is four times farther from B than it is from A. Answer B is just four units from point A. Answer C is just four units from point B.

23. C: The series consists of the squares of consecutive integers, beginning with 1: $1^2 = 1, 2^2 = 4$, and so on. In the fifth position, $5^2 = 25$, so that choice C is correct.

24. A: The sum $3 + 4 + 16 = 23$. The other choices are less. In particular, although it has more terms, choice B, $6 + 4 + 5 + 7 = 22$, which is less than choice A.

25. A: The numbers defined by (I), (II), and (III) are 8; 6; and 15, respectively.

26. A: Setting the cost of shipping equal to the amount received gives us the equation $3,000 + 100x = 400x$. Subtract $100x$ from both sides to get $3,000 = 300x$, then divide both sides by 300 to see that $x = 10$.

27. C: This can be solved as two equations with two unknowns. Since the integers are consecutive, with $p > n$, we have $p - n = 1$, so that $p = 1 + n$. Substituting this value into $p + n = 15$ gives $1 + 2n = 15$, or $n = \frac{14}{2} = 7$.

28. A: In this series, each number is either double the preceding number, or 2 more than the preceding number, and these procedures alternate. Since $36 = 2 \times 18$, the next element of the series will be determined by adding 2. Since $36 + 2 = 38$, the correct answer is A.

29. C: The perimeter of a rectangle of length 6 and width 4 equals $2(6 + 4) = 20$. The perimeter of a square of side 4 equals $4 + 4 + 4 + 4 = 16$. And the area of a square of side 4 equals $4 \times 4 = 16$. Although the units for the measurement of area differ from those of the perimeters, the magnitude of the measurements for (b) and (c) are the same.

30. A: Since there are 100 cm in a meter, on a 1:100 scale drawing, each centimeter represents one meter. Therefore, an area of one square centimeter on the drawing represents one square meter in actuality. Since the area of the room in the scale drawing is 30 cm^2, the room's actual area is 30 m^2.

Another way to determine the area of the room is to write and solve an equation, such as this one: $\frac{l}{100} \times \frac{w}{100} = 30$ cm^2 , where l and w are the dimensions of the actual room

$$\frac{lw}{10,000} = 30 \text{ cm}^2$$

$$\text{Area} = 300,000 \text{ cm}^2$$

Since this is not one of the answer choices, convert cm^2 to m^2:

$$300,000 \text{ cm}^2 \times \frac{1 \text{ m}}{100 \text{ cm}} \times \frac{1 \text{ m}}{100 \text{ cm}} = 30 \text{ m}^2.$$

31. C: Since the pattern repeats the same 4 figures, each multiple of 4 looks like Fig. 4 (4, 8, 12, ... , 28, 32, ...). The figure in the 31st position is one less than 32, so it should look like the figure left of Fig. 4. That figure is Fig. 3.

32. B: Fractions can be simplified by dividing both numerator and denominator by the same number. Divide the numerator and denominator of item (ii) by 10, and the result is 2/3. Divide the numerator and denominator of (iii) by 15, the result is 2/3. Therefore, all three fractions are equal.

33. A: The totals of each set of numbers are: A: 16; B: 17; C: 17; and D: 18.

34. B: Since $\overline{AB}$, $\overline{BD}$, $\overline{CD}$, and $\overline{AC}$ are sides of the square, they are all equal. They are shorter than the diagonals $\overline{AD}$ and $\overline{CB}$. These diagonals have the same length and bisect one another at the point E, which means that $\overline{AE} = \overline{BE} = \overline{CE} = \overline{DE}$, and are equal to half the length of the full diagonals.

35. C: Supplementary angles add to 180 degrees. Therefore, the other angle is equal to the difference between 180 degrees and 34 degrees: $180° - 34° = 146°$.

36. B: A percent is a number divided by 100, so $4\% = \frac{4}{100}$. The decimal 0.04 is also equal to $\frac{4}{100}$. Multiplying both numerator and denominator of $\frac{2}{50}$ by 2 shows that it, too, is equal to $\frac{4}{100}$.

37. B: Each item in the series is 4 greater than the preceding item. Since $16 + 4 = 20$, 20 is the number that belongs in the blank position.

38. D: If the first lap takes 50 seconds, the second one takes 20% more, or $T_2 = 1.2 \times T_1 = 1.2 \times 50 = 60$ seconds, where T_1 and T_2 are the times required for the first and second laps, respectively. Similarly, $T_3 = 1.2 \times T_2 = 1.2 \times 60 = 72$ seconds, the time required for the third lap. To find the total time, add the times for the three laps together: $50 + 60 + 72 = 182$ seconds.

39. D: Segment $\overline{AD} = 48$. Because the length of $\overline{CD}$ is 2 times the length of $\overline{AB}$, let $\overline{AB} = x$ and let $\overline{CD} = 2x$. Since $\overline{AB} = \overline{BC}$, let $\overline{BC} = x$ also. The total length of $\overline{AD} = \overline{AB} + \overline{BC} + \overline{CD} = 48$, so:

$$48 = x + x + 2x$$
$$48 = 4x$$
$$12 = x$$

So, since $\overline{BD} = \overline{BC} + \overline{CD}$

$$\overline{BD} = x + 2x$$
$$= 3x$$
$$= 3 \times 12$$
$$= 36$$

40. D: Following normal order of operations, the expressions within the parentheses must be evaluated first. Expression (I), $(3 \times 4) + 5 = 12 + 5 = 17$. Expression (II), $(4 + 5) \times 6 = 9 \times 6 = 54$. Expression (III), $(3 \times 5) + 6 = 15 + 6 = 21$.

41. B: Translate this word problem into a mathematical equation. Let the number of Janice's phone calls equal x. Let the number of Elaina's phone calls equal $x + 23$. Let the number June's phone calls equal $x + 14$. Add their calls together and subtract 25 calls:

$$= x + (x + 23) + (x + 14) - 25$$
$$= 3x + 37 - 25$$
$$= 3x + 12.$$

42. C: In this series, the number added to the preceding term goes up by one for each term: $41 + 3 = 44$; $44 + 4 = 48$; $48 + 5 = 53$; $53 + 6 = 59$. Since $59 + 7 = 66$, that is the value of the next term.

43. C: The equation that represents the relationship between the position number, n, and the value of the term, a_n, is $a_n = -3n + 8$. Notice each n is multiplied by –3, with 8 added to that value. Substituting position number 1 for n gives $a_1 = -3(1) + 8$, which equals 5. Substitution of the remaining position numbers does not provide a counterexample to this procedure.

44. A: The distance given from the top to the bottom of the tire through the center is the diameter. Finding the distance the bike traveled in one complete roll of the tire is the same as finding the circumference. Using the formula, $C = \pi d$, we multiply 27 by π. From the first mark to the fourth, the tire rolls three times. Then, you would multiply by 3, and the equation would be $3(27\pi)$.

45. D: First: Add the known values together: $5 + 10 + 12 + 13 = 40$. Now, set up an equation with the sum of the known values in the divisor. Then, put the number of values in the dividend.

46. D: Add 19 to both side of the equation:

$$a - 16 + 19 = 8b + 6 + 19$$
$$a + 3 = 8b + 25$$

47. D: In this series, each number is the sum of the two preceding numbers. For example, $3 = 1 + 2$, and $5 = 3 + 2$. Therefore, the number following 13 must be $13 + 8 = 21$, and the next number must be $21 + 13 = 34$. This is known as a Fibonacci sequence.

48. C: The straight line separating section (a) from sections (b) and (c) is a diameter. Therefore, section (a) is equal to one half of the circle. Since (b) and (c) together make up the remaining half of the circle, their sum is equal to section (a). Since b + c = a, it follows that b = a − c.

49. D: $5^2 = 5 \times 5 = 25$, thus (I) is equal to (III). However, $2^5 = 2 \times 2 \times 2 \times 2 \times 2 = 32$, which means (II) is greater than (I) or (III).

50. B: (I) $2 \times 15 - 3 = 30 - 3 = 27$; (II) $3^3 = 3 \times 3 \times 3 = 27$; (III) $\frac{80}{100} \times 30 + 3 = 24 + 3 = 27$. Therefore, all three expressions are equal to 27.

51. B: Whenever the data includes an extreme outlier, such as 39, the median is the best representation of the data. The mean would include that score and heavily skew the data.

52. A: In this series, the number subtracted from the preceding term increases by two for each term: $108 - 4 = 104$; $104 - 6 = 98$; $98 - 8 = 90$; $90 - 10 = 80$. For the next term, subtract 12: $80 - 12 = 68$. Choice A is correct.

Reading

COMPREHENSION

1. B: There is no indication in the passage that the Bennets are interested in becoming friends with Mr. Bingley (choice A), that Mr. Bingley would be a valuable business connection (choice C), or that Mr. Bingley has any prior knowledge of the Bennet daughters (choice D). Mrs. Bennet tells her husband that a new neighbor is moving in: "Mrs. Long says that Netherfield is taken by a young man of large fortune." Mrs. Bennet is sure he will make an excellent husband for one of her daughters: "You must know that I am thinking of his marrying one of them."

2. A: Mrs. Bennet feels that Mr. Bingley is likely to marry one of her daughters. She tells her husband that Mr. Bingley is a "single man of large fortune; four or five thousand a year. What a fine thing for our girls!"

3. B: Mrs. Bennet is annoyed and fed up with her husband's seeming indifference to Mr. Bingley: "'My dear Mr. Bennet,' replied his wife, 'how can you be so tiresome!'"

4. B: The evidence in this selection indicates that marrying a man with money was a primary goal for young women. Mrs. Bennet tells Mr. Bennet that Mr. Bingley is "A single man of large fortune; four or five thousand a year." Mrs. Bennet further indicates that she is thrilled with the news because of Mr. Bingley's potential as a husband for one of her daughters: "What a fine thing for our girls... You must know that I am thinking of his marrying one of them."

5. A: "It is a truth universally acknowledged" means that something is understood to be true by the general public.

6. A: Mr. Bennet is facetiously asking if the idea of marriage (particularly to one of his own daughters) was Mr. Bingley's intention when he agreed to rent Netherfield Park.

7. D: Choices A and C are detail sentences that do not convey the setting or event of the rest of the paragraph. Choice B references other dancers not mentioned anywhere else in the paragraph.

8. C: This is the only choice that expands on Margaritte's feelings about the music and echoes the tension of the event. Choices A and B refer to people (the audience, the other dancers) outside of Margaritte and her experience with the music as she waits for her cue, which is not the point of the passage. Choice D talks about Margaritte's clothing, which is not mentioned anywhere else in the paragraph.

9. A: Choices B, C, and D are details, but do not invoke a particular image.

10. B: This sentence tells what is happening at the moment and reflects on the tension that is apparent throughout the rest of the paragraph. Choice A only tells what is happening at the moment. Choice C refers to a time beyond the time referenced in the paragraph. Choice D introduces other dancers not mentioned previously in the paragraph.

11. B: The other choices are detail sentences and do not express the main idea of the paragraph.

12. C: Of the choices given, this sentence does not add anything to the paragraph's central premise that people should educate themselves about snakes instead of believing that snakes are looking for someone to attack.

13. A: This is the only choice that sums up the tone and purpose of the paragraph.

14. A: is the best choice because the best definition of "sacrilegious" as it appears in paragraph 2 is "absurdly inappropriate." B, C, and D are not the best choices because they do not express proper definitions of "sacrilegious" as it appears in paragraph 2.

15. C: is the best choice because Will's attitude in paragraph 15 is best described as sentimental. A, B, and D are not the best choices because Will's attitude in paragraph 15 is not angry, cheerful, or annoyed.

16. B: is the best choice because personification is used to describe the stars in paragraph 11. A, C, and D are not the best choices because simile, metaphor, and paradox are not used to describe the stars in paragraph 11.

17. A: is the best choice because it best illustrates how Puck's death is an example of irony. B, C, and D are not the best choices because they do not effectively illustrate how Puck's death is an example of irony.

18. D: is the best choice because it is the only option that is a main idea in this story. A, B, and C are not the best choices because they are all supporting ideas, not main ideas in the story.

19. B: The second sentence in the passage notes that comets are distinguishable from asteroids by the presence of comas or tails.

20. C: The third paragraph notes that there are over 3,500 known comets. It also notes that this represents only a small portion of those in existence.

21. C: The second paragraph notes that because they have low mass, they don't become spherical and have irregular shapes.

22. D: The second paragraph notes that some comets may be tens of kilometers across. The passage also notes that comas may be larger than the sun.

23. D: The passage defines single apparition comets as those whose trajectories make them pass the Sun once and then exit our solar system permanently. It also describes most comets as having oval orbits wherein they are nearer to the Sun during part of their orbit, and then move farther away from the Sun *within the solar system* for the rest of the orbit; hence (a) is incorrect. While single apparition comets are only apparent once, they are NOT still in the solar system (b). The passage defines short and long orbital periods, but does not include long orbital periods in that definition (c).

24. B: Lincoln begins this speech by discussing the founding of the U.S. and what the original purpose of the U.S. was. Then, he goes on to talk about how the U.S. is currently engaged in a war intended to fracture the nation, and he states that the battle being discussed was one large tragedy that came out of the war. Next, Lincoln says that his speech and even the memorial itself can't truly honor those who died, and that it's up to those who survived to continue the fight to ensure the nation does not break apart. Answer B best communicates this message.

25. D: The sentence in which this phrase is found is: The world will little note, nor long remember, what we say here, but can never forget what they did here. In this context, the phrase "the world will little note" means that no one outside of those in attendance or possibly those outside the country will pay attention to the speech or the ceremony. This eliminates all of the answer choices except D.

26. A: The ideals of the revolution are addressed in the first paragraph: Four score and seven years ago our fathers brought forth, upon this continent, a new nation, conceived in Liberty, and dedicated to the proposition that all men are created equal. This introduces the point that Lincoln is trying to make about the battle at hand and the war as a whole: the Civil War is threatening the ideas upon which the nation was created.

27. C: There is a comparison between the ideas of the Revolution and the Civil War in this speech. To facilitate understanding of this comparison, Lincoln has to set the stage by telling his audience about the past event he is referencing. This establishes the context of his message.

28. A: This line directly references the idea in the previous paragraph, which is that the U.S. is a nation that was created to ensure liberty and equality. This sentence talks about how the Civil War is testing whether or not a nation that was created to ensure liberty and equality can really survive.

29. B: When President Lincoln argues that the people who died at Gettysburg did not die in vain, he asserts that their passing was not frivolous or unimportant or meaningless.

30. C: The author points out that just because there is a month focused on African American history, this doesn't mean that African American history must be ignored for the rest of the year.

31. C: The author points out in paragraph 3 that the debate about how to meet the need to teach children about African American history can remind parents that this need is not yet fully met.

32. A: In paragraph 4, the author states that the material available is rich and varied.

33. B: Throughout the passage, the author continues to instill hope and encouragement that Black History Month still has a vital role to play in American culture despite opposing attitudes. Therefore, the best choice is emboldening.

34. C: Choice A and D cannot be correct because the paragraph contains only a handful of moments that are important to black history which are narrowed further by occurring in February. While the final paragraph contains only men, you should not make the conclusion of choice B. Nowhere in the passage does the author make a distinction between male and female influence in black history. Many women have made a remarkable difference in black history. Rosa Parks, Barbara Jordan, Diane Nash, and Septima Poinsette Clark are only a few. The number of men or women to make a significant impact on black history is not the author's point. Instead, you should conclude that regardless of a person's background, ethnicity, or position in society, there are many vital moments and people that connect to black history and those should be known by every individual.

35. A: This passage attempts to persuade readers to accept its point of view. While some of the other choices are true of particular statements found in the passage, only choice A is true of the passage as a whole.

36. A: Choice A is best. The <u>chief</u> benefit, in this context, means the main benefit.

37. D: Only choice D can be correctly inferred from the second paragraph.

38. B: Choice B best represents the passage as a whole.

39. D: To <u>mimic</u> is to resemble. Choice D is best.

40. B: The passage mentions the plastics found in the stomachs of dead birds, so choice B is best.

41. B: Choice B best answers the question: The author excludes discussion of plastics' benefits in order to focus on their dangers.

42. B: <u>Durability</u> in this sense means permanence.

VOCABULARY

43. A: <u>Peevish</u> means ill-tempered.

44. B: <u>Mortified</u> means embarrassed.

45. B: <u>Keen</u> is another word for sharp.

46. B: The word with the nearest meaning to the word <u>secluded</u> is remote.

47. A: A <u>perimeter</u> is a boundary.

48. D: <u>Slight</u> can mean insult when used as a noun.

49. A: <u>Monetary</u> means financial.

50. D: <u>Volatile</u> means explosive.

51. A: <u>Ruddy</u> means red.

52. C: In this context, <u>stellar</u> means exceptional or outstanding.

53. B: <u>Spare</u> means extra.

54. A: <u>Shrill</u> suggests that something is high-pitched.

55. D: <u>Enthralled</u> means captivated.

56. A: To <u>recuperate</u> is to heal.

57. C: <u>Meager</u> means insufficient.

58. A: The word with the closest meaning to <u>severe</u> in this context is relentless.

59. D: To <u>replicate</u> is to reproduce.

60. D: To <u>repudiate</u> is to renounce.

61. A: To <u>absolve</u> is to forgive.

62. D: In this context, <u>impregnable</u> means impenetrable.

Mathematics

1. B: The least common multiple, or LCM, is the smallest number that is a multiple of two numbers. Since $2 \times 2 = 4$, and $1 \times 4 = 4$, 4 is the LCM of the two numbers given.

2. C: First write Equation A in slope-intercept form: $y = mx + b$ where m is the slope and b is the y-intercept.

$$5y - 100x = 25$$
$$5y = 100x + 25$$
$$y = 20x + 5$$

Based on the slope-intercept form of Equation A, the slope, $m = 20$ and the y-intercept, $b = 5$.

3. A: An odd number can be considered as an even number N plus 1. Two even numbers added together produce an even number, so the result of adding an odd and an even number must be an even number plus 1, which is odd. For example, $4 + 3 = 7$.

4. D: In scientific notation, the exponent indicates the number of places that the decimal must be moved to the right. For example, $2.3 \times 10^1 = 2.1 \times 10 = 21$. Moving the decimal three places to the right in this problem is equivalent to multiplying by 1,000, so the result is 6,190.

5. B: The perimeter of a square is 4 times the length of a side. Therefore, in this case, the side s must equal $s = \frac{16}{4} = 4$. The area A is found by squaring the length, or $A = s^2 = 4^2 = 16$. Since the area is 16 ft^2, choice B is correct.

6. A: Negative numbers represent segments extending to the left of zero on the number line. Adding a negative number to another negative number extends the segment even further to the left, or into "negative territory". To add two negative numbers, add the magnitudes and retain the negative sign. For example: $(-3) + (-5) = -8$.

7. C: The square root of a number which is raised to the 4th power is the same number raised to the 2nd power. That is, $\sqrt{2^4} = 2^2 = 4$. Since $4 \times 4 = 16$, C is correct.

8. B: The chart indicates that 40% of the total recycled material is paper. Since 50,000 tons of material are recycled every month, the total amount of paper will be 40% of 50,000 tons, or $\frac{40}{100} \times 50,000 = 20,000$ tons.

9. B: Percentage is equivalent to dividing by 100, so that $12.5\% = \frac{12.5}{100} = \frac{1}{8}$.

10. C: The area of a circle is equal to πr^2, where r is the radius. Since the diameter is two times the radius then $\frac{d}{2} = r$, thus:

$$\pi r^2 = 36\pi$$
$$\pi \left(\frac{d}{2}\right)^2 = 36\pi$$
$$\left(\frac{d}{2}\right)^2 = 36$$
$$d = 12$$

11. B: A prime number has only two whole integer divisors, 1 and itself. This is true of 3, 17, and 41. However 6 can be divided by 1, 2, 3, and 6. It is therefore not a prime number.

12. B: The reciprocal of 5 is $\frac{1}{5}$. When numbers are multiplied by their reciprocals, the result is always 1. Thus, $5 \times \frac{1}{5} = 1$.

13. C: Each throw of the dart is an independent event and has no influence on the outcome of any other throw. Every time the dart is thrown, it has a 50% chance of landing on black, irrespective of the results of previous throws.

14. D: The integers are $-4, -3, -2, -1, 0, +1, +2, +3, +4, +5$, and $+6$.

15. A: The answer is expanded to simplify the calculations. The total of choice A is $\$8.00 + \$1.60 = \$9.60$, which is the same as the total calculated in the problem.

16. C: The volume of a cube of side a is given by $Volume = a^3 = a \times a \times a$. In this case, since $a = 3$, the area is $3 \times 3 \times 3 = 27$.

17. B: The verbal description "five times a number m squared" means that m must be squared, and the resulting number multiplied by 5. Choice C is incorrect because the value within the parentheses is evaluated first, so that both 5 and m are squared. This results in a value of $25m^2$, which is incorrect.

18. C: The square root of a number must lie between the square roots of numbers that are larger and smaller than itself. Since $\sqrt{4} = 2$, and $\sqrt{9} = 3$, and since $4 < 6 < 9$, it follows that $\sqrt{6}$ must lie between 2 and 3.

19. C: The area scales with the square of the radius, so if the radius increases in length by a factor of 2, the area will increase by 2^2, or 4. Since $Area = \pi r^2$, if the radius r is replaced with $2r$, this yields $Area = \pi(2r)^2 = 4\pi r^2$, which is 4 times the original area.

20. A: The average, or arithmetic mean, is computed by totaling all the measurements and dividing by the number of measurements. To obtain an average of 75 from 3 measurements, the measurements must total $3 \times 75 = 225$. Since $68 + 73 = 141$, then $225 - 141 = 84$ points are required on the third test.

21. C: The ratio of left- to right-handed players will be the same as the ratio 2:3. Therefore, $\frac{2}{3} = \frac{12}{R}$, so that $R = 18$ right-handed players. The total number on the roster is therefore $12 + 18 = 30$.

22. D: To round to the nearest hundredth, leave two digits to the right of the decimal. Since the third digit after the decimal is greater than 5, round the preceding digit up to 9.

23. B: The y-intercept of the line is $(0, -1)$. Another point on the line is $(1,0)$. Slope is the vertical change over horizontal change which is $\frac{1}{1} = 1$. Plugging this information into the slope-intercept form $y = mx + b$, the equation is $y = x - 1$.

24. D: Rainfall in October increases to 6 inches, from 1 inch in September. This represents an increase of 5 inches. None of the other month-to-month differences are as great.

25. C: Solve for x:

$$3x + 5 - 5 = 11 - 5$$
$$3x = 6$$
$$x = 2$$

26. D: Jamet had $2.75 after all the transactions described. To solve this problem, first subtract $4.25 and then $2.00 from the initial sum of $6.50, leaving $0.25. Then add $2.50, arriving at the final answer of $2.75.

27. D: There are two ways to solve this problem: either convert meters to centimeters and then convert centimeters to inches, or else convert meters to yards, and then convert to inches.

In the first instance, recall that there are 100 centimeters in 1 meter and 2.54 centimeters in 1 inch:

$$19 \text{ m} \times \left(\frac{100 \text{ cm}}{1 \text{ m}}\right) \times \left(\frac{1 \text{ in}}{2.54 \text{ cm}}\right) = \left(\frac{19 \times 100}{2.54}\right) \text{ in} \approx 748 \text{ in}$$

In the second instance, recall that there are 1.094 yards in 1 meter and 36 inches in 1 yard:

$$19 \text{ m} \times \left(\frac{1.094 \text{ yd}}{1 \text{ m}}\right) \times \left(\frac{36 \text{ in}}{1 \text{ yd}}\right) = (19 \times 1.094 \times 36) \text{ in} \approx 748 \text{ in}$$

28. D: Since 16 chairs are empty, and this represents 2/5 of the total enrollment, then the full class must consist of

$$\text{Class} = 16 \div \frac{2}{5} = 16 \times \frac{5}{2} = 40 \text{ students}$$

29. A: To answer this question, we first determine the total cost of the onions and carrots, since these prices are given. This will equal $(2 \times \$3.69 + 3 \times \$4.29) = \$20.25$. Next, this sum is subtracted from the total cost of the vegetables to determine the cost of the mushrooms: $\$24.15 - \$20.25 = \$3.90$. Finally, the cost of the mushrooms is divided by the quantity in lbs to determine the cost per lb:

$$\text{Cost per lb} = \frac{\$3.90}{1.5} = \$2.60$$

30. C: To determine this, first determine the total distance of the round trip. This is twice the 45 miles of the one-way trip to work in the morning, or 90 miles. Then, to determine the total amount of time Elijah spent on the round trip, first convert his travel times into minutes. One hour and ten minutes is the same as 70 minutes, and an hour and a half is 90 minutes. So, Elijah's total travel time was $70 + 90 = 160$ minutes. Elijah's average speed can now be determined in miles per minute:

$$\text{Average Speed} = \frac{90 \text{ miles}}{160 \text{ min}} = 0.5625 \text{ miles per minute}$$

Finally, to convert this average speed to miles per hour, multiply by 60, since there are 60 minutes in an hour: Average speed (mph) = $60 \times 0.5625 = 33.75$. Therefore, his average speed for the round trip was 33.75 mph.

31. A: The percentage of increase equals the change in the account balance divided by the original amount, \$80, and multiplied by 100. First, determine the change in the balance by subtracting the original amount from the new balance: $\$120 - \$80 = \$40$. Now, determine the percentage of increase: $\frac{\$40}{\$80} \times 100 = 50\%$.

32. D: Manipulate the inequality:

$$4x - 12 < 4$$
$$4x < 4 + 12$$
$$4x < 16$$
$$x < 4$$

33. D: Substitute the variables and then carefully follow the order of operations:

$$
\begin{aligned}
4a(3b + 5) + 2b &= 4(-6)(3(7) + 5) + 2(7) \\
&= -24(21 + 5) + 14 \\
&= -24(26) + 14 \\
&= -624 + 14 \\
&= -610
\end{aligned}
$$

34. B: Since the rate, miles per minute, is constant, this can be applied to the whole distance and used to find the total travel time:

$$210 \text{ mi} \times \left(\frac{12 \text{ min}}{10 \text{ mi}}\right) = \left(\frac{210 \times 12}{10}\right) \text{ min} = 252 \text{ min}$$

Now, divide 252 by 60 to get 4 with a remainder of 12. This correlates to 4 hours and 12 minutes.

35. C: Define the variable t as the passed time (in hours) from the time the first airplane takes off. Then, at any time the distance traveled by the first plane is $d_1 = 250t$. The second plane takes off 30 minutes later. So, at any time the distance that it has traveled is $d_2 = 280(t - 0.5)$. The units used for the half hour should remain in hours, not minutes, and they must be negative since the second plane left after the first plane. This plane will overtake the first when the two distances are equal: $d_1 = d_2$ or $250t = 280(t - 30)$.

Result	Next Step
$250t = 280(t - 0.5)$	Use the distributive property
$250t = (280 \times t) - (280 \times 0.5)$	Simplify the parentheses
$250t = 280t - 140$	Add 140 to each side
$250t + 140 = 280t - 140 + 140$	Subtract $250t$ from each side
$250t - 250t + 140 = 280t - 250t$	Divide both sides by 30
$140/30 = 30t/30$	Final result

$$4\frac{2}{3} = t$$

This gives the value of t in hours. So, you have the found an elapsed time of 4 hours and 40 minutes. The first plane left at 2 PM. So, 4 hours and 40 minutes later is 6:40 PM.

36. A: This equation represents a linear relationship of slope 3.60 that passes through the origin, or zero point. The table shows that for each hour of rental, the cost increases by an amount equal to $3.60. This corresponds to the slope of the equation. Of course, if the bicycle is not rented at all (0 hours) there will be no charge ($0), so the line must pass through the origin. Relationship A is the only one that satisfies these criteria.

37. D: In order to determine the number of questions Joshua must answer correctly, consider the number of points he must earn. Joshua will receive 4 points for each question he answers correctly, and x represents the number of questions. Therefore, Joshua will receive a total of $4x$ points for all the questions he answers correctly. Joshua must earn more than 92 points. Therefore, to determine the number of questions he must answer correctly, solve the inequality $4x > 92$.

38. D: Simply count the squares and half squares: $(9 + 9 + 12)(1) + (12)\left(\frac{1}{2}\right) = 30 + 6 = 36$ units

39. D: Use conversion factors to find the meters per revolution:

$$\left(\frac{50 \text{ km}}{\text{hr}}\right) \times \left(\frac{1000 \text{ m}}{\text{km}}\right) \times \left(\frac{\text{hr}}{60 \text{ min}}\right) \times \left(\frac{\text{min}}{500 \text{ rev}}\right) = \left(\frac{50 \times 1000}{60 \times 500}\right)\frac{\text{m}}{\text{rev}} = \frac{10}{6}\frac{\text{m}}{\text{rev}}$$

Note that meters per revolution is the same as the circumference of the tire.

40. D: To solve the equation, first get rid of the denominators by multiplying both sides of the equation by $x(x-3)$ and simplifying the result:

$$\frac{4}{x-3} - \frac{2}{x} = 1$$
$$x(x-3)\left(\frac{4}{x-3} - \frac{2}{x}\right) = x(x-3) \times 1$$
$$4x - 2(x-3) = x(x-3)$$
$$4x - 2x + 6 = x^2 - 3x$$
$$2x + 6 = x^2 - 3x$$

The result is a quadratic equation. Move everything to one side and then solve for x by factoring the left side and applying the zero-product rule:

$$x^2 - 5x - 6 = 0$$
$$(x+1)(x-6) = 0$$

$$x + 1 = 0 \quad x - 6 = 0$$
$$x = -1 \qquad x = 6$$

Therefore, the possible solutions are $x = -1$ and $x = 6$. Since neither of these values will cause division by zero when substituted back into the original equation, they are both valid solutions.

41. C: Since he buys two cups per day for five days, and one cup on Saturday, the total number of cups that Richard buys each week is $(2 \times 5) + 1 = 11$ cups. Since each cup costs $2.25, the amount he spends is $11 \times \$2.25 = \$24.75$.

42. B: Since each mile is equivalent to 2 inches, then 6.5 inches is equivalent to $\frac{6.5}{2} = 3.25$ miles.

43. B: Since five people are dividing $17.90, each person's share is calculated as $\frac{\$17.90}{5} = \$3.58$.

44. B: Calculate $\frac{9}{72} \times 100\% = 12.5\%$.

45. C: The score that has approximately 50% above and 50% below is approximately 500 (517 to be exact). The scores can be manually written by choosing either the lower or upper end of each interval and using the frequency to determine the number of times to record each score, i.e., using the lower end of each interval shows an approximate value of 465 for the median; using the upper end of each interval shows an approximate value of 530 for the median. A score of 500 (and the exact median of 517) is found between 465 and 530.

46. C: Since $220 = 4 \times 55$ miles, the train will require $4 \times 40 = 160$ minutes to travel 220 miles. Since 1 hour = 60 minutes, the time required is $\frac{160}{60} = 2$ hours with 40 minutes left over.

47. D: The price is reduced by an amount equal to 5% of the original price, or $\frac{5}{100} \times \$120 = \$6$, so subtract $6 from the original price of $120 to calculate the sale price: $114.

48. B: The ratio of correct to incorrect answers is 2:3, giving a whole of 5. It takes 12 sets of 5 questions to total 60 questions. To determine how many correct answers Sam gave, multiply 2 by 12, for a total of 24.

49. C: In $\triangle ABC$, the midpoints are marked as D, E, and F. The medians of the triangle are then drawn in as $\overline{AF}$, $\overline{BD}$ and $\overline{CE}$. The medians intersect at a point called the centroid. Based on this intersection, it is the case that $\overline{AG} = 2\overline{GF}$, $\overline{BG} = 2\overline{GD}$, and $\overline{CG} = 2\overline{GE}$. Since we are given that $\overline{BG} = 6x - 4$ and $\overline{GD} = 2x + 8$, we can set up the equation as $6x - 4 = 2(2x + 8)$. Simplifying that equation, it becomes $6x - 4 = 4x + 16$. After subtracting $4x$ from both sides and adding 4 to both sides, the equation becomes $2x = 20$. Divide both sides by 2 to get $x = 10$. Then, the length of $\overline{GD}$ is calculated as $2(10) + 8 = 20 + 8 = 28$.

50. B: Determine the number of gallons used by dividing the distance in miles by the fuel efficiency in miles per gallon: $\frac{629}{34} = 18.5$ gallons of gasoline.

51. B: The listed angles are located in the alternate interior angles position. According to the Alternate Interior Angle Theorem, when a transversal cuts across parallel lines, the alternate interior angles are congruent. Since lines a and b are parallel, it means that $2x + 5 = 3x - 25$. After subtracting $2x$ from both sides and adding 25 to both sides, the equation simplifies to $30 = x$.

52. D: First, add the two straight 150-yard portions. Also, note that the distance for the two semi-circles put together is the circumference of a circle. Since the circumference of a circle is π times the diameter, the length of the circular portion of the track is simply 30π. Then, add this to the length of the two straight portions of the track.

$$\text{Perimeter} = 30\pi + (2 \times 150) \approx 394.25$$

Therefore, the perimeter of the entire track is approximately 395 yards.

53. D: Rafael's profit on each computer is the difference between the price he pays and the price he charges his customer: $800 - $450. If he sells n computers in a month, his total profit will be n times this difference: $n(800 - 450)$. However, it is necessary to subtract his fixed costs of $3000 from $n(800 - 450)$ to find his final profit per month.

54. D: The slopes of perpendicular lines are reciprocals and have the opposite sign. In the figure below, line A has a slope of $-\frac{1}{2}$, and line B has a slope of 2.

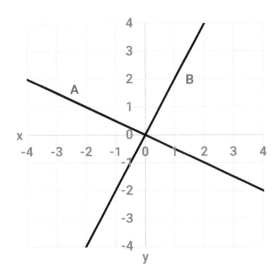

55. B: Any color can be drawn the first time, leaving five marbles. At this point, only one of the five is the same color as the one that was drawn the first time. The odds of selecting this marble are one chance in five, or 20%.

56. D: Expanding the factors demonstrates the equivalence:

$$\begin{aligned}(x - 4)(x + 7) &= x^2 + 7x - 4x - 28 \\ &= x^2 + 3x - 28\end{aligned}$$

57. A: Nancy spent a total of $3.15 + $6.75 = $9.90. Subtracting $9.90 from $17.25 yields $7.35.

58. C: When the dress is marked down by 20%, the cost of the dress is 80% of its original price. Since a percentage can be written as a fraction by placing the percentage over 100, the reduced price of the dress can be written as $\frac{80}{100}x$, or $\frac{4}{5}x$, where x is the original price. When discounted an extra 25%, the dress costs 75% of the reduced price. This results in the expression $\frac{75}{100}\left(\frac{4}{5}x\right)$, which can be simplified to $\frac{3}{4}\left(\frac{4}{5}x\right)$, or $\frac{3}{5}x$. So the final price of the dress is three-fifths of the original price.

59. B: The first wall has an area of $10 \times 18 = 180$ square feet. Two men working for 8 hours is equivalent to 16 man-hours of work. Thus, each man paints $\frac{180}{60} = \frac{90}{8}$ square feet per hour. The new wall is $27 \times 10 = 270$ square feet. It will require $\frac{270}{90/8} = \frac{270 \times 8}{90} = 24$ man-hours to paint. Since there are three men, each is responsible for $\frac{24}{3} = 8$ man-hours.

60. D: If x is the cost of the pen, then, $2x$ is the cost of the book and $4x$ is the cost of the calculator. Vivian has spent $x + 2x + 4x$, or $7x$. She started with $50 and had $15 left, so $50 - 7x = \$15$. Solving for $x = \frac{\$35}{7} = \$5$, and the cost of the calculator was $4x = \$20$.

61. B: If x represents the width of the box, its length is equal to $2x$. Since the sides of a square are equal, $2x - 3 = x + 3$, and $x = 6$. So, the box is 6 inches wide.

62. C: For each die there is a 1 in 6 chance that a 6 will be on top. The reason is that the die has 6 sides. The probability that a 6 will show for each die is not affected by the results from another roll of the die. In other words, these probabilities are independent. So, the overall probability of throwing 3 sixes is the product of the individual probabilities: $P = \frac{1}{6} \times \frac{1}{6} \times \frac{1}{6} = \frac{1}{6^3} = \frac{1}{216}$

63. C: At 10%, Richard is paid $140 \times 10\% = \frac{10 \times \$140}{100} = \$14$ for every phone he sells. To make $840, he must sell $\frac{\$840}{\$14} = 60$ phones.

64. C: In scientific notation, the negative exponent means that the decimal point must be moved to the left. Therefore, $2 \times 10^{-2} = 0.02$. The positive exponent moves the decimal point to the right. Therefore $5 \times 10^3 = 5,000$. Since $0.02 \times 5,000 = 100$, C is correct.

Language

USAGE, PUNCTUATION, AND GRAMMAR

1. C: The longest word recorded in an English dictionary are "Pneumonoultramicroscopicsilicovolcanokoniosis."

Error: Subject-verb disagreement

The subject of this sentence is the singular noun "word," so the plural verb "are" disagrees with the subject. The verb used here should be the singular "is."

2. B: The largest catfish ever catch is 646 pounds, the size of an adult brown bear.

Error: Incorrect verb tense

The verb "catch" is not in the appropriate tense. It should be written in the past tense, "caught."

3. C: Though a highly influentially anthropologist, Claude Levi-Strauss often took criticism for spending little time in the field studying real cultures.

Error: Adverb / adjective error

The adverb "influentially" is being used to modify the noun "anthropologist." Since adverbs cannot modify nouns, "influentially" should be written in adjective form: "influential."

4. C: It is easy to get confused when calculating time differences between time zones a useful way to remember them is that the Atlantic Ocean starts with A, as in A.M., and the Pacific Ocean starts with P, as in P.M.

Error: Run-on sentence

Choice C contains two complete thoughts, each with its own subject and predicate. The second complete thought begins, "a useful way to remember them...." A sentence composed of two complete thoughts joined together without appropriate punctuation is called a "run-on." A period or semicolon should appear between the phrases "time zones" and "a useful way."

5. C: The surrealists were a group of artists who believed that art should reflect the subconscious mind, their images are often very dreamlike, showing businessmen falling like rain over a city and melting clocks.

Error: Comma splice

There are two complete sentences here joined by only a comma. A period or semicolon should replace the comma after "mind."

6. B: "Orange is my favorite color, but not my favorite fruit." said Lisa.

Error: Punctuation

The period that appears at the end of the quote should be a comma.

7. B: The deepest canyon, too.

Error: Fragment

This phrase contains a subject, but it does not contain a predicate, which makes it a sentence fragment.

8. A: Pocahontas spent the last year's of her young life in England under the name Rebecca.

Error: Apostrophe

The apostrophe in the word "year's" is unnecessary. The sentence should read, "Pocahontas spent the last years...."

9. A: The Pima Indians of Arizona have remarkably high rates of diabetes and obesity some scientists believe the gene that causes this present-day health crisis was actually of great value to the Pima's ancestors who had to be able to retain glucose during periods of famine.

Error: Run-on sentence

A sentence composed of two complete thoughts joined together without appropriate punctuation is called a "run-on." A period or semicolon should appear between "obesity" and "some scientists."

10. C: Director Alfred Hitchcock make over 60 films in his career.

Error: Subject-verb disagreement

The subject "Alfred Hitchcock" is a singular subject, which requires a singular verb. "Make" should be "makes."

11. D: No error.

12. A: The earliest recording of a human voice was made by Thomas Edison in 1877, when they recorded himself reciting "Mary Had a Little Lamb."

Error: Pronoun-antecedent agreement

Thomas Edison is singular, so the plural pronoun "they" is incorrect. It should read "he."

13. B: Our basement floods once a yearly.

Error: Adjective/adverb

Here the adverb "yearly" is incorrectly used. It should be replaced with the noun "year."

14. D: No error.

15. B: The spread of Islam began around 600 AD and reached from the Middle East to North Africa, Spain, Central Asia, and India?

Error: Punctuation

Since this is a declarative sentence and not a question, the question mark should be a period.

16. C: The names of the days of the week originate in either Latin or Saxon names for deities, Sunday, for instance, is Saxon for "Sun's Day," while Thursday derives from "Thor's Day."

Error: Comma Splice

There are two complete sentences here joined by only a comma. A period or semicolon should replace the comma after "deities."

17. D: No error.

18. A: Ironically, the namesake of the Nobel Peace Prize, Alfred Nobel, are most noted for his invention of dynamite in the 1860s.

Error: Subject-verb disagreement

The subject of this sentence is the singular noun "namesake." The plural verb "are" is incorrect. It should be replaced with the singular verb "is."

19. A: Loud sounds can causing damage to the hair cells that turn sound waves into electrical signals, which the brain perceives as sound.

Error: Verb tense

The verb "causing" is the progressive tense, which is the incorrect tense for this sentence. The sentence should read, "Loud sounds can cause...."

20. C: Carbon monoxide Poisoning can cause disorientation and delirium, and it can induce a coma.

Error: Capitalization

The word "poisoning" does not need to be capitalized because it is not a proper noun.

21. D: No error.

22. A: They closed the parking deck at midnight, so we could not get no cars out until morning.

Error: Double negative

The phrase "could not get no" is an example of a double negative. The phrase should read, "could not get any ...."

23. A: Joni designed the grocery stores sign, but Evan painted it.

Error: *Apostrophe*

Since the sign belongs to the grocery store, an apostrophe should be used to indicate possession. The sentence should read, "...the grocery store's sign...."

24. D: No error.

25. C: Twenty-four leaders of the Nazi party was brought to trial at the end of World War II in what became known as the Nuremberg Trials.

Error: *Subject-verb disagreement*

The subject of this sentence is the plural noun "leaders," which requires a plural verb. "Was" is a singular verb. The sentence should use the plural verb *"were."*

26. C: Water is called "hard water" if it do not quickly create lather upon contact with soap because of mineral compounds dissolved in the water.

Error: *Subject-verb disagreement*

The pronoun "it" is singular, and the verb "do" is plural. The sentence should read, "if it does not quickly create...."

27. B: Ice crystals in the atmosphere, which can create a halo around the sun or moon.

Error: *Sentence fragment*

This sentence contains a subject, but it does not contain a predicate, which makes it a fragment. *Rule of thumb*: Watch out for words such as "which" or "that" in a sentence because the verb that comes afterward *oftentimes does not function* as the main verb of the sentence. One way to correct this sentence would be to delete the comma and the word "which." "Ice crystals in the atmosphere can create a halo around the sun or moon" is a complete thought because it contains a subject, "Ice crystals," and a main verb, "can create."

28. B: Atomic clocks keep time by measuring the vibrations of Atoms and molecules.

Error: *Capitalization*

The word "Atoms" should not be capitalized because it is not a proper noun.

29. A: Heat was once believes to be a type of fluid called "caloric," which flowed into objects and raised their temperature.

Error: *Verb tense*

The verb phrase "was once believes" uses two different tenses: past and present. It should read, "Heat was once *believed*...."

30. B: Apart from a sine wave created by an electronic device, most sounds are not "pure" because they contain many different vibrations at different frequencies pure tones vibrate at only one frequency.

Error: *Run-on sentence*

This sentence contains two complete thoughts without punctuation separating them. The second one begins with the words "pure tones vibrate...." A period or semicolon should be inserted before these words.

31. A: Arthur, realizing that bugs were turning the roots of his zucchini plants to mush.

Error: *Sentence fragment*

These words form an incomplete thought; it does not contain a subject and verb. *Rule of thumb*: Watch out for verbs ending in –ing. These verbs *cannot* be the main verb of a sentence *on their own*. They need another verb (called a "helping verb"), such as "was." The following sentence is a complete thought because the –ing verb is not alone: "Arthur *was realizing* that bugs were turning the roots of his zucchini plants to mush."

32. D: No error.

33. D: No error.

34. A: The narwhal is a member of the dolphin family, easily recognized by its long, spiraling tusk, it is often compared to the mythical unicorn.

Error: *Comma splice*

There are two complete thoughts here, joined together with a comma. The second complete thought begins with the words "it is often...." To correct this sentence, replace the comma after "tusk" with a period or semicolon.

35. C: The first Ferris' Wheel was built in Chicago, Illinois.

Error: *Apostrophe*

The apostrophe at the end of "Ferris" is incorrect because it is not a possessive noun.

36. A: Trees in the Olympic rain forest in northwest Washington State is covered with a thick green moss that is nourished by the 150 annual inches of rainfall.

Error: *Subject-verb agreement*

The subject of the sentence is "trees," which is a plural form; the verb "is" does not agree with the subject because it is singular. The main verb in this sentence should be "are." *Rule of thumb:* Watch out for sentences that have a lot of words between the subject and verb. Often, these sentences contain subject-verb verb errors.

37. D: No error.

38. C: I was, hoping to avoid the customs official who was yelling at all of the other travelers.

Error: *Comma*

The comma between "was" and "hoping" is incorrect. A single comma should not come between a helping verb and an –ing verb.

39. A: Reykjavik is the Capitol of Iceland.

Error: Capitalization

The word "Capitol" does not need to be capitalized because it is not a proper noun.

40. D: No error.

SPELLING
41. D: No error.

42. C: "Graitful" should be spelled "grateful."

43. C: "Sower" should be spelled "sour."

44. B: "Sinator" should be spelled "senator."

45. A: "Groshery" should be spelled "grocery."

46. A: Though "nite" has become a common informal spelling, the formal spelling of the word is "night."

47. C: "Alway" should be spelled "always."

48. C: "Spays" should be spelled "space."

49. D: No error.

50. D: No error.

COMPOSITION

51. A: The sentence, "<u>Many people have proposed explanations for this drop</u>," provides an introduction to the short explanations that follow. It should come after the first sentence.

52. B: The third sentence of this passage refers to "these insecticides," but there is no earlier reference to any insecticides in the paragraph. The sentence, "Insects that carry the disease can develop resistance to the chemicals, or insecticides, that are used to kill the mosquitoes," needs to be placed after sentence 2 for sentence 3 to make sense.

53. B: Since the second part of this sentence goes on to list examples that help support the point made in the first sentence, "for instance" is the best transitional phrase.

54. C: The second part of the sentence adds additional evidence to prove the claim made in the first part. "In fact" is the best transition to introduce supporting evidence.

55. A: The second part of the sentence contrasts with the first. "However" is the most appropriate transition to use to help create that sense of contrast.

56. A: All of the sentences except sentence A contain errors. Sentences B and C contain verb errors; sentence D is a run-on sentence.

57. B: All of the sentences except sentence B contain verb errors.

58. A: Sentence A contains no errors. Sentence B is less clear than sentence A because it is awkwardly written in the passive voice. Sentence C contains a subject-verb agreement error. Sentence C switches pronouns from "We" to "I" in mid-sentence.

59. C: Sentence 4, regarding Jefferson's affair with one of his slaves, is not directly relevant to the main topic at hand, which is Jefferson's debts.

60. B: Sentence 2, regarding Feynman's musicianship, is of little relevance to the discussion of the atomic theory.

How to Overcome Test Anxiety

Just the thought of taking a test is enough to make most people a little nervous. A test is an important event that can have a long-term impact on your future, so it's important to take it seriously and it's natural to feel anxious about performing well. But just because anxiety is normal, that doesn't mean that it's helpful in test taking, or that you should simply accept it as part of your life. Anxiety can have a variety of effects. These effects can be mild, like making you feel slightly nervous, or severe, like blocking your ability to focus or remember even a simple detail.

If you experience test anxiety—whether severe or mild—it's important to know how to beat it. To discover this, first you need to understand what causes test anxiety.

Causes of Test Anxiety

While we often think of anxiety as an uncontrollable emotional state, it can actually be caused by simple, practical things. One of the most common causes of test anxiety is that a person does not feel adequately prepared for their test. This feeling can be the result of many different issues such as poor study habits or lack of organization, but the most common culprit is time management. Starting to study too late, failing to organize your study time to cover all of the material, or being distracted while you study will mean that you're not well prepared for the test. This may lead to cramming the night before, which will cause you to be physically and mentally exhausted for the test. Poor time management also contributes to feelings of stress, fear, and hopelessness as you realize you are not well prepared but don't know what to do about it.

Other times, test anxiety is not related to your preparation for the test but comes from unresolved fear. This may be a past failure on a test, or poor performance on tests in general. It may come from comparing yourself to others who seem to be performing better or from the stress of living up to expectations. Anxiety may be driven by fears of the future—how failure on this test would affect your educational and career goals. These fears are often completely irrational, but they can still negatively impact your test performance.

> **Review Video: 3 Reasons You Have Test Anxiety**
> Visit mometrix.com/academy and enter code: 428468

Elements of Test Anxiety

As mentioned earlier, test anxiety is considered to be an emotional state, but it has physical and mental components as well. Sometimes you may not even realize that you are suffering from test anxiety until you notice the physical symptoms. These can include trembling hands, rapid heartbeat, sweating, nausea, and tense muscles. Extreme anxiety may lead to fainting or vomiting. Obviously, any of these symptoms can have a negative impact on testing. It is important to recognize them as soon as they begin to occur so that you can address the problem before it damages your performance.

> **Review Video: 3 Ways to Tell You Have Test Anxiety**
> Visit mometrix.com/academy and enter code: 927847

The mental components of test anxiety include trouble focusing and inability to remember learned information. During a test, your mind is on high alert, which can help you recall information and stay focused for an extended period of time. However, anxiety interferes with your mind's natural processes, causing you to blank out, even on the questions you know well. The strain of testing during anxiety makes it difficult to stay focused, especially on a test that may take several hours. Extreme anxiety can take a huge mental toll, making it difficult not only to recall test information but even to understand the test questions or pull your thoughts together.

> **Review Video: How Test Anxiety Affects Memory**
> Visit mometrix.com/academy and enter code: 609003

Effects of Test Anxiety

Test anxiety is like a disease—if left untreated, it will get progressively worse. Anxiety leads to poor performance, and this reinforces the feelings of fear and failure, which in turn lead to poor performances on subsequent tests. It can grow from a mild nervousness to a crippling condition. If allowed to progress, test anxiety can have a big impact on your schooling, and consequently on your future.

Test anxiety can spread to other parts of your life. Anxiety on tests can become anxiety in any stressful situation, and blanking on a test can turn into panicking in a job situation. But fortunately, you don't have to let anxiety rule your testing and determine your grades. There are a number of relatively simple steps you can take to move past anxiety and function normally on a test and in the rest of life.

> **Review Video: How Test Anxiety Impacts Your Grades**
> Visit mometrix.com/academy and enter code: 939819

Physical Steps for Beating Test Anxiety

While test anxiety is a serious problem, the good news is that it can be overcome. It doesn't have to control your ability to think and remember information. While it may take time, you can begin taking steps today to beat anxiety.

Just as your first hint that you may be struggling with anxiety comes from the physical symptoms, the first step to treating it is also physical. Rest is crucial for having a clear, strong mind. If you are tired, it is much easier to give in to anxiety. But if you establish good sleep habits, your body and mind will be ready to perform optimally, without the strain of exhaustion. Additionally, sleeping well helps you to retain information better, so you're more likely to recall the answers when you see the test questions.

Getting good sleep means more than going to bed on time. It's important to allow your brain time to relax. Take study breaks from time to time so it doesn't get overworked, and don't study right before bed. Take time to rest your mind before trying to rest your body, or you may find it difficult to fall asleep.

> **Review Video: <u>The Importance of Sleep for Your Brain</u>**
> Visit mometrix.com/academy and enter code: 319338

Along with sleep, other aspects of physical health are important in preparing for a test. Good nutrition is vital for good brain function. Sugary foods and drinks may give a burst of energy but this burst is followed by a crash, both physically and emotionally. Instead, fuel your body with protein and vitamin-rich foods.

Also, drink plenty of water. Dehydration can lead to headaches and exhaustion, especially if your brain is already under stress from the rigors of the test. Particularly if your test is a long one, drink water during the breaks. And if possible, take an energy-boosting snack to eat between sections.

> **Review Video: <u>How Diet Can Affect your Mood</u>**
> Visit mometrix.com/academy and enter code: 624317

Along with sleep and diet, a third important part of physical health is exercise. Maintaining a steady workout schedule is helpful, but even taking 5-minute study breaks to walk can help get your blood pumping faster and clear your head. Exercise also releases endorphins, which contribute to a positive feeling and can help combat test anxiety.

When you nurture your physical health, you are also contributing to your mental health. If your body is healthy, your mind is much more likely to be healthy as well. So take time to rest, nourish your body with healthy food and water, and get moving as much as possible. Taking these physical steps will make you stronger and more able to take the mental steps necessary to overcome test anxiety.

Mental Steps for Beating Test Anxiety

Working on the mental side of test anxiety can be more challenging, but as with the physical side, there are clear steps you can take to overcome it. As mentioned earlier, test anxiety often stems from lack of preparation, so the obvious solution is to prepare for the test. Effective studying may be the most important weapon you have for beating test anxiety, but you can and should employ several other mental tools to combat fear.

First, boost your confidence by reminding yourself of past success—tests or projects that you aced. If you're putting as much effort into preparing for this test as you did for those, there's no reason you should expect to fail here. Work hard to prepare; then trust your preparation.

Second, surround yourself with encouraging people. It can be helpful to find a study group, but be sure that the people you're around will encourage a positive attitude. If you spend time with others who are anxious or cynical, this will only contribute to your own anxiety. Look for others who are motivated to study hard from a desire to succeed, not from a fear of failure.

Third, reward yourself. A test is physically and mentally tiring, even without anxiety, and it can be helpful to have something to look forward to. Plan an activity following the test, regardless of the outcome, such as going to a movie or getting ice cream.

When you are taking the test, if you find yourself beginning to feel anxious, remind yourself that you know the material. Visualize successfully completing the test. Then take a few deep, relaxing breaths and return to it. Work through the questions carefully but with confidence, knowing that you are capable of succeeding.

Developing a healthy mental approach to test taking will also aid in other areas of life. Test anxiety affects more than just the actual test—it can be damaging to your mental health and even contribute to depression. It's important to beat test anxiety before it becomes a problem for more than testing.

> **Review Video: <u>Test Anxiety and Depression</u>**
> Visit mometrix.com/academy and enter code: 904704

Study Strategy

Being prepared for the test is necessary to combat anxiety, but what does being prepared look like? You may study for hours on end and still not feel prepared. What you need is a strategy for test prep. The next few pages outline our recommended steps to help you plan out and conquer the challenge of preparation.

STEP 1: SCOPE OUT THE TEST

Learn everything you can about the format (multiple choice, essay, etc.) and what will be on the test. Gather any study materials, course outlines, or sample exams that may be available. Not only will this help you to prepare, but knowing what to expect can help to alleviate test anxiety.

STEP 2: MAP OUT THE MATERIAL

Look through the textbook or study guide and make note of how many chapters or sections it has. Then divide these over the time you have. For example, if a book has 15 chapters and you have five days to study, you need to cover three chapters each day. Even better, if you have the time, leave an extra day at the end for overall review after you have gone through the material in depth.

If time is limited, you may need to prioritize the material. Look through it and make note of which sections you think you already have a good grasp on, and which need review. While you are studying, skim quickly through the familiar sections and take more time on the challenging parts. Write out your plan so you don't get lost as you go. Having a written plan also helps you feel more in control of the study, so anxiety is less likely to arise from feeling overwhelmed at the amount to cover.

STEP 3: GATHER YOUR TOOLS

Decide what study method works best for you. Do you prefer to highlight in the book as you study and then go back over the highlighted portions? Or do you type out notes of the important information? Or is it helpful to make flashcards that you can carry with you? Assemble the pens, index cards, highlighters, post-it notes, and any other materials you may need so you won't be distracted by getting up to find things while you study.

If you're having a hard time retaining the information or organizing your notes, experiment with different methods. For example, try color-coding by subject with colored pens, highlighters, or post-it notes. If you learn better by hearing, try recording yourself reading your notes so you can listen while in the car, working out, or simply sitting at your desk. Ask a friend to quiz you from your flashcards, or try teaching someone the material to solidify it in your mind.

STEP 4: CREATE YOUR ENVIRONMENT

It's important to avoid distractions while you study. This includes both the obvious distractions like visitors and the subtle distractions like an uncomfortable chair (or a too-comfortable couch that makes you want to fall asleep). Set up the best study environment possible: good lighting and a comfortable work area. If background music helps you focus, you may want to turn it on, but otherwise keep the room quiet. If you are using a computer to take notes, be sure you don't have any other windows open, especially applications like social media, games, or anything else that could distract you. Silence your phone and turn off notifications. Be sure to keep water close by so you stay hydrated while you study (but avoid unhealthy drinks and snacks).

Also, take into account the best time of day to study. Are you freshest first thing in the morning? Try to set aside some time then to work through the material. Is your mind clearer in the afternoon or evening? Schedule your study session then. Another method is to study at the same time of day that

259

you will take the test, so that your brain gets used to working on the material at that time and will be ready to focus at test time.

STEP 5: STUDY!

Once you have done all the study preparation, it's time to settle into the actual studying. Sit down, take a few moments to settle your mind so you can focus, and begin to follow your study plan. Don't give in to distractions or let yourself procrastinate. This is your time to prepare so you'll be ready to fearlessly approach the test. Make the most of the time and stay focused.

Of course, you don't want to burn out. If you study too long you may find that you're not retaining the information very well. Take regular study breaks. For example, taking five minutes out of every hour to walk briskly, breathing deeply and swinging your arms, can help your mind stay fresh.

As you get to the end of each chapter or section, it's a good idea to do a quick review. Remind yourself of what you learned and work on any difficult parts. When you feel that you've mastered the material, move on to the next part. At the end of your study session, briefly skim through your notes again.

But while review is helpful, cramming last minute is NOT. If at all possible, work ahead so that you won't need to fit all your study into the last day. Cramming overloads your brain with more information than it can process and retain, and your tired mind may struggle to recall even previously learned information when it is overwhelmed with last-minute study. Also, the urgent nature of cramming and the stress placed on your brain contribute to anxiety. You'll be more likely to go to the test feeling unprepared and having trouble thinking clearly.

So don't cram, and don't stay up late before the test, even just to review your notes at a leisurely pace. Your brain needs rest more than it needs to go over the information again. In fact, plan to finish your studies by noon or early afternoon the day before the test. Give your brain the rest of the day to relax or focus on other things, and get a good night's sleep. Then you will be fresh for the test and better able to recall what you've studied.

STEP 6: TAKE A PRACTICE TEST

Many courses offer sample tests, either online or in the study materials. This is an excellent resource to check whether you have mastered the material, as well as to prepare for the test format and environment.

Check the test format ahead of time: the number of questions, the type (multiple choice, free response, etc.), and the time limit. Then create a plan for working through them. For example, if you have 30 minutes to take a 60-question test, your limit is 30 seconds per question. Spend less time on the questions you know well so that you can take more time on the difficult ones.

If you have time to take several practice tests, take the first one open book, with no time limit. Work through the questions at your own pace and make sure you fully understand them. Gradually work up to taking a test under test conditions: sit at a desk with all study materials put away and set a timer. Pace yourself to make sure you finish the test with time to spare and go back to check your answers if you have time.

After each test, check your answers. On the questions you missed, be sure you understand why you missed them. Did you misread the question (tests can use tricky wording)? Did you forget the information? Or was it something you hadn't learned? Go back and study any shaky areas that the practice tests reveal.

Taking these tests not only helps with your grade, but also aids in combating test anxiety. If you're already used to the test conditions, you're less likely to worry about it, and working through tests until you're scoring well gives you a confidence boost. Go through the practice tests until you feel comfortable, and then you can go into the test knowing that you're ready for it.

Test Tips

On test day, you should be confident, knowing that you've prepared well and are ready to answer the questions. But aside from preparation, there are several test day strategies you can employ to maximize your performance.

First, as stated before, get a good night's sleep the night before the test (and for several nights before that, if possible). Go into the test with a fresh, alert mind rather than staying up late to study.

Try not to change too much about your normal routine on the day of the test. It's important to eat a nutritious breakfast, but if you normally don't eat breakfast at all, consider eating just a protein bar. If you're a coffee drinker, go ahead and have your normal coffee. Just make sure you time it so that the caffeine doesn't wear off right in the middle of your test. Avoid sugary beverages, and drink enough water to stay hydrated but not so much that you need a restroom break 10 minutes into the test. If your test isn't first thing in the morning, consider going for a walk or doing a light workout before the test to get your blood flowing.

Allow yourself enough time to get ready, and leave for the test with plenty of time to spare so you won't have the anxiety of scrambling to arrive in time. Another reason to be early is to select a good seat. It's helpful to sit away from doors and windows, which can be distracting. Find a good seat, get out your supplies, and settle your mind before the test begins.

When the test begins, start by going over the instructions carefully, even if you already know what to expect. Make sure you avoid any careless mistakes by following the directions.

Then begin working through the questions, pacing yourself as you've practiced. If you're not sure on an answer, don't spend too much time on it, and don't let it shake your confidence. Either skip it and come back later, or eliminate as many wrong answers as possible and guess among the remaining ones. Don't dwell on these questions as you continue—put them out of your mind and focus on what lies ahead.

Be sure to read all of the answer choices, even if you're sure the first one is the right answer. Sometimes you'll find a better one if you keep reading. But don't second-guess yourself if you do immediately know the answer. Your gut instinct is usually right. Don't let test anxiety rob you of the information you know.

If you have time at the end of the test (and if the test format allows), go back and review your answers. Be cautious about changing any, since your first instinct tends to be correct, but make sure you didn't misread any of the questions or accidentally mark the wrong answer choice. Look over any you skipped and make an educated guess.

At the end, leave the test feeling confident. You've done your best, so don't waste time worrying about your performance or wishing you could change anything. Instead, celebrate the successful completion of this test. And finally, use this test to learn how to deal with anxiety even better next time.

Important Qualification

Not all anxiety is created equal. If your test anxiety is causing major issues in your life beyond the classroom or testing center, or if you are experiencing troubling physical symptoms related to your anxiety, it may be a sign of a serious physiological or psychological condition. If this sounds like your situation, we strongly encourage you to seek professional help.

Tell Us Your Story

We at Mometrix would like to extend our heartfelt thanks to you for letting us be a part of your journey. It is an honor to serve people from all walks of life, people like you, who are committed to building the best future they can for themselves.

We know that each person's situation is unique. But we also know that, whether you are a young student or a mother of four, you care about working to make your own life and the lives of those around you better.

That's why we want to hear your story.

We want to know why you're taking this test. We want to know about the trials you've gone through to get here. And we want to know about the successes you've experienced after taking and passing your test.

In addition to your story, which can be an inspiration both to us and to others, we value your feedback. We want to know both what you loved about our book and what you think we can improve on.

The team at Mometrix would be absolutely thrilled to hear from you! So please, send us an email at tellusyourstory@mometrix.com or visit us at mometrix.com/tellusyourstory.php and let's stay in touch.

Additional Bonus Material

Due to our efforts to try to keep this book to a manageable length, we've created a link that will give you access to all of your additional bonus material:

mometrix.com/bonus948/hspt

Printed in the USA
CPSIA information can be obtained
at www.ICGtesting.com
LVHW052039300923
759761LV00007B/189